Writing Children's Books For Dummies

KT-427-889

Tips for Editing

At some point after you have a solid draft of your children's book, you must begin the editing process. Although we cover these points in detail in Chapter 13, here's a quick overview of the salient points to keep in mind.

- ✔ If a sentence doesn't contribute to plot or character development, delete it.
- ✔ Make sure your characters don't all sound the same when they speak.
- ✔ If you have a page or more of continuous dialogue, chances are it needs tightening.
- ✔ When starting a new scene or chapter, make sure to briefly establish context.
- ✔ When changing place or time, provide brief transitions to keep your story moving smoothly.
- ✔ Make sure to keep the pace moving from action to action, scene to scene, chapter to chapter.
- ✔ If you find yourself using a lot of punctuation (!!!), CAPITAL LETTERS, *italics,* or **bold,** chances are your words are not working hard enough for you.
- ✔ When you can find one word to replace two or more words, do it.
- ✔ Don't be afraid to introduce a new word, just make sure to define it right away.
- ✔ Watch excessive use of adjectives, adverbs, and long descriptive passages.
- ✔ After you choose a point of view for a character, stick to it.
- ✔ If your character has not changed at the end of your story, chances are he is not yet fully fleshed out.
- ✔ If your character talks to himself or does a lot of wondering aloud, he needs a friend to talk to.
- ✔ If you're bored with a character, your reader will be, too.
- ✔ If you can't tell your story in three well-crafted sentences: the first one covering the beginning, the second one alluding to the climax (the middle), and the last one hinting at the ending — you may not have one yet.
- ✔ If you find yourself overwriting because you're having trouble expressing exactly what you mean, sit back and say it aloud to yourself, and then try again.

Children's Book No-Nos

Just as writing children's books has a unique set of rules, here are ten things you should never do. Never

- ✔ Write books that preach or lecture.
- ✔ Talk down to children as if they are small, idiotic adults.
- ✔ Write books that have no real story (nor a plot with beginning, middle, end).
- ✔ Use art that is totally inappropriate for the story or vice versa.
- ✔ Pack picture books with text.
- ✔ Pack nonfiction books with too much text and too few visuals.

- ✔ Create characters who are boring or uninteresting.
- ✔ Create main characters who have a problem they don't solve or who don't change throughout the course of the story.
- ✔ Tell instead of showing by using narrative as a soapbox.
- ✔ Anthropomorphize animals and use alliterative names (Squishy Squirrel, Morty Mole — Wretched Writer).

Writing Children's Books For Dummies®

Twelve Commandments for Writing Younger Children's Books

The rules for writing younger children's books (ages 2–8) are different from the rules for writing books for middle graders, young adults, or adults. Keep the following dozen commandments in mind when writing a younger children's book. (As with most commandments, you may be able to dance around one or two, but you'd better have a dang good reason.)

- It's okay to be different, but it's not easy.
- Bad guys never win.
- Good guys must win in the end.
- Extremes rule (the world is black or white, not both — most children ages 10 and under can be quite literal).
- People can change from essentially good (with faults) to pretty bad (with some good points) or vice versa, but they can't be both at the same time.
- It's fine for something to be scary, but it can never touch your body.
- Little people can triumph over big people.
- Poopoo, peepee, tushies, passing gas, burping, underwear — they're all hilarious.
- Turning things upside down is funny — as long as those things make sense in the first place right side up.
- Magic can occur as a logical reaction to an action.
- Regular children can perform extraordinary feats.
- Regular children can go on implausible missions sanctioned (or not) by adults in charge.

Promotion

After you've written a book, you have to sell it. Try to accomplish one of these tasks each week:

- Set up an interview on a local radio or TV show.
- Do readings in a bookstore, school, or library.
- Submit your book for an award or prize.
- Think up a crazy publicity stunt and set it in motion.
- Brainstorm new promotional ideas with a professional children's book publicist — and then start working on one.

Age Levels for Book Formats

Publishers generally assign age groups for readers of various formats (see Chapter 2), as follows. It's okay to veer off a year or so in either direction when assigning a target audience age range to your work.

- Board books: Newborn to age 3
- Picture books: Ages 3–8
- Coloring and activity (C&A) books: Ages 3–8
- Novelty books: Ages 3 and up, depending on content
- Early, leveled readers: Ages 5–9
- First chapter books: Ages 6–9 or 7–10
- Middle-grade books: Ages 9–12
- Young adult (YA) novels: Ages 12–18

Copyright © 2005 Wiley Publishing, Inc. All rights reserved. Item 3728-8.

For more information about Wiley Publishing, call 1-800-762-2974.

For Dummies: Bestselling Book Series for Beginners

Writing Children's Books

FOR

DUMMIES®

Writing Children's Books FOR DUMMIES®

by Lisa Rojany Buccieri and Peter Economy

WILEY

Wiley Publishing, Inc.

Writing Children's Books For Dummies®

Published by
Wiley Publishing, Inc.
111 River St.
Hoboken, NJ 07030-5774
www.wiley.com

Copyright © 2005 by Wiley Publishing, Inc., Indianapolis, Indiana

Published simultaneously in Canada

For general information on our other products and services, please contact our Customer Care Department within the U.S. at 800-762-2974, outside the U.S. at 317-572-3993, or fax 317-572-4002.

For technical support, please visit www.wiley.com/techsupport.

Wiley also publishes its books in a variety of electronic formats. Some content that appears in print may not be available in electronic books.

Library of Congress Control Number: 2005923239

ISBN-13: 978-0-7645-3728-8

ISBN-10: 0-7645-3728-8

Manufactured in the United States of America

10 9 8 7 6 5 4

1O/RV/QU/QV/IN

WILEY

About the Authors

Lisa Rojany Buccieri is a publishing executive with over 15 years' experience in the industry. Lisa has also written nearly 40 children's books and co-written a *New York Times*-bestselling adult nonfiction hardcover, *Fund Your Future* (Berkley, 2002), with Julie Stav. Her books have received various accolades, such as reaching Number 1 on the *Publishers Weekly* bestseller list two years in a row (*Make Your Own Valentines,* PSS/Penguin) and winning the American Bookseller's Pick of the List (*Giant Animal Fold-Outs: Kangaroo & Company*, PSS/Penguin). *King Arthur's Camelot* (Dutton) was selected to be a Book of the Month Club selection; *Child* Magazine chose her *Exploring the Human Body* (Barron's) as one of its Best New Parenting Books; and *The Magic Feather* (Troll) won a Parent's Choice Silver Honor Award. Lisa is currently spearheading a new children's book packaging and publishing division at Americhip Books, focusing on integrating light, sound, animation, paper engineering, and other cutting-edge technologies with stories and art. She has been Editorial/Publishing Director for Golden Books, Price Stern Sloan/Penguin Group USA, Intervisual Books, Gateway Learning Corp (Hooked on Phonics), and others. She speaks about children's publishing, writing, and editing at U.C.L.A. Writer's Program Extension courses and other venues and is currently working on a book of fiction for grown-ups. Lisa also runs her own company, Editorial Services of Los Angeles, in which she helps other writers make their work the best it can be. You can contact her at www.editorialservicesofla.com.

Peter Economy is a veteran author with nine *For Dummies* titles under his belt, including two second editions. Peter is coauthor of *Home-Based Business For Dummies, Building Your Own Home For Dummies, Consulting For Dummies, The Management Bible, Why Aren't You Your Own Boss?, Enterprising Nonprofits: A Toolkit for Social Entrepreneurs,* and many more books. Peter is also Associate Editor of *Leader to Leader,* the award-winning journal of the Leader to Leader Institute. Check out Peter's Web site at www.petereconomy.com.

Dedication

To writers and illustrators everywhere, aspiring and published, who use their creativity, imagination, perseverance, and courage to write children's books that make a difference.

Authors' Acknowledgments

We would like to thank all the busy publishing professionals, teachers, librarians, book buyers, and bookstore owners who agreed to be interviewed for this book: Lesleigh Alchanati, Michael Cart, Cindy Chang, Michael Green, Sharon Hearn, Chuck Hurewitz, Bitsy Kemper, Leslie McGuire, Erin Molta, Stephen Mooser, Chuck Murphy, Glenn Murray, Judy Ostarch, Susan Patron, Susan Goldman Rubin, Barney Saltzberg, Lauri Smith, Deborah Warren, Doug Whiteman, and Debra Mostow Zakarin. Your words of wisdom and experience are deeply appreciated — and any errors are all our fault. We are also grateful to the authors, illustrators, and publishers who gave us permission to reprint book covers and interiors. Thanks as well to the folks at Wiley who cared enough to make this book the best it could be: Joyce Pepple, Tracy Boggier, Jen Bingham, Tricia Sprietelmeier, Corbin Collins, and the amazing Tere Stouffer. Laura Backes, your comments were right on target — thank you!

Lisa's additional thanks: I take off my hat to my co-writer, Peter Economy, whose unfailing sense of humor, wisdom, and patience kept me going. Heartfelt thanks to Donna Becker, Director of Temple Beth Haverim's Early Childhood Center, and all the teachers there, for generously giving me those extra hours so I could finish the book. To those who attend my writers' workshops, I bow to you for continually amazing me and for never giving up on yourselves. Gobs of thanks are due to my mom who gives me big breaks on a regular basis — you make it easier for me to be a good parent. Aba, your generosity allows me little freedoms all writers cherish, thank you. Big, fat hugs of gratitude go to my closest girlfriends, you know who you are, for those monthly dinners and coffee breaks in Malibu that nourish my soul. Thanks to Kristian, a better person I have never met; you are my angel, my inspiration, and one of the best writers I know. And to Olivia, Chloe, and Genevieve — the lights of my life — may the readers of this book supply you with quality reading entertainment for many years to come.

Peter's additional thanks: A thousands thanks are not enough to acknowledge the debt of gratitude I owe my coauthor Lisa Rojany Buccieri for putting her heart and soul into this book. You are a joy to work with — a real pro — and I am honored to be your writing partner and friend. And to my wife Jan and children Peter J, Skylar Park, and Jackson Warren — you're what this book is all about!

Publisher's Acknowledgments

We're proud of this book; please send us your comments through our Dummies online registration form located at www.dummies.com/register/.

Some of the people who helped bring this book to market include the following:

Acquisitions, Editorial, and Media Development

Project Editor: Tere Stouffer

Acquisitions Editor: Tracy Boggier

Copy Editor: Corbin Collins

Editorial Program Assistant: Courtney Allen

Technical Editor: Laura Backes

Editorial Manager: Michelle Hacker

Editorial Supervisor: Carmen Krikorian

Editorial Assistants: Hanna Scott, Melissa S. Bennett

Cartoons: Rich Tennant (www.the5thwave.com)

Composition Services

Project Coordinator: Adrienne Martinez

Layout and Graphics: Andrea Dahl, Denny Hager, Joyce Haughey, Barry Offringa, Lynsey Osborn, Heather Ryan, Mary Gillot Virgin

Special Art: Kathryn Born

Proofreaders: Laura Albert, Leeann Harney, Jessica Kramer, TECHBOOKS Production Services

Indexer: TECHBOOKS Production Services

Publishing and Editorial for Consumer Dummies

Diane Graves Steele, Vice President and Publisher, Consumer Dummies

Joyce Pepple, Acquisitions Director, Consumer Dummies

Kristin A. Cocks, Product Development Director, Consumer Dummies

Michael Spring, Vice President and Publisher, Travel

Kelly Regan, Editorial Director, Travel

Kathleen Nebenhaus, Vice President and Executive Publisher, Consumer Dummies, Lifestyles, Pets, Education

Publishing for Technology Dummies

Andy Cummings, Vice President and Publisher, Dummies Technology/General User

Composition Services

Gerry Fahey, Vice President of Production Services

Debbie Stailey, Director of Composition Services

Contents at a Glance

Table of Contents

Introduction

1f you've gone through the trouble and expense of buying this book, we're going to take a wild guess that you dream of writing your own children's book and getting it published. Your desire may come from a deep-seated yearning to communicate with young people or to share experiences with them. Or it may stem from an interest in a subject that you think children may also be interested in. Regardless of where your desire comes from, we want to help you turn that desire into a well-written, saleable manuscript. Our goals in writing this book are to help you understand the children's book writing process and give you the tools you need to turn your children's book dream into reality. Many people think writing a children's book is child's play. Actually, it's not. Writing a children's book takes a lot of hard work.

We've seen plenty of people just like you attempt to tackle the process of writing a children's book. Some haven't the slightest idea where to start. Others have a good idea where to start, but don't know what to do with their manuscript after they've written it. Still others have published a children's book or two, but would like to try writing a new type of children's book. Good news: We understand the process and what it takes to move through it with as little stress as possible. In the pages that follow, we provide you with the very best advice our many years of experience have to offer.

About This Book

There's a lot more to writing a children's book and getting it published than simply knocking out a manuscript and mailing it to a publisher. If you're serious about getting your book published, then you need to understand the entire children's book process and how to deal with the different challenges that present themselves along the way. Where do you start? Who at a publishing house does what? How do you get your manuscript in front of an editor? How do you help market your book after it's published? This book answers these questions, and hundreds more like them — and all in an easy-to-use reference that you can take with you anywhere.

We also include interviews with extremely knowledgeable veterans of the children's book industry — authors, editors, agents, illustrators, publicists, and more — in each chapter to provide you with their own unique perspectives and experience.

We divide each chapter into sections, and each section contains information about some part of the process, such as:

- ✔ The basics of the children's book market — who your buyers are (and who they're not)
- ✔ The many different formats of children's books, from board books to picture books to chapter books
- ✔ Elements of good writing explained, from writing good characters to setting up a strong plot to transitioning from scene to scene
- ✔ Writing exercises to spark your creativity
- ✔ How to get an agent or publisher interested in your book
- ✔ How to help publicize your book after it's published

Conventions Used in This Book

We use the following conventions throughout the text to make everything consistent and easy-to-understand:

- ✔ All Web addresses appear in `monofont`.
- ✔ New terms appear in *italics* and are closely followed by an easy-to-understand definition.
- ✔ **Bold** text indicates keywords in bulleted lists or highlights the action parts of numbered steps.

What You're Not to Read

We've written this book so that you can find information easily — and readily understand what you find. We also simplify it so you can identify "skippable" material. *Sidebars* are the shaded boxes that appear here and there. They share fun facts, but nothing that's essential to the success of your children's book. Many of the sidebars include interviews with veterans of the children's book industry — authors, editors, agents, illustrators, publicists, and more — who provide you with their own unique perspectives and experiences.

Foolish Assumptions

We wrote this book with some thoughts about you in mind. Here's what we assume about you, our reader:

- You've long been dreaming about writing your own children's book and getting it published.

- You may have already written a children's story but are not sure how to ready it for submission. You may have already had a children's book published, but would like to experiment with a different type of children's story. Or you may even be an experienced children's book author who is looking for new perspectives on the industry.

- You're looking for a comprehensive guide that demystifies the children's-book-writing process by focusing on the information that's most important for you to know.

- You would like to improve your writing skills.

- You're willing to take the time to become knowledgeable about the conventions in the children's book world that will separate you from the wannabes.

- You're interested in exploring different publishing options.

- You want to know what you need to do to find an agent or publisher.

Foolish of us, maybe, but we assume that you trust us to do our very best when writing this book. We hope you enjoy reading it, discover new approaches and processes, and move your dream of writing a children's book closer to reality.

How This Book Is Organized

This book is divided into six parts — jump in wherever you want. The following sections explain what you'll find where.

Part 1: The ABCs of Writing for Children

In this part, we introduce you to the world of children's books and take an in-depth look at the many different formats of children's books as well as who actually buys children's books and why.

Part II: Immersing Yourself in the Writing Process

Above all, writing a children's book involves *writing*. In this part, we help you get a jump on the writing process, looking at how to set up your workspace, develop great story ideas, and build upon your great ideas with research.

Part III: Creating a Spellbinding Story

A spellbinding story includes a plot that makes sense and doesn't leave out details that make the story believable, characters you care about and root for, dialogue that sounds real, a setting that transports you to a different world, and so on. This part helps you create all of that and more, whether you're writing a picture book, a chapter book, or a work of nonfiction.

Part IV: Making Your Story Shine

In this part, we show you how to rewrite and edit your manuscript yourself and where to get outside help. We also look into formatting and illustrating your manuscript. Finally, we give you some information about where to find other writers and great teachers.

Part V: Getting Published and Promoting Your Book

After you've written your book, it's time to sell it. In this part, we consider the pros and cons of working with literary agents versus approaching publishers directly yourself. We provide detailed information on book deals and contracts and give you some quick tips on dealing with copyright law. We also take a close look at the publication process and where your manuscript goes when your editor starts it off on its publication journey.

We consider how to deal with the sad reality of rejection and when it may be time to look into self-publishing. We wrap up this part by discussing how you can promote and publicize your book.

Part VI: The Part of Tens

This part includes quick resources that provide information in an easy-to-digest fashion. Explore some tried-and-true, classic children's book storylines, and understand the very best ways to promote your book. Above all, have fun. (And sell lots of books.)

Icons Used in This Book

To make this book easier to read and simpler to use, we include some icons in the margins that can help you find and fathom key ideas and information.

These tidbits provide expert advice to help you save time, money, or frustration in the book-writing process.

This icon highlights important information to store in your brain for quick recall at a later time.

Avoid mistakes by following the sage words of advice that appear by this icon.

This icon tells you that we're covering a topic that is new and innovative in the children's book industry.

Where to Go from Here

The great thing about this book is that *you* decide where to start and what to read. It's a reference you can jump into and out of at will. Just head to the table of contents or the index to find the information you want.

If you're new to the business of writing children's books, you may want to start at the beginning of this book and work your way through to the end. You'll find a wealth of information and practical advice. Simply turn the page and you're on your way!

Part I
The ABCs of Writing for Children

The 5th Wave   By Rich Tennant

"Is this where the breakout session for children's book authors meets?"

In this part . . .

The world of children's books can be a bewildering and foreign place for the aspiring author. The diversity of this world's products — and customers — is unequaled in any other corner of the publishing world. In this part, we provide you with a broad overview of the world of children's books. After covering the basics, we take a very detailed look at all the different formats of children's books — from board books to chapter books to young adult novels, and much more — and delve deeply into the children's book market.

Chapter 1

The Basics of Writing Children's Books

For many, dreams of writing a children's book remain just that — dreams — because they soon find out that writing a really good children's book is *hard*. Not only that, but actually getting a children's book published is even harder. If you don't know the conventions and styles, if you don't speak the lingo, if you don't have someone to advocate for your work, or if you don't come across professionally, you'll be hard pressed to get your manuscript read and considered, much less published.

We wrote this book to help you as you go through the process of writing your children's book and getting it published. In many of the chapters, we provide insightful, candid interviews with publishing pros who answer common questions with incredible candor and honesty and, often, a great sense of humor.

Every bestselling children's book author started with a story idea — just like yours. Many of today's most successful writers were rejected time after time, until they finally found someone who liked what they saw and decided to take a chance. Follow your dreams. Never give up. When your children's book is published one day, we'll be cheering for you.

Knowing Your Format and Audience

Before you do anything else, figure out what kind of children's book you're writing (or want to write). Manuscripts are published in several tried-and-true formats, with new ones being developed every year. Formats involve the physical characteristics of a book: page count, trim size (width and height), whether it's color or black and white, has lots of pictures or lots of words, or is hardcover or softcover. There are also lots of genres your book may (or may not) fall into. So, figuring out your format and genre will help you determine exactly how to write your book — see Chapter 2 for more.

You also need to ask yourself: Who is my audience? Believe it or not, *children* isn't the correct answer. Children of a particular age bracket, say *newborn to age 2,* or *ages 3 to 8* may come closer to defining the target age you're trying to reach, but are they really the ones who buy your book? Because books are ushered through the process by grown-ups — edited by editors, categorized by publishers, pushed by sales reps, shelved and sold by booksellers, and most often purchased by parents and other adults — your audience is more complicated than you may think. In Chapter 3, we tell you all about the different people you need to impress before you get your book in the hands of children.

Getting to a Good Writing Zone

If you thought you could just grab a pen and paper and jump right in to writing, you're right! But you also may want to consider what will happen when your life starts to intrude on your writing time. How do you work around the children needing to be fed and your desk being buried under mounds of bills and old homework? How do you figure out when it's best to write? In Chapter 4, we talk about finding a space of your own for writing and making that space conducive to productivity and creativity. We also emphasize the importance of making a writing schedule and sticking to it.

After you figure out how to get to work, you have to decide what you're going to write about. Coming up with an interesting idea for a story isn't necessarily as easy as you may think. In Chapter 5, we provide lots of ways to boot up your idea factory and get you started. If you get stuck, we also have ways to get you unstuck.

As soon as you've got your good idea, you'll want to get out for a little bit and research. Every good book is built on a good idea and good research to make sure the idea fits with the audience. We cover the hows and whys of researching your audience, of figuring out what children like and what is important in the lives, and then researching the topic itself in Chapter 6.

Transforming Yourself into a Storyteller

Children's books are all about great, memorable characters. Whether it's a child who can fly, a big, bad wolf, a boy and a slave floating down the Mississippi River, or a smelly green ogre, characters are the heart and soul of children's books. So how can you create characters who jump off the page and into your readers' hearts? And how do you make sure they have a supporting cast that does what they are supposed to do? In Chapter 7 we delve into how to build and flesh out great characters and how to avoid stereotyping and other typical pitfalls. We even add some exercises that help you practice your character-building skills.

What exactly is a plot, and how does one figure out what constitutes a beginning, a middle, and an end? And what the heck is a step sheet and will it help you structure your story? That's the territory of Chapter 8, where we talk about conflict, climax, and resolution and how to get started on that all-important first draft.

We then provide some tips and step-by-step advice for writing good dialogue for your characters to make sure that they sound as realistic (and as age appropriate) as you intended them to be. We also look at ways to keep them sounding different from one another. All that can be found in Chapter 9.

One way to engage young readers is to write about people they can relate to and set your story in places that intrigue them. We give you some pointers on how to really create interesting settings that ground your story in a particular context and draw in your reader in Chapter 10.

Many writers find joy in using words as their own little playthings (we know we do). Word play, rhyming, rhythm — the music inherent in words well matched — is indeed exciting to read and even more fun to write. Children delight in poetry and music. If you've forgotten just what makes a youngster giggle out of control, we use Chapter 11 to remind you what children of different ages find hilarious. We also discuss how to choose and stick to a consistent point of view while creating a tone that works for you.

We wrap up this section with an in-depth look at writing creative nonfiction (true) stories or a how-to book. Chapter 12 is chock-full of good advice on jump-starting that nonfiction project by choosing a kid-friendly topic, organiz-ing your ideas into a comprehensive outline or plan, and fleshing out your ideas with all the right research.

Polishing Your Gem and Getting It Ready to Send

After you've written your first (or tenth) draft, you may be ready for the rewriting or editing process. Rewriting and editing aren't just exercises to go through step-by-step; they are processes in which the writer gets to know his story inside and out. Characters are fleshed out, the story is honed and sharpened, the pacing is fine-tuned, and the writing is buffed and polished. In Chapter 13, we guide you through the steps of rewriting and editing, address-ing in detail how to fix everything from dialogue issues to awkward writing, advising when to adhere to the rules of grammar (and when it's okay not to), and giving you a few simple questions to ask yourself that will make the process much smoother and less complicated. The chapter also gives you editing tips from the pros and tells you how they work with their writers to help them make their books the best they can be.

Perhaps you've been through the writing and rewriting and editing processes and are ready to push your duckling story out into the pond and see if she'll swim. Your work is about to encounter a lot of professional publishing folks, and first impressions carry a lot of weight. In Chapter 13, we also talk about how to format your work before you send it out, taking care to make it look as professional and enticing as possible.

And what about illustrations? Should you illustrate your book yourself or should you partner with or hire an illustrator to create the pictures you envi-sion to complement and enhance your manuscript? The answers may sur-prise you. In Chapter 14, we address illustrations and illustrators, how to find them, and how to work with them.

Often in the process of rewriting and editing their work, writers find that they need another set of eyes to confirm (or reject) their thoughts about their manuscript. You may have general questions such as, "Is this really final or does it need work?" You may have specific questions about your characters or your storyline. To help you feel less alone, we include a chapter on joining the children's book writing community, whether you join (or start) a local writers' group, go to book writer's conferences, or go back to school. Chapter 15 gives you the scoop on feedback of all types. We want you to be aware of what these specific events, venues, and services can and should offer you before you take the plunge and pull out your checkbook (or your typed and double-spaced manuscript).

Submitting, Selling, and Promoting Your Book

All dressed up and lots of places to go! What a marvelous place to be: You have a well-written, carefully edited, perfectly formatted manuscript that you are ready to launch on its first (or seventeenth) journey out into the big, bad world of agents and publishers. But what in the heck are you supposed to do next?

In Chapter 16, we talk about where you start looking for someone who will best represent your interests and do all the photocopying, cover-letter writing, submitting, tracking, and negotiating on your behalf. An *agent* can be a necessary and welcome addition to your family of writing supporters, and the good ones are well worth the 15 percent they typically charge to take your career from amateur to professional. Finding the right one, getting her attention, and then negotiating your contract is a process unto itself, and we've got your back to make sure you understand what you're getting yourself into.

Whether an agent is in your future or you decide to submit directly to the publishers yourself, you'll know what to do next when you read Chapter 17. Finding the right match and submitting only to the "right" publishing houses is an art form itself and requires in-depth research and quite a bit of sleuthing. We also provide tips on how to make yourself stand out from the pack with scintillating query letters and proposals that get you noticed. And if you choose to work with a packager instead, we talk you through the opportunities open to writers who seek packagers and licensors as publishing partners. When all your efforts pay off, and you're about to enter into a legal agreement with a publisher, you need to know which rights are most important to protect and what issues you need to negotiate before you sign and date your first publishing contract. Chapter 17 can help there, too.

Rejection hurts, no matter who you are or where you are in your publishing career. Yet why is it that some writers tell tales about getting rejected dozens of times and still manage to get published, while others send something out to one or two publishers and then toss their manuscript in a drawer to gather dust while they move on to another, less painful hobby? Developing a tough hide isn't easy, but it's absolutely necessary when you're a writer. In Chapter 17, we offer ways of combating the rejection blues and moving onward and upward, including publishing your story yourself.

You may know what an editor does (sort of), but perhaps you have no idea how a book gets transformed from the stuff you pulled out of your printer into the lovely hardcover or softcover package you see sitting on the book-store shelf. Who decides which illustrations will accompany your text, and how will the illustrator know what he's supposed to show on each page? What is the next process your beloved manuscript will now take? In Chapter 18, we let you in on where a manuscript goes once it's inside a publishing house.

Improving your chances of getting published

We've worked in the publishing industry for a long time, and we've got a pretty good idea of what works and what doesn't. Here are some insider tips that can significantly improve your chances of getting published. Some of these tips involve very specific advice, such as getting feedback before submitting, and less concrete (but just as important) tips about the etiquette of following up with publishers and how to behave if rejected.

Act like a pro. If you act like you're an experienced and savvy children's book writer, people perceive you as being an experienced and savvy children's book writer. And because the children's book industry tends to be more accepting of those people who already "belong to the club" than of the newbies pounding on the door to be let in, you'll greatly improve your chances of getting published by behaving as if you already belong. Some examples of this include sending a one-page query letter that addresses all the salient points, submitting your manuscript edited carefully, and formatting your manuscript properly (all discussed in Chapter 13).

Create magic with words. Writing a fabulous children's book isn't easy. Children's book editors have very finely tuned senses of what constitutes a well-written book and what will sell in the marketplace. If you want to get your book published, your writing must be top notch — second-best isn't good enough. If you're still learning the craft of writing, by all means engage the services of a professional children's book editor or book doctor to help fix up your manuscript before you submit it to a publisher for consideration — or get some reliable and knowledgeable feedback. Head to Chapter 13 for advice on hiring an editorial service and Chapter 15 for ways of getting additional good feedback.

Research thoroughly. To get published, your book needs to be both believable and factually correct (especially if you're writing nonfiction). If you're sloppy with the facts, your editor won't waste much time with your manuscript before it gets pitched in the round file. (Chapter 6 keeps you up on the latest developments in the world of children and ways to research your topic.)

Follow up — without stalking. After you submit your manuscript or proposal, expect to follow up with the agent or editor to whom you submitted it. But keep in mind that agents and editors are very busy people, and they probably receive hundreds of submissions every year. Be polite and persistent, but avoid stalking the agent or editor by constantly calling or e-mailing for status. Making a pest of yourself will buy you nothing except a one-way ticket out of the world of children's books. See Chapter 18 for more on when and how to follow up.

Accept rejection graciously. Every children's book author — even the most successful and famous — knows rejection and what it's like to wonder whether her book will ever be published. But every rejection provides you with important lessons to be applied to your next submission. Take these lessons to heart and move on to the next opportunity. Head to Chapter 18 for more on rejection.

Practice until you're perfect. There's no better way to succeed at writing than to write, and no better way to get better at submitting your manuscripts and proposals to agents or publishers than to submit. Don't let rejection get in the way of your progress; keep writing and keep submitting. The more you do, the better you'll get at it — *it* being everything you discover in Parts II and III. And remember: Hope means always having a manuscript being considered somewhere.

Promote like crazy. Publishers love authors with a selling platform — that is, people who have the ability to publicize and promote their books as widely as possible. By showing your prospective publishers that you have the ability to promote your books — in the media, through your networks of relationships, and more — you'll greatly increase your chances of being published. (For more on promotion, see Chapters 19 and 21.)

Give back to the writing community. Pros give back to their profession, to their readers, and to their communities. They volunteer to participate in writing groups or conferences to help new or unpublished authors polish their work and get published; they do free readings in local schools and libraries; and they advocate for children in their communities. When you give back like a pro, you improve your standing in the children's book industry, which increases your chances of getting published. And besides all that, you establish some good karma, and that can't hurt.

After you have your book in your hand, how can you be sure anyone else ever will? Getting a book published is only part of the process toward success. And guess what? The efforts your publisher is planning on making on your behalf may not impress you. Delving into marketing and publicizing will make your book sell over the long run. In Chapter 19, we talk to publicity professionals who let us in on their secrets, and we give you lots of ideas of how to get your book noticed. Marketing, planning, and promotion take you from book signing to lecture — all starring you and your fabulous children's book.

So if you're ready to begin examining the process that all writers must enter, jump right in or tiptoe on over. We're ready for you.

Chapter 2

Children's Book Formats and Genres

· ·

In This Chapter

▶ Getting to know different children's book categories and formats

▶ Acquainting yourself with different genres

· ·

Children are as different as the many different books that cater to their diverse interests and desires. Because of this, children's books offer a wealth of diversity in formats, shapes, sizes, intended audiences, and genres. In this chapter, we explain the different formats and genres children's books fall into. We also show you a dozen examples of book covers to give you a feel for the children's book market.

Children's Book Categories and Formats

Children's books can be grouped into two large *categories:* fiction and nonfiction, both of which we talk about in depth in Part III of this book. Diving further in, you'll see that children's books are also divided into *formats,* which are based on the various ages the books serve, as well as the book's size and shape, and its content, such as whether the book has more pictures than words, or vice versa. Some examples of formats include picture books, board books, chapter books, and young adult books, all of which we describe in this section.

Formats help publishers group their titles by age appropriateness (that is, where children are developmentally) or physical characteristics or both, which, in turn, helps children's book readers know what type of books are suitable for particular age ranges, interests, or goals. These format separations and identifications follow each title from conception through in-house production in the publishing company and to the sales team and bookseller, who often organizes the books by format right in the store. So even the customers, who may not even know they're buying a certain format, find books presented to them in formats.

The parts of a book

Before we go dropping lots of terminology on you, we wanted you to have the most basic parts of a book at your fingertips. Being at least a little familiar with these terms will help you when you are communicating about your book to other publishing professionals.

✔ **Cover:** The *cover* of your book is the face your book presents to the world after it is published. It can be a *hardcover* book, meaning that it has paper glued over hard cardboard on all three sides (front cover, back cover, and spine); or it can be a *softcover* book, meaning that it has thicker bond cardstock (like postcard) paper for all three sides. A book's front cover usually has a title, the author's name, the illustrator's name, and some graphic image. The back cover can have *sell copy* (words that describe what the book is about in brief and why it's so great), the publisher's name, copyright info, a barcode, a price, and other information that helps retailers categorize and sell it.

For many board books and novelty books, the text and images begin right away on the *inside front cover*.

✔ **Spine:** The *spine* is the part of the book that usually hides the *binding* of the book or where the pages are glued or sewn together. The spine is between both covers and usually carries, at minimum, the title, the author's (and illustrator's) last names, and the publisher's name or logo.

✔ **Jacket:** A *jacket* is a separate piece of heavier stock removable paper that may be wrapped around the cover and tucked under the front and back covers of the book. The jacket often repeats all the information and images found on the front cover, but sometimes the book's actual covers may be blank (often the case in picture books and hardcover YA (young adult) novels), with the jacket providing all the images and publishing information including the title, credits, sell copy, author and illustrator bios, and the dedication.

✔ **Pages:** *Pages* are the sheets of paper onto which your story is printed. Illustrations also appear on the pages. Most books are published in *signatures* (groups) of 8 pages each, because of how the pages are printed, folded, and then cut at the bindery, so that's why you may notice that most children's books have pages in denominations of 8: such as 24- or 32-page picture books, 48- or 64-page first chapter books, and so on.

✔ **Trim (or trim size):** *Trim* is the size of the book. *Page trim* refers to the size of the book's interior pages. *Cover trim* refers to the size of the cover, which may be larger than or the same size as the page trim.

✔ **Endpapers:** Most of the time, *endpapers* are not part of the books as printed. They are the double leaves of paper added at front and back of the book before it is bound. The outer leaf of each page is pasted to the inner surface of the cover (this is known as the *pastedown*), the inner leaves (or free endpapers) forming the first and last pages of the book when bound. Endpapers are mostly of heavier stock paper than the rest of the text pages and are often decorated or illustrated with mini-illustrations.

✔ **Front matter:** *Front matter* refers to the material that comes before the text or story of a book including title and copyright pages, a table of contents, an introduction, a dedication, and acknowledgments.

✔ **Spread:** The left page and the right page of an open book constitute a *spread*. So instead of referring to these two pages by their page numbers, you may refer to them as spreads.

Always refer to your work's title and the format *together* — in the same sentence — as in, "*Alphababies* is a board book that uses photographs of babies to teach the alphabet to toddlers." That way, the person reviewing your work can immediately identify the format into which your book falls.

Many writers can't figure out their format until they have their story down and are in the editing process, way down the road from this point. But others find it helpful to know the parameters of the various formats ahead of time to help them make decisions along the way about a writing style appropriate for the age group, plot complexity, word count, and other elements that go into defining a format. And knowing about formats does not mean you cannot start writing without figuring out which format your book should be. Nor does it mean that you can squeeze any story into any format.

Books with Pictures

What we loosely refer to as "books with pictures" include any of the formats that focus mainly on heavy illustration and few words. These formats include board books, picture books, coloring and activity books, and novelty books. These books are perfect for babies and growing toddlers. Usually, parents read these to their kids, rather than the kids reading the books themselves.

Board books

Get yourself a chunky book with a heavy stock, rounded corners, and bright, eye-catching pictures, and you've got yourself a *board book* (see Figure 2-1). Perfect gifts for little ones, these books are for the youngest readers — so young, in fact, that they don't even read yet! *Goodnight Moon* and *Runaway Bunny,* both by Margaret Wise Brown (both HarperFestival), *Jamberry* by Bruce Degen (HarperFestival), and *Hug* by Jez Alborough (Candlewick Press) are all stellar.

Many board books today are written by their illustrators. This is because the text is usually so short and the pictures do most of the storytelling. Sandra Boynton and Rosemary Wells are board book author/illustrators who are worthy of study. However, if you are determined to sell a board book based on text only, in a market totally inundated with concept books and simple stories about everyday experiences, the text must be very unique indeed. The only way for you to make sure yours stands out is to study what is already out there so you can create an original concept and story.

The basics of board books

Board books get their name because they're made of *cardboard* or *chipboard,* which makes their pages stiffer and heavier than regular paper — and able to withstand use by small hands that don't have the fine motor development to turn regular paper pages without tearing them. Board books are perfect for kids ages 0 to 3 years old.

Figure 2-1:
Halloween,
Be My
Valentine,
Easter Egg
Surprise,
and
Monsters.

By Salina Yoon. Reprinted courtesy of Price, Stern Sloan, a division of Penguin Young Readers Group.

Most of these books are 10 to 14 pages long, with very little text, if any. We're talking a few sentences at most, and sometimes only one word to a page. These books vary in size, from 2 × 3 inches to 14 × 16 inches.

Other variations of books for children of the same age range — newborn to age 3 — are made of different materials, such as cloth books (which may include zippers, buttons, laces, pockets, and other pleasing fabrics — see Figure 2-2), vinyl bath books, and books cut into interesting shapes.

Writing great board books

Terrific topics for board books include early learning concepts, such as shapes and colors and daily experiences like mealtime and naptime. But you don't need a lot of words to get your concepts across. Board books are the perfect place to use simple rhyming text, using sometimes as little as one word per page and lots of bright, colorful pictures to keep baby's attention.

In order to write a good board book you need to make sure that your content is unique. The only way to ascertain that is to research what's out there and take a good look at the board books that continue to sell and sell and sell, such as the ones we mentioned. They all share a few elements in common:

✔ Choose simple concepts or storylines appropriate for babies and toddlers.

✔ Write minimal text per page, often only a word or two.

✔ Make sure the text is illustratable (no overly complex concepts such as gravity or black holes).

 ✔ If you are the illustrator, present clear and evocative illustrations that, if the words were to disappear, can tell the story by themselves.

 ✔ Keep to the K.I.S.S. rule: Keep It Simple, Silly!

Picture books

Picture books, like the one shown in Figure 2-3, are most often hardcover, heavily illustrated storybooks that cover almost every topic under the sun. They can be fiction or nonfiction, told in poetry or prose, and aimed at the literary or the mass/commercial markets. Teachers and parents with children from preschool age through early elementary years use picture books to speak to children about everything and anything the children might be experiencing at the moment: holidays, new siblings, moods, a fascination with birds or princesses — you name it, picture books cover it.

Figure 2-2:
Fleecy
Puppy.

Illustrated by Patti Jennings. Reprinted courtesy of Price, Stern Sloan, a division of Penguin Young Readers Group.

One of the most popular picture books in the last few years is Ian Falconer's *Olivia* (Atheneum/Anne Schwartz Books), a perfect example of picture book writing and illustrating in which the author/illustrator manages to create a fleshed-out character who looks and feels and behaves just like the kid next door — even though she is a pig. The minimal text, limited color palette, and evocative yet restrained illustrations all work together in just the way they should in a picture book. Other bestsellers, all very different from one another include Dr. Seuss's *Oh, the Places You'll Go!* (Random House Books for Young Readers)*, How I Became a Pirate* by Melinda Long (Harcourt Children's Books), *Walter the Farting Dog* by William Kotzwinkle and Glenn Murray (North Atlantic Books), and *Where the Wild Things Are* by Maurice Sendak (HarperCollins).

Picture book basics

Picture books are perfect for readers 3 to 8 years old. Generally with 24 or 32 pages (though some are 16, others are 48) pages, and anywhere from 100 to 1,500 words, these books can capture the vastly different interests and attention spans of kids this age. Picture books most often measure in at 8½ × 11 inches.

Figure 2-3:
Skippyjon Jones.

By Judy Schachner. Reprinted courtesy of Dutton Children's Books, a division of Penguin Young Readers Group.

Why is the standard length of a picture book 32 pages? Thirty-two pages fits best on a big sheet of two-sided paper for most printing presses.

Other picture book varieties include the following:

✔ Softcover storybooks that are 8 inches × 8 inches are called *eight by eights* or *8x8s* in the industry. They're usually 8, 16, or 24 pages long, often star licensed characters, and come in pairs — if not series — of books. Sometimes these are also referred to as *picturebacks.* You can often find them in spinner racks at bookstores and markets.

Licensed characters are characters generally culled from popular television shows, toys, and movies. Some that have been around for a while and will probably stick around for a while more include Elmo, Barbie, and Bob the Builder.

✔ Board book adaptations of picture books are titles that have already had a successful run as a picture book and get a second life as a board book. In general, these *picture boards* are huge board books with the same text and illustrations as the original picture books (with sometimes an editorial nip and tuck here and there, but usually not enough to be noticeable to the casual reader).

✔ Softcover picture books (see Figure 2-4) come in many sizes and shapes besides 8x8s. It used to be that all picture books had a *first run* (the first printing of the book) as hardcovers. If the hardcover picture book was successful, then the publisher would follow up with the cheaper softcover. Nowadays picture book originals are often published directly into a softcover format, often referred to as *picturebacks.*

Figure 2-4:
Countdown to Grandma's House and *Grandpa Lets Me Be Me.*

By Debra Mostow Zakarin, Illustrated by Stacy Peterson. Reprinted courtesy of Grosset & Dunlap, a division of Penguin Young Readers Group.

Becoming a picture book author

Although word count is a wild card, some picture books, like Monique Felix's *Story of the Little Mouse Trapped in a Book* (Simon & Schuster Children's Publishing) have no words, and some are packed with words from the top of a page to the bottom, page after page. So we can give you a good rule: Less is more. The best picture books are those whose spare, well-chosen text and well-structured stories complement the illustrations, with no fat left over.

As we mentioned before, topics for picture books are nearly infinite, with the caveat that the subject matter must be appropriate for children in the age range of 3 to 8 years old. Some picture books may be more juvenile, others for more mature readers within the range.

To break into the picture book market, you have to write a stellar story. You need to master the elements of writing in Part III, and when you're done, make sure your picture book

- ✔ Captures the essence of your story in no more than 1,500 words.

- ✔ Makes every word work really hard, eliminating all descriptive baggage and every unnecessary word.

- ✔ Replaces ordinary words with richer, more evocative ones where possible without getting wordy or too adult.

- ✔ Has a strong, multidimensional main character that a child can relate to.

- ✔ Takes your main character through a satisfying story arc including a beginning (sets the stage), a middle (crisis), and an end (resolution).

- ✔ Conveys concrete visual imagery in a series of action and dialogue throughout — that move the plot ahead.

Other books with pictures

Although picture books and board books seem to dominate the field in illustrated books, that perception is not accurate. There are other major players in the category — coloring and activity books, coloring books, activity and how-to books, novelty books, and graphic novels — one of which, coloring and activity (also known as *C&A*) probably outsells all the others combined in terms of units sold.

Coloring, activity, and how-to

With pictures to color and lots of activities, from mazes, dot-to-dots, hidden pictures, word scrambles, crossword puzzles, coloring and activity books offer kids fun — plain and simple. And some activity books are educational, as shown in Figure 2-5. Although the sky is truly the limit when it comes to making a great coloring, activity, or how-to book, we do know some of the usual winning topics in such books:

- Have a well-known main character or set of characters hosting the book's content (this can be as simple as having a known or licensed character on the cover).

- Stick to one set of activities; for example, all games (word games, dot-to-dots, word searches, word scrambles, mazes, and the like) or all coloring or all preschool learning but not a mishmash of everything.

- Do not try to be storybooks.

- Keep it simple and age-appropriate.

Figure 2-5:
Cool Yule! A Creative and Crafty Christmas! and *Happening Hanukkah: Creative Ways to Celebrate.*

By Debra Mostow Zakarin, Illustrated by Debra Ziss. Reprinted courtesy of Grosset & Dunlap, a division of Penguin Young Readers Group.

The cool thing about coloring and activity books on the market today is that they often come with innumerable and novel extras such as punch-outs, stickers, crayons, paints, glow-in-the-dark markers — you name it. These extras actually cross-classify these C&A books as novelty books, which we talk about in the next section.

Mad Libs (those great fill-in-the-word-blank games published by Price Stern Sloan) are fabulous for good, clean fun at sleepovers. Almost any arts and crafts book by Klutz (Klutz Press) keeps kids busy for hours. Dozens and dozens of choices are on the Klutz rack, including *Braids & Bows,* and *Glove Compartment Science: Experiments, Tricks, and Observations for the Backseat Scientist.* (Consider getting one of these books for yourself on a road trip to drown out the cries of "Are we there yet?" and "He touched me!") Any activity you can think of — mazes, card games, chess — that kids enjoy spending time doing or creating can be made into an activity or how-to book.

Traditional C & A book authors are often in-house editors at publishing houses or established writers with specific educational experience, firmly rooted in the publisher's stable of workhorse writers. Very rarely do new authors break into this work. Another bummer: This writing is often *uncredited* work; that is, you won't get to see your name on the cover.

Novelty books

A *novelty book* is one that goes beyond just words and pictures on flat pages. It is often three-dimensional and always *interactive* (interactive here meaning that the child must engage more than just his eyes in the experience). From pop-ups to pull-tabs, from juggling balls to paper dolls, innovative novelty books can really engage the imagination. (See Figures 2-6 and 2-7 for examples.) When any type of children's book has something besides just flat paper and images in it, it moves into the novelty category.

"Wow me, please!" says editor Erin E. Molta

Erin E. Molta is an editor who handles mostly novelty books at one of the biggest children's publishing houses. Read on to discover what she looks for in novelty book submissions.

WCBFD: What formats, aimed at the youngest readers, sell the most year after year?

EEM: It's not so much the format but the author. Straight board books by Sandra Boynton sell continually, lift-the-flap board books by Karen Katz, as do classic board books reprinted from best-selling picture books, such as Eric Carle's *Papa, Please Get the Moon for Me* (Little Simon).

WCBFD: What are your favorite formats for the youngest readers to develop new writers into and why?

EEM: Again, the manuscript dictates a format, though we have certain formats that we consistently publish — mostly holiday or seasonal titles, like Sparkle N Twinkle or Sparkle N Shimmer series. They are holiday based and have glitter and/or sequins on each spread.

WCBFD: What formats for the youngest readers are you always looking for new ideas for?

EEM: The buzzwords these days are *new* and *innovative*. Everybody wants something different. So it can't just be a flap book, it must be a flap book with touch-and-feel or sound or pop-ups and foil, glitter, acetate — and it has to be able to be produced really inexpensively, too!

WCBFD: What are the most common pitfalls occurring to new writers who submit to you and in what formats do those pitfalls seem to occur most?

EEM: Everybody thinks they can write for children. It's easy, right? But most people are writing as an adult to a child rather than for — or with — a child. Kids want the text to be on their level. It doesn't mean it has to be childish — just child-appealing and childlike.

WCBFD: What formats seem to be up-and-coming for 2005 and beyond?

EEM: New and innovative! The key to a successful format for the youngest reader is how it is integral to the text and art. If you have flaps in a book but there's no incentive to lift them and once you do, you don't care, then that is a bad use of the flap as a technique to further the story and enhance the reading experience. I'm looking for truly interactive books, where a child can spin a wheel to find an answer or press a button, or something pops up to stimulate understanding.

WCBFD: What do you look for in a submission that would make you immediately excited?

EEM: New and innovative! I'm looking for the perfect integration of an interactive element and lively text. Say you have animals and it's counting and the animals are night creatures — rather than on the farm (I'm sick of farm animal books). Or you're doing a book on colors, but it's in outer space. There are zillions of books about colors, shapes, counting, and opposites but something out of the ordinary sparks my interest!

WCBFD: What would make you reject a submission almost immediately?

EEM: Tell me you read it to your students, grand-kids, or even your very own children and they loved it. Of course they did! Would any kid say they didn't? Poor spelling doesn't help either, nor do farm animals.

WCBFD: How do new formats get developed? Do most of your ideas for new formats come from submissions, in-house, packagers, or combinations? Tell me how the process works for you.

EEM: We get ideas for new formats from brainstorming in-house or from packagers. I usually will come up with a format and see if I have a manuscript that fits *or* I get a manuscript and try to come up with a format that will make it stand out on the bookstore shelves! It's very much a collaborative process — taking a little bit of what's been done and tweaking it to make it new and innovative!

Graphic novels

Graphic novels are books with lots of pictures *and* words aimed at older readers. Graphic novels are aimed at middle-graders (ages 7 to 10), tweens (children who are between being children and being teenagers, usually 9 to 12), young adult readers (12 and up), and even adults. They all have graphics, which can come in the form of black and white illustrations, color illustrations, or captured video/TV/movie photos on almost every page. Most often, the illustrations look more comic-book-like than full-page picture book illustrations.

In graphic novels, the text does not appear in freestanding blocks but in dialogue bubbles or with a line around it, like in comic books, near the relevant image. They often come in what is called *digest sized* (5½ inches wide × 8½ inches high — about the size of a piece of paper folded in half) or slightly smaller at 6⅗ × 4⅖ — as well as bigger and smaller. Becoming a graphic novel writer generally requires the ability to illustrate in the style of graphic novels or comics. Another option is to pair up with someone who has that talent. We discuss more about illustrating your work in Chapter 14.

Graphic novels today are very different from their comic book ancestors and are not simply just collections of comics. Graphic novels tell more complex, sophisticated, and lengthy stories than comics do and they often have more realistic subject matter than traditional comic books.

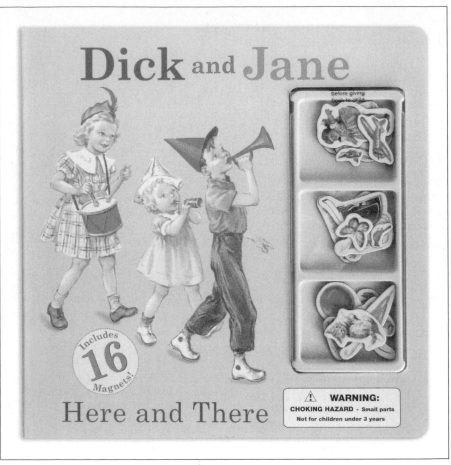

Figure 2-6:
Dick and Jane: Here and There.

Many hugely talented writer/illustrators are making their mark in graphic novels, best known to non-aficionados as the heavily illustrated format made famous by Art Spiegelman, creator of the Pulitzer-Prize winning *Maus* (Pantheon). As Spiegelman did, some new graphic novel creators are using the format for overt or sly political, social, and cultural commentary. For younger readers, Dav Pilkey's *The Adventures of Super Diaper Baby: The First Graphic Novel* (Blue Sky Press/Scholastic, Inc.) is a stellar entry for middle-graders.

From the stories by A. A. Milne with illustrations by Andrew Grey. Reprinted courtesy of Dutton Children's Books, a division of Penguin Young Readers Group.

Figure 2-7:
The Magical Pop-Up World of Winnie-the-Pooh (back cover photo).

Books with Lots of Words

In this section, we take a look at books that focus more on telling a story through words. This category includes early readers, first chapter books, middle-grade books, and young adult (YA) books.

Early readers

Early readers (see Figure 2-8) are developed for children who are first learning their letters or perhaps even sounding out their first words. Experts in reading, teaching, learning, or curricula create particular programs around the theory of reading that the publisher has chosen to embrace, often a phonics-based or whole-language-based theory (depending on what is most in fashion at the moment).

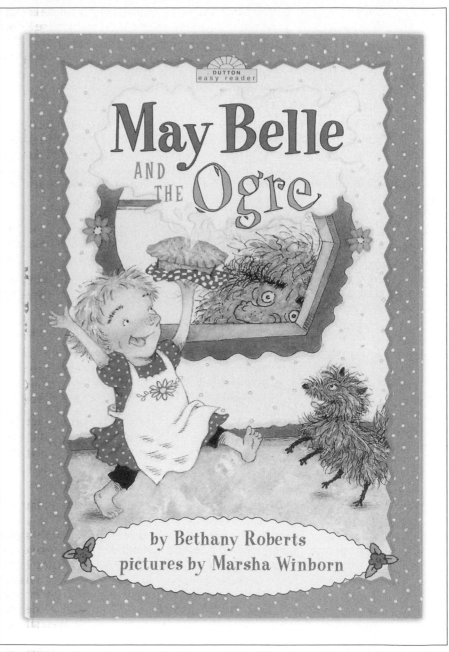

Figure 2-8:
May Belle and the Ogre.

By Bethany Roberts, pictures by Marsha Winborn. Reprinted courtesy of Dutton Children's Books, a division of Penguin Young Readers Group.

Developing an early reader program in a publishing house includes creating vocabulary lists and deciding on parameters for story development and illustration, page counts, and more — all designed to make the child's first reading experiences satisfying and logically progressive, and to encourage more reading.

Early reader basics and age levels

With anywhere from 10 pages to 64 pages, the amount of information and the word count varies greatly, but one thing normally stays the same: the size. Most early reader books come sized at 6 inches × 9 inches. Early reader books (also known as *leveled readers* or *easy-to-reads*) are best for kids between the ages of 5 and 9, though they are divided into five levels, depending on the reading level of each child.

- ✓ **Level 1:** For readers who are just getting started, who know the alphabet, and are excited about reading their first books. Sometimes labeled for ages 3 to 6.

- ✓ **Level 2:** For readers who can recognize and sound out certain words but who may still need help with more complex words. Often labeled for ages 4 to 6.

- ✓ **Level 3:** For readers who are ready to tackle easy stories all by themselves. For kindergarten through third graders.

- ✓ **Level 4:** Many programs introduce chapter breaks here for children who are ready to jump into "bigger kid" books but are not yet ready for middle-grade topics or length. For second and third graders.

- ✓ **Level 5:** If the program goes this far, these books are actual chapter books. Not unusual to find third and fourth graders still reading these. with a few black-and-white illustrations scattered throughout.

Knowing how to write early readers

It's no easy task to turn word lists into fascinating stories. Indeed, writing truly good leveled readers requires a talent for minimalism, perfect word choice, a well-honed sense of whimsy and fun, and an understanding of how to keep plot, pacing, and character development on the move with the turn of each page. We go more into the latter elements of writing in Part III, but we maintain that to be able to write well in this format, you have to research the style, tone, and contents of each publisher's early reader series and then practice until you get better at it. Most publishers offer guidelines for submission into their programs that you can access on their Web sites.

Leveled readers can be fiction or nonfiction and cover topics that are often found in the curriculum taught in school for particular age ranges. As nationwide testing in reading comprehension and reading skills starting at the earliest grades becomes more prevalent, we expect even more curriculum-based reading programs to surface, supplementing what teachers are presenting in the classrooms.

First chapter books

A first chapter book is often a child's first real foray into reading books without full-color illustrations. It's often a very exciting time in a child's life when they get to go the section in the bookstore or library that houses the big-girl and big-boy books. The subject matter is more mature, and the stories in first chapter books are more complex — as are the characters and their relationships with one another. Most, if they are illustrated at all, contain a few black and white images scattered randomly throughout. The plots are more complicated, and the pacing is maintained much more directly through story developments and conflict more than through illustration or subtle suggestion. Some popular first chapter book series include *The Magic Tree House* by Mary Pope Osborne (Random House) and Paula Danziger's *Amber Brown* series (Penguin Books).

The basics on first chapter books

As a child moves from Level 5 early readers to first chapter books, the books are longer, the illustrations switch from color to black and white, and the stories and vocabulary generally progress in complexity. These books are generally for kids in the 7 to 10 age range. With approximately 128 pages, first chapter books come in hardcover or softcover digest size which is usually around 5½ × 8½ inches.

Writing first chapter books

As with any other format, writing good first chapter books requires skill, and practice helps you develop that skill. First you must read, read, read examples of the format to get a feel for the ways in which the characters are developed, the story is created and fleshed out, the plot is kept progressing, and the pacing and interest are maintained at steady levels. You need to have an appreciation for children in the target age group of 7 to 10 years old (what they like, what they don't like, what they glom onto and what they are likely to reject) — we discuss how to figure out some of that in Chapter 6. When researching first chapter books, you will notice that they mostly contain about 10 or 11 chapters of about 8 to 10 pages each.

Middle-grade books

Middle-grade fiction and nonfiction books (such as the example in Figure 2-9) are what many people remember reading from our childhoods. These are the first books we read that were long and detailed and complex and that dealt with subject matter that was much more intriguing and issues that were potentially much more divisive than the children's picture books. Some classic middle-grade books include *Stuart Little* and *Charlotte's Web* both by

E. B. White (both HarperTrophy), *The Secret Garden* by Frances Hodgson Burnett (HarperTrophy), *James and the Giant Peach* by Roald Dahl (Knopf Books), and *The Phantom Tollbooth* by Norton Juster (Yearling).

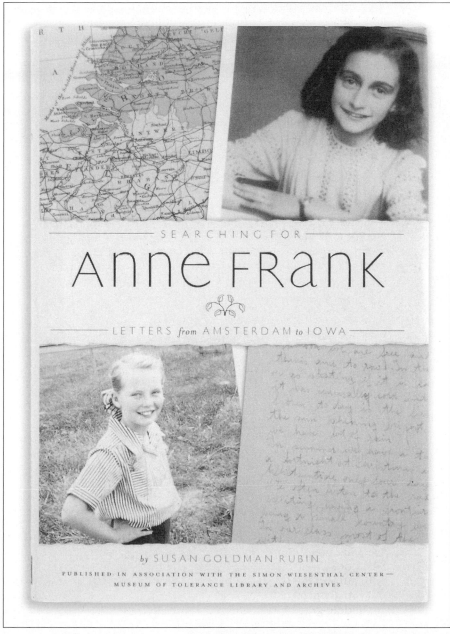

Figure 2-9:
Searching for Anne Frank: Letters from Amsterdam to Iowa.

By Susan Goldman Rubin (Harry N. Abrams, 2003). Reprinted courtesy of the author.

Consider some of the issues covered in these classics: In *Charlotte's Web*, Wilbur, the main character, is a runt of a pig who is about to be killed before the farmer's daughter saves him; not lost or hidden or given away, but *killed!* This is big-kid stuff. Then think about the word play and complex relationships found in *The Phantom Tollbooth*. *The Secret Garden* delves into death and sickness (physical and emotional), not to mention social class discrepancies between the pampered, high-class protagonist and the maid's brother. Middle-grade books are often a child's first peek into the real world, where people die, are irredeemably bad, have to solve real problems, and often fail — even at the end of the book.

Getting down to the middle-grade basics

With anywhere from 96 to 156 pages typically, middle-grade books are written for 8 to 12 year olds and they normally come in the small $5\frac{1}{2} \times 8\frac{1}{2}$ size. They can be hardcover or softcover, and the classics often exceed 156 pages. Many are developed into series, such as the *Series of Unfortunate Events* series by Lemony Snicket (HarperCollins), but just as many are *one-offs* (meaning they are never developed into series, but stand alone).

Writing for the middle-grades

You can't rely on lots of photographs or illustrations to help tell your story here. The distinguishing factor that most children become aware of as they master this format is that these books have few or no interior illustrations. If illustrations are included at all, they're often limited to black-and-white sketches at chapter breaks.

Gary Paulsen is a good example of the fluidity of age levels and labeling. While many bookstores categorize his fiction in the young adult section of the store, you are just as likely to find his books shelved with the middle-grade books. So which format are his books? Young adult novels or middle-grade fiction? Up for grabs.

Want to break into writing for this age group? What makes good middle-grade fiction good also makes YA novels good — and also makes grown-up books good:

- ✔ Strong, interesting, uniquely drawn characters who have a problem and try to solve it
- ✔ Stories that grab you from the get-go and don't let you go till you've turned the last page
- ✔ Writing that uses language to paint pictures in the mind — writing with style and voice (which we delve into in detail in Part III)
- ✔ A unique voice that stands out

✔ A clear grasp of the audience and their concerns (older tweens and teenagers are serious about their lives and problems and issues, and people who write for them have to treat the subject matter seriously)

✔ An ability to go back into space and time and put yourself into the shoes of a protagonist of that age without ever sounding like an adult or a younger child — a balancing act of the highest order

You may start to notice that many of the skills required to break into children's book writing for any format or age group are starting to sound alike. And you would be right on target. As we discuss in Part III, the basic elements of good writing are the same for any format. Although the subject matter, topics, complexity, vocabulary, images, and other parts of the content change from format to format and age level to age level, the skills you need to develop are basically the same. Good writing is good writing.

Young adult books

Young adult (or YA) books are just what they sound like: books aimed at readers in their middle to later teens. And although it used to be a common belief that young adults only read teen magazines and grown-up novels, bookstores are now creating separate sections devoted to material they believe addresses the issues, concerns, and interests of young adults.

It's not that there were never young adult sections in bookstores and libraries. There were. But they were usually mixed right in with the board and picture books — the "baby" books. Now these venues often physically separate out the books and the space to give teens their own hangouts. See Figures 2-10 and 2-11 for examples of YA novels.

Some classic young adult titles include *Go Ask Alice* by the no-longer-anonymous Beatrice Sparks (Simon Pulse), Brian Jacques's *Redwall* series (Philomel Books), *Catcher in the Rye* by J. D. Salinger (Little, Brown), Francesca Lia Block's *Weetzie Bat* books (HarperTrophy), *The Chocolate War* by Robert Cormier (Laurel Leaf), *Speak* by Laurie Halse Anderson (Penguin), *The Hobbit* by J. R. R. Tolkien, *King of the Mild Frontier* by Chris Crutcher (Greenwillow), and *Forever* by Judy Blume (Atheneum).

Young adult basics

Young adult books are for those 12- to 18-year-olds who want to read novels about issues they face everyday or fantasies they wish they did. With anywhere from 128 to 300 pages, these books come in sizes ranging from 4¼ × 6¾ (also known as mass market or rack-sized books — you know, the fat paperback size that only used to be sold at supermarkets and drug stores) or 6¼ × 9¼ tall (about the same size as standard grown-up hardcovers).

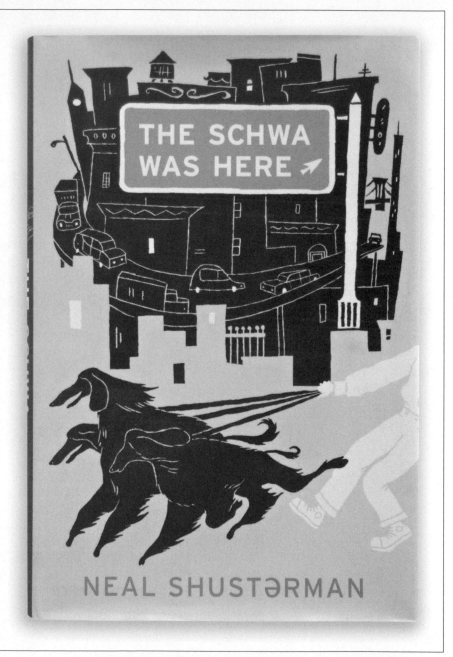

By Neal Schusterman. Reprinted courtesy of Dutton Children's Books, a division of Penguin Young Readers Group.

Figure 2-10:
The Schwa Was Here.

Figure 2-11:
Guitar Girl.

By Sarra Manning. Reprinted courtesy of Dutton Children's Books, a division of Penguin Young Readers Group.

Young adult books are often cross-shelved with grown-ups' books, and sometimes the only distinction between the two is that the protagonists of young adult novels are usually teenagers. The issues confronted in YA novels are often of a complex, politically marginalized, or incendiary nature (gay teenagers, straight teens in gay-parent families, cross-gendered teenagers, pregnant teens considering their options, teens experimenting with drugs and not completely messing up their lives or dying because of it, teens falling in love with older adults and acting on it, and the like). The protagonists are not always winners at the end, and are most often, if they are human, buried in drama and trauma. If they are not human, their issues often parallel those of human teenagers: trying to fit in, making a difference, finding love, scouting out acceptance, breaking out of their parentally imposed limitations, seeking independence, proving their worth, and so on. With few exceptions today, the protagonists of YA novels have lost their innocence, but that does not mean they have lost hope or strength or their ability to imagine a better life, a better self, a better world. One thing's for sure — nothing is boring in the good YA novels today.

Some YA books are considered *crossovers,* meaning that they can serve as both a young adult book and a contemporary adult book. An example of a crossover title is Carl Hiaasen's Newbery Honor-winning *Hoot* (Knopf), which, though designed as a young adult novel, is also found in the adult section with his other books. (More on children's book awards in Chapter 3.)

Writing young adult books

Young adult books are filled mostly with words and rarely have any illustrations. So if you're hankering to break into the young adult field, you have to be ready to write well and to do it for 200 pages or more. Again, the criteria are similar to those required for writing good middle-grade fare, repeated here with some real differences noted:

- Strong, interesting, uniquely drawn characters who have a problem — only they might not try very hard to solve it, in fact they might wallow in it for awhile

- Stories that grab you from the get-go and don't let you go till you've turned the last page — and how!

- Writing that uses language to paint pictures in the mind and writing with style and voice (which we delve into in detail in Part III)

- A unique voice that stands out — some might argue this is the most important element of good YA fiction

- A clear grasp of the audience and their concerns (teenagers are serious about their lives and problems and issues, and people who write for them have to treat the subject matter seriously) — the tweens have been kicked out of the target audience in YA novels except as pesky siblings and the like

✔ An ability to go back into space and time and put yourself into the shoes of a protagonist of that age without ever sounding like an adult or a child — the balancing act of the highest order still holds here, perhaps even more than with middle-grade fiction

✔ An understanding of contemporary issues and pop culture and its effect on teens (this does not mean that we are recommending you use slang or wear pants with the waist hanging down to your knees for you to be able to nail a character, but you should be at least a little bit hip to what its like to be a teen today)

Dr. Donald Freeman, an aspiring YA writer, actually took our advice and sat down to read a dozen successful YA novels; he came up the following list of similarities in most of them:

✔ Word counts generally fall between 50,000 and 70,000 words.

✔ The main protagonist is in every scene, with limited point of view (see Chapter 11), whether the story is told in the first or third person.

✔ He or she is already between 10 and 16 years of age at the beginning of the story, and anything that happened before is revealed either in flashback or dialogue.

✔ The story begins at a moment of crisis.

✔ The protagonist's repeated efforts to rectify matters tend to backfire, but can also lead to unexpected benefits: new friendships, improved self-awareness, and so on.

✔ The hero or heroine finds him- or herself in contention with an initially intimidating and harsh-seeming older adult, yet their relationship ends up being positive and rewarding.

✔ The parent figures are either ineffectual and in need of help themselves, or else they are entirely out of the picture.

✔ There are no *deus ex machina* (convenient, fairy godmother-like) or Horatio Alger (Pollyanna-ish) resolutions; rather, success ultimately crowns the protagonist's often bumbling and misguided efforts as helped along by others such as buddies or the adult (non-parent) figure.

✔ Overt sex is usually avoided.

✔ The protagonist is bright and energetic, but is initially hampered by lack of sophistication.

✔ Belonging (literal or figurative) and the quest to attain belonging are all-important and often define the theme.

✔ Much of the action involves a quest (or at least a lot of moving around).

✔ Both adults and peers experience a mixture of charm and alienation over the protagonist's "differentness," and it is his or her main developmental task to become socially effective without sacrifice of essential individuality.

Not every single one of these applies to any single YA book, but it is surely a good list of attributes to aspire to in your writing.

Genres for Different Readers

In this section, we take a look at some of the most common *genres* of children's books — that is, the general nature of major children's book categories. Then, if there is a distinctive style, form, or content that comprises the very nature of certain genres, we talk about those, too. Next we dip into the series pool, where single characters can take off into multi-book adventures.

Conventions of a genre are customs or rules widely accepted because they've been in use that way for a long time. Basically, conventions are expectations a reader has for a genre because that's what he's used to reading; for example, it is a widely accepted convention that a book that falls into the mystery genre will have a problem that has to be solved, and a solution that is not readily apparent right off the bat, requiring discovery by the protagonist. Sometimes you will want to stick to those conventions, and sometimes you will want to veer away from them to make your story more interesting. Either way, it helps to know what genres are out there.

Most children's writing is divided into two main categories: Fiction and non-fiction. *Fiction* is writing based on made-up characters in a real-world setting, and it's a big plate that other derivative (and delicious!) morsels may fall on. *Nonfiction* is writing based on real facts, people, places, or events — see Figure 2-12.

If you aren't writing plays, poetry, or nonfiction, chances are you're writing fiction.

Under these two larger categories of fiction and nonfiction fall most of the other genres of children's books. Genres are like big buckets into which a bunch of books that are written with certain similar conventions are thrown. For example, mystery fiction is a genre, as is action/adventure. We are going to take a look at a lot of genres in the following sections.

By Susan Goldman Rubin (Crown, 2004). Reprinted courtesy of the author.

Figure 2-12:
*Art Against
the Odds:
From Slave
Quilts to
Prison
Paintings.*

Science fiction

Writers of *science fiction* can manipulate settings to fit narratives or make up
out-of-this-world settings altogether. Sci-fi writers rely on the utter *suspension
of disbelief,* which is a fancy way of saying that you gotta believe what you
read no matter how implausible it may seem. If the writer of science fiction
does his job, he sets up the story and characters in such a way that he seems

to be describing something that can occur in the not-so-distant future because it's based on things that already exist today. Science fiction takes existing scientific principles and theories and uses them in the plot. It's meant to be understood literally, not metaphorically, and its characters ought to be believable even if the setting isn't.

Subgenres of sci-fi include apocalypse, space travel, utopia/dystopia, and messianic works. One of Peter's favorite books when he was in first grade (although it's hard to find today) was Louis Slobodkin's *The Space Ship Under the Apple Tree* (MacMillan). Current popular sci-fi titles include the upper-middle-grade (nearly YA) books *The House of the Scorpion* (Atheneum) by Nancy Farmer, *Ender's Game* by Orson Scott Card (Tom Doherty Associates), and Madeleine L'Engle's *A Wrinkle in Time* (Yearling).

Fantasy

Like science fiction writers, authors of *fantasy* can manipulate settings to fit their narratives, and they, too, rely on the utter suspension of disbelief. Although often grouped with science fiction, fantasy is truly a different genre. Fantasy relies on the notion that real people in real settings can encounter magical things and can often perform magic. In other words, some people have special powers, while others don't. It can also involve mythical creatures such as fairies and unicorns, as well as talking animals that may or may not interact with humans.

Fantasy and science fiction can also be combined. This is especially popular for middle-grade and young adult readers. One example would be Philip Pullman's *His Dark Materials* series (Laurel Leaf). It has technological aspects to the plot as well as fantasy-type characters. Subgenres of fantasy include King Arthur tales and sword-and-sorcery tales.

Great examples of classic contemporary children's fantasy include Roald Dahl's *Charlie and the Chocolate Factory* and *Matilda* (Viking Books) and, of course, J. K. Rowling's *Harry Potter* series (Arthur A. Levine Books).

Related to fantasy is the rich array of fairy tales, fables, folktales, myths, and legends. What they all have in common is that they come from old traditions of storytelling that can be traced to particular countries of origin; a few of the originating sources that are mined again and again include the Brothers Grimm, Charles Perrault, Hans Christian Andersen, Aesop, Russian folk tales, and Greek mythology. In fact, nearly every culture has a storytelling tradition that can be researched for material. These stories inspire writers every year to try to improve upon or change them in some unique way, writing that is referred to as *adaptation*.

Horror and ghost stories

Horror stories and *ghost stories* are the creepy, goose bump-inducing stories that make you leave the flashlight on under your sheets — even when you're done reading.

Good ghost stories always suck you in because they are grounded in reality. After you really fall for the characters and the setting (as if the story were about the family next door), the plot springs something otherworldly on you. Neil Gaiman's *Coraline* (HarperCollins) is an example of good writing in the genre. To break into writing horror you need to demonstrate an appreciation for otherworldy content and hold-your-breath pacing — and you need to stick to formats for middle-graders and older.

Action/adventure

Often targeted to boys with very stylized, masculine covers, *action/adventure* focuses on young boys and girls who combat nature, industry, bad adults, and other evils. You usually find action/adventure stories in early readers, middle-grade books, young adult books, and graphic novels.

The best action/adventure stories are characterized by engaging, well-thought-out plots and a main character who is smart, self-reliant, and cunning. They have true a true danger element and often take place in territory unfamiliar to the reader. Gary Paulsen is a master of the genre and books of his such as *Hatchet* (Atheneum) and *The River* (Delacorte) are great examples.

Subgenres of action/adventure include thrillers and espionage (usually involving a spy who must protect her imperiled country, school, or family against an enemy), mysteries, crime-solving stories, and detective novels. And though lots of younger children's books have action and adventure in them, this genre is usually found in chapter books, middle-grade fiction, and YA fiction.

Historical fiction

Who needs to look further than one's own history to find exciting stories of heroes and heroines from all over the globe? Based on real events or on real people in history, *historical fiction* offers the best of both worlds if written well: exciting stories and stealthy learning. *My America* (Scholastic) is a successful middle-grade series in this category. These books do well because they are well-written and because teachers, parents, and children support the subject matter they cover. Historical fiction works well with picture books, chapter books, middle-grade, and YA.

To write good historical fiction it's important to keep in mind that the time and place provide the setting for the story, but the plot and characters are still the most important elements. Don't let the setting or time period take center stage. And remember that the characters live in this time, so they wouldn't remark upon how different it is from our time period, or even notice what we'd consider strange or different.

Biography

Biographies are told in the third person and involve a lot of research. Biographies of historical, cultural, and scientific figures past and present can be very literary, whereas biographies of current hipsters and celebrities tend to read like *Teen People* magazine — and both have their readership. The subjects of biographies for children in the past were usually historical figures taught as part of the school curricula. Today, anyone who has made a mark on history — even entertainment and sports figures — may merit a biography.

The best biographies always reveal the most about the central figure's character and include enough details and tidbits about the character's personal life to make the reader feel as if he is getting a realistic and comprehensive look at another person's life. Popular literary picture book biographies include Mordicai Gerstein's *The Man Who Walked Between the Towers* (Roaring Brook), *Snowflake Bentley* by Jacqueline Briggs Martin (Houghton Mifflin), and Kristin Armstrong's *Lance Armstrong: The Race of His Life* (Grosset & Dunlap).

Learning/educational

The most skilled writers disguise learning in the most elegant manner so that the reader doesn't even know she's learning. As a genre, you mostly find *learning/educational* in board books, picture books, early readers, C & A books, how-to-books, activity books, and middle-grade nonfiction.

David Macaulay's *The New Way Things Work* (Houghton Mifflin) is a best-selling example of a children's learning/educational book that's so well-written adults were grabbing it out of their children's hands and hiding in the other room to read it in peace.

Workbooks, subject-based readers, leveled readers, and supplementary school materials fill up stacks and stacks of shelves in most chain bookstores, so if you have an educational or teaching background, you can likely find work writing for children. *Historical-figure biographies, activity,* and *how-to* all fall into this genre. Issue-based books on puberty, sex, divorce, race, adoption, understanding gays/lesbians, and all the hot-button issues of the day for children and teens generally are included as well, though a lot of fiction also covers these topics.

American Girls Publications has a few great entries in this category, such as *The Care & Keeping of You: The Body Book for Girls* by Valorie Lee Schaefer and *Help! The Absolutely Indispensable Guide to Life for Girls* by Nancy Holyoke (both Pleasant Company Publications). Or try *From Boys to Men: All About Adolescence and You* by Michael Gurian and Brian Floca (Price Stern Sloan). Often, when elections come around, publishers try to get children involved in the process with books such as *Take a Stand: Everything You Never Wanted to Know About Government* by Daniel Weizmann (Price Stern Sloan), which a lot of teachers buy (as do parents who forget the difference between the Senate and the House of Representatives).

Religion and diversity

Religion as a genre includes stories related to the Bible, biblical characters, Christianity, Judaism, Islam, Buddhism, and any other religious affiliation and its attendant holidays, characters, or tenets. This genre permeates nearly every format of books — from board books to Bible story compilations for the middle grades. Diversity and multiculturalism are also big topics in schools found in this genre, so titles that focus on these issues are often found in this section in the bookstore. Books such as Charles Schultz's *Charlie Brown Christmas* (Little Simon) and Maria Shriver's *What's Heaven?* (Golden Books) fall into this genre.

The potential problem with poetry

It is a well-accepted truism that most children's book editors feel pretty strongly about rhymed text. From those that despise it or merely tolerate it to those who adore it, editors are pretty picky about rhyme. Why? Because, authors often sacrifice the story for the sake of the rhyme. They skimp on plot and character development and throw in extra words just to make the rhyme work. The story should come first; the rhyme secondary. A good rhyming story will often sell, but it has to be written as tightly as a story in prose.

If you are going to write poetry, take it from us: Dr. Seuss did a fabulous job with the particular rhyme schemes he used in his books, and he continues to sell tens of thousands of books a year despite not being among the living anymore. But if you want to rhyme, don't use Seussian meter, make up your own.

It's all about the homework: A president describes a writing pro

If you want to know what it takes to stand out, listen to Doug Whiteman, President of Penguin Books for Young Readers. Having been in the publishing business for two decades, Doug started out as a book sales rep and worked his way to the top. He's a publishing exec who still loves reading as much as he did when he first came to the company so many years ago.

WCBFD: Since we're talking about genres and series for children in this chapter, can you tell us how important you think it is that a writer understands the conventions of a children's book genre and that she sticks to what the readers expect?

DW: That's a really good question, because we have different filters that we're selling to, each of whom has its own expectations. Our accounts and their buyers certainly expect things to fit into traditional molds, as do many parents, and many times I've seen books stopped cold if they couldn't be easily classified in a traditional way. Having said that, kids themselves are looking for the truly unique and original. So, the best answer to your question is, understand the conventions and know that we will have to package and position your book in a relatively traditional way in order to get past the filters, but give us some sneaky originality inside the covers so that the kids are captivated.

WCBFD: As one of the largest publishing companies, with lots of different divisions that publish different kinds of books, what kinds of books are always hot?

DW: It seems to me that we're becoming increasingly cyclical, so there's very little that's *always* hot. Picture books, for example, seem to go into downturns every ten years or so, and we're in a downturn now. Series books are extremely cyclical. And nothing is more cyclical than licensed publishing, which goes up and down like a roller coaster every few years. Probably the steadiest category is fantasy; everyone likes to think that *Harry Potter* has "made" fantasy into a bestselling genre, but the truth is that people like Philip Pullman and Brian Jacques were selling huge numbers long before J. K. Rowling came along.

WCBFD: What kinds of books are most always *not* hot?

DW: Picture books with long texts, expensive books based on holidays that can't command high price points (like Halloween), and books that have depressing endings! I can't think of a genre, though, that's never hot.

WCBFD: What turns a one-off children's book title into a contender for a series?

DW: A wonderful character (or characters). People can enjoy a great book that doesn't have an impactful, memorable character, but a great character can supersede an otherwise mediocre book, leaving your readers clamoring for more.

WCBFD: If you could project into the next decade, what genre of books could you see being most successful?

DW: For one thing, I think picture books are going to bounce back pretty aggressively in 2006, based on the demographic studies and budgetary projections I've seen. More specific to subject matter, I see people increasingly looking for true "escapist" fiction, so I'm putting my money on fantasy, futuristic books, and books that have a lot of humor.

WCBFD: Any advice for new writers?

DW: Just what I've said already: Do your homework, and *listen!*

Girl-oriented series books

The Baby-Sitter's Club (Scholastic) is probably one of the most famous series of girl-oriented titles. The Olsen Twins, Mary-Kate and Ashley, have more than one series to their names, and the list continues to grow with books focusing on what's still considered traditional "girly" fare, such as horses, ice skating, romance, and the like. Some famous middle-grade girl-oriented series include *Trixie Belden* (Random House), *Nancy Drew* (Putnam) (and the old classic middle-grade series aimed specifically at boys, *The Hardy Boys* [Putnam]), *Lizzie McGuire* (Disney Press), *Pony Pals* (Scholastic), *W.I.T.C.H.* and *From the Files of Madison Finn* (both Volo), the *Little House on the Prairie* (HarperCollins) books — all fiction — and *American Girl* (Pleasant Company Publications) which includes fiction and nonfiction series. A classic in the young adult series category is Louisa May Alcott's *Little Women* (Signet Classics).

Though girl-oriented fiction is an actual category, boy-oriented fiction does not seem to be. At least not in the bookstores. We attribute this to the old and very worn (not to mention outdated!) adage that boys won't read books with girl protagonists but girls will read anything. We doubt this is true anymore (if it ever was true), but we suppose that perception is everything because you won't see a boys' fiction section in many bookstores, but you can often find a girl's fiction one. Really!

Licensed character series books

Licensed character series start out life basically in one of two ways: as characters in books, or as characters in products, TV, or other media. Then when they become popular, they are licensed (loaned out for a price) into other media and products.

Publishers are almost always the people who assign TV and movie-based books to writers, so chances are that unless you're the best friend of one of the stars or are tied to the original movie or TV show, you won't be writing a movie or TV tie-in.

Chapter 3

Understanding the Children's Book Market

*Y*ou may think that a writer of children's books would be writing solely for children. However, the children's book universe is populated by all sorts of grown-ups who essentially serve as gatekeepers, judging your book at each stage of the publications process, determining whether your book passes muster and may be allowed to proceed on to the next step, or whether it sits waiting by the portals.

The chain of book business professionals whom you have to impress before even one child will see your book looks more or less like this:

Agent → Editor → Marketing Pro → Sales Rep → Bookseller or Librarian or Teacher → Parent → Child

You can read about how to impress your agent in Chapter 16, and the editor, marketing pro, and sales rep are all discussed in Chapter 18. But the booksellers, librarians, teachers, and parents are different beasts altogether — and important beasts at that. So how do you get your book to speak to them, so ultimately it can end up grasped tightly between two little-kid hands?

In this chapter, we explore the gatekeepers your book must first pass: booksellers, librarians, teachers, and parents. Then we take a look at your target audience: children, and we look at what kids like, what they don't like, and how you can tap into the latest trends and maybe even write the book that rocks the ages.

Of the many grown-ups who stand between you and your audience (children), booksellers, parents, teachers, and librarians are the most powerful. All of the children without pocket change or an allowance of their own will be out of your reach if you can't get these adults on your side. So how do you ingratiate yourself with them?

Book Buyers

In a retail store, the *book buyers* are the people who sit down with the sales representatives from the publishing companies and decide which books they are going to take, for which stores, and in what quantities.

Large chains, such as Barnes & Noble, may employ an entire department of buyers. Or, at the other end of the spectrum, a buyer may be the owner of an independent bookstore with only one or two locations.

The requirements of each of these buyers may be quite different from one another, and publishers must adjust their selling approaches to the buyers' unique needs. For example, an independent bookstore buyer may have the time to look a little more carefully at each book in detail. They want to see bright illustrations and little text for board books. Other buyers may want more early readers, for children ages five to seven, that have different and interesting stories from what's already been written. One buyer may be on the lookout for middle-grade fiction books that target little boys, because there are so few out there, and another book buyer may insist that the book must be a good read and age-appropriate, and beyond that nothing else matters.

Lauri Smith, Dutton's Books

Lauri Smith, a buyer for Dutton's Books — an independent bookstore with three locations in Los Angeles — oversees purchasing for the children's sections in two of the stores. As a result of her many years of experience in the industry, she has very clear reasons for buying — and rejecting — certain titles. The characteristics that make her want to buy a children's book are both objective and subjective. If you want to sell your books in her store, be sure to pay close attention to her advice. Lauri tells us,

If a board book has more than three sentences per page I will not buy it because the author and illustrator are trying to get across more than is appropriate for the age group this format targets, which is babies and toddlers. What matters in board books are the illustrations and colors that are vibrant. I like to see something beyond concept books, such as books that rhyme (rhyming *well* is important) and books that are soothing to the child. Besides *Good Night, Gorilla* by Peggy Rathmann (G. P. Putnam's Sons), the adaptations of regular picture books into board books are disappointing in general because there is too much text crammed onto the page.

Lauri goes on to discuss what, in her opinion, does not work in picture books. She feels, for example, that it's hard to write a picture book biography or one based on historical facts because they get too bogged down with text. Picture books, she says, should immediately get into the story and the problem that has to be solved as opposed to drowning the reader in facts. A favorite title for Lauri is *Sector 7* by David Wiesner (Clarion Books). Funny thing about this Caldecott Honor winner is that it is a wordless picture book!

Lauri also has ideas about areas she feels could use more titles:

> Another opportunity I see for new writers lies in early readers for ages 5 to 7. We could use more interesting stories that are short, don't have a lot of text, and that use words that are appropriate for the age group so readers can feel accomplished. *Buster* by Denise Fleming (Henry Holt and Co.) is a good example because the story is good, it is short, and there is a problem that has to be solved. In general, please no more early readers about dogs, kittens, and bears — enough already!

With middle-grade fiction, Lauri needs to be pulled into a good read that is not boring or too involved for the age group, which she identifies as grades three through six.

> Watch out with subjects, such as sex and violence, that could be questionable to parents and are not appropriate for preteens. And I'm seeing a glut of fantasy titles. *Ida B.: . . . and Her Plans to Maximize Fun, Avoid Disaster, and (Possibly) Save the World* by Katherine Hannigan (Greenwillow) is a good example of an involving story that has a good strong protagonist who is a real individual with issues to overcome. Oh, and there are more girl books than boy books, so I'm always on the lookout for riveting stories featuring boys as main characters.

> So much of the middle-grade series fiction published today really seems to disintegrate in terms of storyline and writing style beyond the third or fourth title. There are some exceptions such as the *Magic Tree House* series (Random House Books for Young Readers), because that series teaches children about different eras in history and has well-developed protagonists. But the writing in most series fiction does not hold up for 10 or 12 books. Good standalone titles are preferable.

Lauri finds young adult books hard to categorize, as do other book buyers.

> Young adult is a hard category because a lot of authors are almost writing for adults. Do these go into regular fiction or into the children's area? Regardless, you cannot have enough YA titles focusing on going to high school and the diverse experiences kids have there, such as not fitting in, romantic problems, and issues in which the teenager would have to take a side and figure out what he or she would do in that situation. Make it personal and real for teenagers, and they will respond!

Sharon Hearn, Children's Book World

Sharon Hearn, owner of Children's Book World in Los Angeles, an independent bookstore specializing in children's books, is also very specific about what she considers worth buying. For fiction, Sharon says,

> First and foremost, it must be a good read. If it's not, then nothing else matters.

For picture books, she wants the story and the artwork to be well matched. The illustrations should enhance the story. They both must be good, and at least one of them needs to be outstanding. With so many board books to choose from, Sharon insists that there be something special for it to be included in her store's collection. Board books must have great art, minimal text, and if there's a novelty aspect to it, it needs to enhance the presentation, not be gratuitous. Novelty books or books-plus must have value as a book first, and a toy second.

For middle-grade and YA fiction, Sharon is equally discerning:

> There are so many great contemporary classics and standard classics that new fiction must be able to complete with what's already out there. There are an infinite number of appropriate themes, and plot is important, but the book must be an outstanding read. The writer should have a unique voice and a solid writing style that makes the reader want to continue turning the pages.

With nonfiction, "There can never be too much information," Sharon says, "but how the material is presented in terms of layout and format is vital. It needs to be user-friendly for children, and there should not be a mass of text without visuals and clear, easy-to-follow organization of the text."

A chain bookstore buyer may share some independent bookstore buyers' discerning tastes, but the chain bookstore buyer has also to consider specific sections within children's books that he has to fill, which size books will fit in those sections, which books may go well in the store's book displays, and how often a section will have to be replenished with new product to keep it from looking stale to frequent customers.

How the chains buy books

Buyers for chain retailers that don't specialize in books, such as Target or Wal-Mart, may also have additional parameters a book must meet:

✔ Does the book fit in the *planogram* (an aisle-long rack with tiered, face-out shelves fitting specific size books)?

✔ Is the book's orientation appropriate for its size? (Sometimes taller, portrait-oriented books work better than wider, landscape-oriented ones.)

✔ Does it target the store's primary audience that parents buy for, which is ages 0 to 5?

✔ Is it priced right to survive up to a 50-percent markdown if the sell-through is poor?

✔ Does it look mass market enough for the audience or is it too trade-y in appearance?

✔ And how will it compete against all the licensed books, which comprise a large portion of the books sold in these venues?

With a chain store buyer, it's often more than just what's inside the book. The physical size and appearance of the book take on great importance, too.

Find out as much as you can about the book business, because after you become a published writer, this business becomes yours, too! So get out to those bookstores, those chains, and those warehouses and study their offerings. Someday, your book may be the one you pick up.

Librarians

Every book buyer looks at content to one extent or another, but public librarians and school librarians are among the most discerning when choosing books for their collections. The American Library Association (www.ALA.org) offers lots of reference tools on how to build a library collection, but every librarian has his own methods.

Susan Patron, Los Angeles Public Library

Susan Patron, Children's Services Juvenile Materials Collection Development Manager at the L.A. Public Library, must choose books that serve a large and diverse community in the library system serving the city of Los Angeles, with a huge system of branches. Each branch serves its own community and has its own budget, so although she compiles a big selection of books of all types, not every branch will buy every title.

For example, if she is looking at a book on skateboarding, she first looks at her existing collection to see whether what's current addresses the range of her target audience (meaning appropriate for readers ages 5 to 11, the readers most likely to want to read about skateboarding) or if she could use a new book not already in the collection. For nonfiction, she asks whether the book is well researched, whether the pictures are appropriate for the audience, whether the contents are arranged logically, whether it is readable, and whether the text and illustrations are well matched. Susan wants a book that reflects the author's passion for the subject:

> Children want a lot of variety on the page: the text not too dense and illustrative material that is clearly marked and ample. All ages of readers now want to see a lot of illustrations or photographs, much more than with nonfiction in the past.

Susan goes on to say that if the nonfiction can be used to supplement school assignments, it should include a table of contents and an index — and short is better than long, as kids will invariably select a thin book over a thick one. An example she gives is *What If You Met a Pirate?* by Jan Adkins (Roaring Brook Press).

In terms of picture books, Susan searches for an original idea that has not been done before, or if it has, that it's being done with a new twist:

> A child protagonist has to solve the problem, not the adult or some fantasy creature, and the story should be told from a child's perspective. The pictures and words should work well together, and every page should offer enough interest, suspense, drama, or humor to keep the reader (or listener) turning the pages. Linda Ashman's *How to Make a Night* (HarperCollins) infuses a well-worn subject, bedtime, with fresh originality and vitality and is entirely child-centered.

In terms of younger middle-grade fiction, kids are interested in stories about friendship, siblings, animals, and school. These subjects are explored in chapter books over and over, and Susan finds that the most popular books work because they're written from the heart and have a unique voice. This audience loves humor and strong protagonists. Susan's pick among current titles at this level is Helen Fox's *Eager* (Wendy Lamb Books), a page-turner about a robot who is almost human.

Susan says the library also purchases lots of board books for babies and toddlers, including ones with flaps and diecuts. The best board books have very few words, but the text directly relates to the very young child's experience. To facilitate access, children's librarians actually place board books in baskets on the floor because they want the target audience to be able to find them. An example of a book that perfectly addresses its audience's experience is *Where's Spot?* by Eric Hill (Penguin Books for Young Readers).

It's the perfect two-year-old's book because over and over again the text repeats a two-year-old's favorite word: 'NO!' It's funny, suspenseful, interactive, and reassuring because by the end we know that Spot's mom cares more about Spot than anything in the world and will find him no matter what. Sandra Boynton, Lucy Cousins, and Rosemary Wells produce brilliant board books to engage babies and very young children.

Susan says her library even loves pop-up books, which we thought would be a no-no due to their fragility. (But as we figured, novelty books with pieces that can be separated from the book are not purchased.)

Even if a pop-up or novelty book is likely to be ephemeral in the collection, we will often buy it for display and story time. We want kids to see how fun and inventive and beautiful books can be. Well-done pop-up books, like those of David A. Carter and Robert Sabuda, are great for story time because they project to a group and can be seen at the back of the room. Plus, they are often packed with audience-pleasing surprises.

Libraries occasionally even buy coloring books and activity books, but very selectively. For example, Susan says that if they relate to topics or information kids are asking for with school assignments, the library will provide them as supplementary material.

There's a coloring book about the Los Angeles landmark, Olvera Street, that we provide to our kids because it has a lot of accessible information.

Public librarians can be a writer's best friend. We want books that engage and delight children, books that make them want to read for pleasure, and we love to help writers in their research — whether it's tracing the source of a folktale or checking what's in print on a given subject.

She says she hopes new writers will enlist the help of their local children's librarian in becoming knowledgeable and informed about the current field of children's literature.

Michael Cart, critic, editor, lecturer

Michael Cart, critic, editor, lecturer, and former Director of the Beverly Hills Public Library, still spends a lot of time reading and evaluating books for young adults. In his words:

After 55 years of avid reading, I find the thing I look for more than any other is freshness and originality. Give me a story I haven't read a gazillion times before and I'm a happy chappie! Also, because I think it's imperative that every kid be able to see his or her face reflected in the pages of a good book — especially if that kid has been marginalized for whatever reason (race, religion, place of national origin, sexual identity, etc.) — I look for books that feature characters who have been absent from traditional YA fiction. I also look for books that are creatively venturesome, that play with considerations of structure, voice, and narrative strategy. Some recent favorites include *Under the Wolf, Under the Dog* by Adam Rapp (Candlewick Press) and *The Fire-Eaters* by David Almond (Delacorte Books for Young Readers).

As for nonfiction, I look for high-interest, non-curriculum-related topics that may be offbeat but that will capture the attention of teens with limited time for reading. To that same end I look for books with strong narrative content and also for books that are eye-catching in terms of design and visual content.

Michael recommends *Witch-Hunt* by Marc Aronson (Atheneum) and *Dangerous Planet* by Bryn Barnard (Crown Books for Young Readers) as good examples of nonfiction to check out.

Teachers

Teachers have various concerns and issues they want books in their classroom to address. Of course, for teachers of middle school and higher, a lot depends on the subject taught, but many teachers buy books across a wide range of subjects.

For example, a preschool director will buy a lot of books dealing with the behaviors, experiences, and concerns of preschoolers. *Hands are Not for Hitting* by Martine Agassi (Free Spirit Publishing), *Teeth Are Not for Biting* by Elizabeth Berdick (Free Spirit Publishing), and *The Way I Feel* by Janan Cain (Parenting Press) are all good examples of books a preschool director might make available to her teachers. A contemporary classic addressing an issue of grave concern to all 2-year-olds is *Everyone Poops* by Taro Gomi (Kane/Miller Book Publishers).

We asked one of our favorite teachers, Lesleigh Alchanati — a mother of seven-year-old triplets who is now also a library media specialist — what kinds of books she looks for as a teacher of kindergarten through eighth graders. She tells us that the age of the child determines her needs and whether or not she is choosing a book to get a child to read or to supplement the core curriculum. For the former, in the primary years, kindergarten through third grade, Lesleigh informs us that, if she is looking for picture books to read to the class,

Obviously, pictures are vital, and they must be eye-catching. Humor is an absolute gift, because it draws the child in. And if the protagonist does obviously dumb or silly things, so much the better.

Lesleigh also appreciates picture books that contain *subtle* (notice the emphasis) moral messages or topics that can lead to meaningful discussions in the classroom and that may stimulate the children's analytical skills. She also purchases a lot of books dealing with issues the children are going through in their own lives: new siblings, moving, best friend problems, and the like.

For the middle primary years, she says,

> The pictures are not so much an issue any more, but humor still reigns. And books with main characters their age involved in interesting and exciting things that fourth through sixth graders could relate to are always appreciated. On the other hand, the children of this age also like to read a lot of fantasy that is completely removed from real life.

And we find that not much has changed for teenaged readers:

> Kids this age are invariably caught up in a world in which they are the center of the universe. They think everything in their lives generally sucks and that their life is really hard, that nothing is fair. As such, they like to read about kids who have it worse. So books such as *It Happened to Nancy: by an Anonymous Teenager, A True Story from Her Diary* by Beatrice Sparks (Avon), *Go Ask Alice* also by Beatrice Sparks (Simon Pulse/Aladdin), and *A Child Called "It:" One Child's Courage to Survive* by Dave Pelzer (HCI) — these are the kinds of stories they really get into: real-life, horrible things that happen to average boys or girls. I think these kinds of books actually make these readers feel better — that they can overcome, even if just for a moment.

When the curriculum calls for supplemental reading, Lesleigh likes to tie in books with whatever her students are learning in history. For instance, eighth graders learning American history might be assigned *My Brother Sam Is Dead* by James Lincoln Collier (Scholastic), *Johnny Tremain* by Esther Forbes (Yearling Newbery), or *Across Five Aprils* by Irene Hunt (Berkley). Says Lesleigh,

> Many English teachers assign monthly book reports to get children to try out different types of books; and they usually assign a specific genre per month. Other teachers might assign books by topic or issue to get the children to discuss issues. This is done by assigning four to six children the same book, and then the children identify and discuss issues in the context of the story. This is referred to as a *literature circle*.

Lesleigh adds that fictional books with ethical issues are favorites as well. Titles include *Standing Up to Mr. O* by Claudia Mills (Hyperion) (about the use of animals in research, animal dissections in educational contexts, and vegetarian lifestyle); *Phoenix Rising* by Karen Hesse (Puffin) (about nuclear power, a nuclear radiation leak, radiation contamination); and *Among the Hidden* by Margaret Peterson Haddix (Aladdin) (about population control and the extermination of children). Lesleigh also values books that deal with self-esteem issues such as *Staying Fat for Sarah Byrnes* by Chris Crutcher (Harper Tempest) and *The Skin I'm In* by Sharon G. Flake (Jump at the Sun). Many of these are appropriate for readers in the upper middle grades to early young adults.

Teachers we know and love are always looking for books to supplement, enhance, and reinforce the curriculum. If you are a writer unsure of a topic, go ask a teacher what subjects she can always use more reference for. You may hear that she needs more nonfiction works targeted to sixth graders on subjects such as the history of hairstyles, or fiction starring females in the 1600s, or perhaps she wants books on holidays for fourth and fifth graders — whatever holes exist in the juvenile publishing spectrum, teachers and librarians will be the ones most keenly aware of them.

Parents

As parents and writers, we, Lisa and Peter, occupy an interesting space on the oxymoron spectrum: We probably own more children's books than most people, but we're also likely to be much more discerning regarding the children's books we allow into our homes and our children's lives.

Parents of the very youngest readers (the ones who prefer to use their books as teething toys rather than reading them) buy books that have great art, are bright and eye-catching, and are made of tasty board material. So if you as a new writer aim to create a board book, make sure it focuses on a baby's experiences and has art bright enough to distract baby from inhaling that pile of dust bunnies in the corner.

It's not until your child starts really paying attention to the content of the books that you have to be very, very, very careful of which books you buy. Because if you buy a book that you will not enjoy reading 5,000 times in a row, you only have yourself to blame. So this is where great story and excellent art really come into play. And at about the same time that your child begins to request certain books at bedtime, she will also sneakily start to change personality, exhibiting strange and terrifying behaviors that often send her sprawling all over the floor, limbs flailing, voice at glass-shattering decibels, mouth foaming.

As your child grows, your taste in books may be less issue oriented and more media oriented, such that you find a lot of licensed books (based on popular television, film, cartoon, or toy characters) creeping into your collection. Or not. And issue-oriented books for older children are just as important as they were back when your child was cleaning the floor with her squirming belly. This is what parents look for most: books told from a child's perspective, starring unique child protagonists who can help their own children become better people, dealing with their issues in a positive and hopeful manner.

So if you want to appeal to parents, get down and dirty — literally, get down into the sandbox and listen to what's really going on in children's minds and hearts. And then write from that perspective, writing what a child wants to hear, not what you as a parent feel he has to hear.

Thinking Like a Kid

Something happens to children when they grow up: They forget what it is like to have magic in their lives. They forget that an ant on the sidewalk can be a source of endless entertainment and speculation (hey — put down that magnifying glass and its 5,000-degree beam of sunlight). They forget that the need to right injustices and make things fair is as necessary as breathing. They forget that most of the world is black and white, with unbreakable divisions between what is right and what is wrong, what is good and what is bad. They forget that you don't need sauce to make food taste good.

And most pivotally, adults forget that for children, the line between fantasy and reality is blurred. What may seem miraculous or outlandish to an adult is simply part of life to a child.

As a result of this amnesia, many new writers (and sorrowfully, quite a few published writers — but not the truly successful ones) write down to children. They write about what they think children should learn, lecture, chide, preach, and tell stories instead of showing a storybook world.

So how do you, as a new writer, write for children and not for your own peers? Keep reading. We're going to discuss a little about what children want — and, of course, what they don't want.

Speaking to children on their level doesn't mean speaking down to them or using baby talk. It means getting into their heads and their lives and writing about what is relevant and of interest to them.

And the winner is . . .

Everyone has favorite books that they carry around in their memories from the time they were small. What's yours? If you don't remember the title, do a little digging on the Internet and try to find it. When you pick it up, we guarantee you that it will bring you whooshing right back into your footie PJs and into the mindset you should be in when writing for children.

To get you started figuring out what's great in children's books we list the Caldecott and Newbery winners from the last decade, books that rocked our worlds.

Caldecott Medal winners: The Caldecott is awarded by the Association for Library Service to Children, a division of the American Library Association, to the artist of the most distinguished American picture book for children.

- **1996:** *Officer Buckle and Gloria,* by Peggy Rathman (Putnam)
- **1997:** *Golem,* by David Wisniewski (Clarion)
- **1998:** *Rapunzel,* by Paul O. Zelinsky (Dutton)
- **1999:** *Snowflake Bentley,* by Jacqueline Briggs Martin, illustrated by Mary Azarian (Houghton)
- **2000:** *Joseph Had a Little Overcoat,* by Simms Taback (Viking)
- **2001:** *So You Want to be President?,* By Judith St. George, illustrated by David Small (Philomel)
- **2002:** *The Three Pigs,* by David Wiesner (Clarion/Houghton Mifflin)
- **2003:** *My Friend Rabbit,* by Eric Rohmann (Roaring Brook Press/Millbrook Press)
- **2004:** *The Man Who Walked Between the Towers,* by Mordicai Gerstein (Roaring Brook Press/Millbrook Press)

- **2005:** *Kitten's First Full Moon,* by Kevin Henkes (Greenwillow)

Newbery Medal winners: The Newbery Medal is awarded by the Association for Library Service to Children, a division of the American Library Association, to the author of the most distinguished contribution to American literature for children.

- **1996:** *The Midwife's Apprentice,* by Karen Cushman (Clarion)
- **1997:** *The View from Saturday,* by E. L. Konigsburg (Jean Karl/Atheneum)
- **1998:** *Out of the Dust,* by Karen Hesse (Scholastic)
- **1999:** *Holes,* by Louis Sachar (Frances Foster)
- **2000:** *Bud, Not Buddy,* by Christopher Paul Curtis (Delacorte)
- **2001:** *A Year Down Yonder,* by Richard Peck (Dial)
- **2002:** *A Single Shard,* by Linda Sue Park (Clarion Books/Houghton Mifflin)
- **2003:** *Crispin: The Cross of Lead,* by Avi (Hyperion Books fro Children)
- **2004:** *The Tale of Despereaux: Being the Story of a Mouse, a Princess, Some Soup, and a Spool of Thread,* by Kate di Camillo, illustrated by Timothy Basil Ering (Candlewick Press)
- **2005:** *Kira-Kira,* by Cynthia Kadohata (Atheneum)

Going after what kids like — regardless of mom and dad

Sometimes writing about what children like may offend adults. J. K. Rowling's *Harry Potter* series, because it has magic, witchcraft, and other (what some consider to be) subversive or pagan content in it, has been banned in many areas of the United States. *Walter the Farting Dog* by Glenn Murray and William Kotzwinkle (North Atlantic Books) faced many adult editors who laughed uproariously behind closed doors but did not have the guts to publish it until one took a chance — and the book hit the bestseller list.

And as we mentioned before, *Everyone Poops* by Taro Gomi (Kane/Miller Book Publishers) is fabulously silly and irreverent, like all the best children's books, besides being packed with true facts about poopoo across species — and Japan had the gumption to publish it way before the United States did. So you have a choice: You can play it safe with topics children love (and adults don't mind) or you can take a chance with topics children love (and adults mind). Entirely up to you.

Here are some things children respond to, adults be darned:

- Extremes rule (the world is black or white, not both).
- It's okay to be different, but it's not easy.
- Bad guys can't win.
- Good guys must win.
- People can change from good to bad or vice versa, but they can't really be both at the same time.
- It's fine for something to be scary, but it can never touch your body.
- Little people can triumph over big people.
- Poopoo, peepee, tushies, passing gas, burping, underwear — all are hilarious.
- Turning things upside down is funny — as long as those things make sense in the first place right side up.
- Magic can occur as a logical reaction to an action.
- Regular children can perform extraordinary feats.
- Regular children can go on implausible missions sanctioned (or not) by adults in charge.

These are only a few of the norms that inhabit children's lives. When writing for children, remember that their world is not constrained by the same limitations and consequences that ours is. In general, unless they have been abused or suffered extreme peril, children have not yet learned to be cynical or hopeless. There is always a chance for everything to work out — and that chance is lurking just behind the next page.

Knowing what kids don't like

Here's the rundown of what kids don't embrace:

- Books that preach or lecture
- Books that talk down to children as if they are small, idiotic adults
- Books that have no real story (nor a plot with beginning, middle, end)
- Books where the art is totally inappropriate for the story or vice versa
- Picture books so packed with text you wonder what happened to the editor
- Nonfiction books so packed with text and so lacking in design and visuals that you wonder what happened to the book designer
- Books whose main characters are boring or uninteresting
- Books whose main characters have a problem they don't solve themselves and, hence, they don't change as characters
- Books that tell instead of showing, using narrative as a soapbox

Tapping into the trends

Because children's book publishing is part of the larger world of commerce, it follows that it is necessarily affected by what happens in the world around us.

You can target a trend that you think may make a great children's book, but be prepared to have competition. Just as you can never predict what will happen in the future, neither can you control the timing of world events or capricious fashions and how they might positively or adversely affect a story you're writing. Alternatively, you can write more universal, timeless stories that will speak to many generations of children.

Like almost every other business steeped in entertainment or education, children's book publishing falls victim to trends and cycles. One year fantasy is the "It" genre, the next year novelty learning books push it out of fashion.

Part II

Immersing Yourself in the Writing Process

The 5th Wave   By Rich Tennant

"Look I hammered out news stories for over 35 years. If I want to hammer out a children's book, I will."

In this part . . .

In order to write creatively and efficiently, you need to set up your writing workspace to be free from the chattering TV, spilled juice, and screaming children. This part shows you how to make a room of your own that is conducive to both creativity and productivity.

And when you've settled into your writing space, you can begin to work on ideas, big and small. Before you start writing, you get to research both the children who will read your story and the subject matter of your story itself.

Chapter 4

Setting Up Your Workspace

. . . .

In This Chapter

▶ Understanding the writing mind

▶ Finding your best time to write

▶ Sticking to a schedule

▶ Setting up your writing area

. . . .

Guess what? Before you can revel in all those copies flying off the bookstore shelves — you have to write a book! For some fortunate writers, this is the easy part; for others, it's like waiting at the dentist's office.

If you're a natural for the job — someone from whom the words spill out by the gallon — then you probably have little use for this chapter. But if you're wondering how to get started, you may need to gain some understanding of how best to prepare for writing up a storm.

So that's exactly what we show you in this chapter. We first explore the best times for individual writers to perform their task, and then we take a look at the tools and the rules you need to create an environment that will leave you little choice but to be creative. So, dear reader — read on!

Finding Your Time to Write

Effective writers know when they're most productive and create a writing schedule around those times — then they stick to it. In this section, we help you pinpoint when *you're* most productive. Then we give you some pointers on creating that schedule to make you want to work on your writing.

When are you most productive?

Are you a night owl? A morning person? Are you at your best after you've had a cup of coffee and a chance to read the morning paper or after you've run five miles? Is your house quiet for long periods of time, or is the atmosphere routinely punctuated with noise and distractions — kids running up and down the hallway, subway trains clamoring outside your window, or a construction project next door?

The answers to these questions and others like them determine when you're most fertile and inventive as a writer. Zero in on when you're most productive and then do the majority of your writing during that period of time.

Although Peter is pretty good at knocking out one or two thousand words at the drop of the hat when necessary, he knows he is much more productive at certain times of the day, and in certain environments, than at others. For example, as these very words are hitting the page, it's 1:33 a.m. in Peter's home office. Aside from the Smashing Pumpkins songs blasting from his computer speakers, it's dead quiet. No kids running around, no phones ringing, no cement trucks on the way to the new house being built down the street. The only distraction is that pumpkin pie and can of whipped cream in the fridge calling his name.

Lisa finds that early mornings are best, when the kids are still asleep, before the day really starts for the rest of the family, or in the evenings when everyone is abed. Closing the doors to her home office/library, sipping a cup of coffee, and surrounding herself with her favorite dictionary and thesaurus often helps to get her started. Her desk has to be free of clutter and there must be no e-mails to answer so she can stay focused. Having inspirational art on the walls, often culled from children's book art galleries or illustrators she has worked with who have sent their work as gifts, also helps her get into the mood. Turning off the phone is a must.

Every successful writer has a sweet spot — the time when he or she is most productive. Check out these tips for finding yours:

- ✔ Try writing for an hour at different times of the day and night — in the morning, in the afternoon, in the evening, and late at night. When do you feel the most creative and prolific? Be sure to give every possible time a try before you settle into a routine.

- ✔ Shift your writing time around specific everyday events in your life: before or after breakfast, before or after you shower or exercise, before or after you watch TV. Play with your schedule and see what feels good to you.

✔ Take a laptop computer or a big pad of paper with you to work and try going early to the office or getting away from it to a park or cafe to do some writing during your lunch hour.

Not all writers function the same way. Some enforce strict writing schedules at the same time every day; others make sure to devote a certain amount of hours daily to their craft, sneaking them in whenever they can. And some writers vary the amount of time they spend writing. Whatever you choose, make sure it works best with when you're most productive writing-wise and with your daily schedule.

Stick to a writing schedule

We're all at the beck and call of our schedules, but if we give writing a high enough priority in our lives, we can be sure to set aside a place for it on our daily to-do list. If you want to be a serious writer — and a successful children's book author — you can't leave your writing to chance. Include writing in your schedule and then do it!

Unfortunately, in many ways this is the hard part. Why? Because it requires discipline and focus.

But try we must. Here's why:

✔ By setting aside a specific time every day to write, you soon make writing a habit. And, as we all know, habits are hard to break (and when it comes to writing, that's a good thing).

✔ After you settle into a writing routine, you take a large amount of the stress of the writing process off your shoulders. You can relax knowing that this special time is devoted only to writing — everything else is just going to have to wait until later. And a relaxed writer is often a more effective and prolific writer.

✔ When you set a definite, regular time to write, you indicate to others (family, friends, and coworkers) that this time is for you and your writing — and to not bother knocking when your keyboard is a-rocking.

Buy an appointment calendar, daily planner, or electronic organizer and use it. Calendars and planners are absolutely essential tools for keeping organized and on track during the course of the day. Lisa can never be sure that she does not have other obligations if she does not fill in space in her daily planner with the words *writing time*. It doesn't matter so much what kind of organizer you use, so long as you use it regularly.

Make sure this is what you want to do

Think about how your writing feels after a few weeks of sticking to your trial schedule? Are you relaxed? Energized? Distracted? Creative? Asleep? Assess your temporary schedule to find a time that works for you.

You may sincerely want to make writing a priority in your life, perhaps going so far as to schedule it into your days. But when the time comes to write, something always gets in the way — taking care of the kids, paying bills, or watching a favorite TV show. If this is the case, ask yourself whether writing a children's book is truly important to you. If the answer is yes, recommit to the process and prioritize it in your life. If the answer is no, then consider waiting a few weeks or months (or even years) before you take up your children's book again. Sometimes taking a break can give you a lot more energy for your project when you come back to it.

You may simply have a temporary writer's block when the words don't seem to flow no matter what you do with your schedule. We discuss how to deal with that particular problem in Chapter 5.

Optimizing Your Writing Environment

Just as important as finding the right time to write is finding the right place to write. Even if you have zeroed in on the very best time of the day to avoid distractions and focus on wordsmithing, it will do you no good if your writing environment is, for one reason or another, unsuitable for the task at hand. Here we consider some of the things that can help you find your special place and share some tricks of the trade for making that place even more conducive to writing.

Find your own special place

Every writer needs a place to write that is comfortable and cozy, stimulates creativity, and has the tools for writing. Have a look at some possible places to write:

- A dedicated office in your home
- Another room in your home, such as a den, dining room, or family room — we strongly advise against using your bedroom as your special writing place if you have a spouse or significant other who routinely occupies it with you

- ✔ An outdoor balcony or deck
- ✔ Your backyard
- ✔ A local library
- ✔ A coffee house or cafe
- ✔ A bookstore with tables and chairs available for patron use
- ✔ A park
- ✔ A train or bus station or airport
- ✔ A shopping mall or shopping center
- ✔ At the beach or by a lake or river

The point is that anyplace can be your special place — you just have to keep looking until you find it. Instead of just settling at the first place you land, try a variety of different locations until you find the one that feels just right. You'll know it when, all of a sudden, everything clicks and the words flow like a spring shower.

Keep in mind that many of these locations require you to either take a laptop computer along with you or write the good, old-fashioned way: with a pen or pencil and a pad of paper. You can then type your story into your desktop computer when you get back home. Either way is fine; just do what feels best to you.

Get ergonomic

To write effectively and effortlessly, it helps if everything in your environment supports and facilitates your writing efforts. When you find yourself in an uncomfortable chair at a desk, you may have a very hard time getting much writing done.

If you've been in the corporate world, you know how important *ergonomics* — adapting a job to the people who have to do it through design of equipment and procedures — is in ensuring that employees work at their full potential. These same principles apply just as much to you in your home office or den or dining room as they do to the people working in that big skyscraper downtown. You should therefore take ergonomics into account when purchasing new computers, desks, chairs, telephones, lighting, and other office equipment.

Your computer monitors need to be large, with adjustable angles and tilts. Keyboards should have long cords, adjustable feet, and wrist rests, if possible. Desktops should be deep enough and high enough — and matte-finished to reduce glare. You need a sturdy swivel chair that is easily adjustable and provides sufficient back and arm support. And desk lighting, telephones, document holders, and even computer mice have guidelines that can help make your work environment comfortable and conducive. Check out the U.S. Occupational Safety and Health Administration Web site (www.osha.gov) for a full checklist of things to consider.

Organize your workspace

What's the old saying? An organized mind is a happy mind? We're not sure if that's the old saying or not, but it sounds pretty good to us. Although different people have different preferences when it comes to the amount of organization they need in their lives, many people work better and more effectively when they are organized. If you find yourself distracted when you work, or constantly looking for a stack of paper that you printed out a couple of hours ago but that is now lost on your desk, get organized and see what happens. When everything in your workspace has its own place and it's there when and where you need it — and when your area isn't cluttered with books, paper, envelopes, kids' toys, dog bones, and who knows what else — then you may just find that you're a far more productive writer.

So how does your workspace look? Like a tornado hit it? Consider some tips for getting organized — sooner rather than later.

- ✔ **Clean up your desk.** With work and family to juggle, it can be very difficult to set aside any time at all to write, much less get organized. And the busier you get, the less time you have to clean up the old coffee cups, the wadded up pieces of paper, the books, folders, empty envelopes, and all the other things that seem to naturally make their home on your desk. As all this stuff piles up, however, it becomes harder for you to write, not only because you have less space in which to work, but because things start getting lost — never to be seen again.

- ✔ **Separate obligations.** If you use your writing desk to pay bills, run your philanthropic endeavors for the children's schools, or conduct your other home business, separate out those obligations from your writing ones. Get file holders that physically keep other tasks separated from your writing and that can be moved out of the way if they prove distracting.

- ✔ **Clean up your office.** Just as your desk will accumulate progressively deeper layers of stuff, so too will your office careen out of control if you neglect it. Empty boxes, stacks of shoes, tossed waste paper that missed the basket, old candy bar wrappers — all will find their way into your office. The solution? Clean it!

✔ **Revisit your office layout.** Does the layout of your office make the most sense? Does it support you in your writing efforts and is it easy to keep organized? Consider where you have your desk, your chairs, your computer, your filing cabinet, and anything else and make sure it's all in the best place.

✔ **Schedule regular organizing sessions.** Don't just clean up your office once every couple of years — when things get so bad that you can't even move. Schedule a regular time to clean up — say every Saturday afternoon, or on the first of the month. Be sure to make an appointment with yourself by scheduling it in your appointment calendar or planner.

✔ **Get organized now!** This one speaks for itself. Don't just think about getting organized, *get* organized. Right now! The sooner you get it over with, the sooner you can start writing.

Hang up and log off

Your telephone or cell phone can be one great big distraction that can keep you from focusing on doing the writing that needs to be done.

Ignoring a ringing phone is almost impossible. (We've all been conditioned to drop whatever we're doing and to leap up to grab it whenever we hear its unique ring or chime.) So unplug it or turn off the ringer if you keep getting interrupted when you should be writing.

If you have become addicted to e-mail, shut it down so that when new missives come in, you're blissfully unaware and continue your writing.

Hang your DANGER! KEEP OUT! sign

You probably think we're joking about this one. We're not. Sometimes, ensuring that you're not subjected to constant interruptions means taking drastic action — including doing things like hanging a "DANGER! KEEP OUT!" sign on your closed office door.

What? You don't have one handy, and you're not feeling very artistic? No problem. Take a trip down to your local hardware supply store or big-box office supply retailer and pick up a keep out sign. You'll probably have a number of different variations to choose from. Lisa likes the ones with the pictures of the rabid, slavering dogs on them. The effect on your potential interrupters will be immediate and measurable. Suddenly, your friends and family will think twice about throwing open your door to see whether you're really working. Just be sure to explain what the sign means to your young ones.

Interview with Debra Mostow Zakarin, author

Successful children's book writer Debra Mostow Zakarin talks about how she keeps focused on writing in the midst of a thousand other distractions.

WCBFD: Many new writers think that there is some inspirational Zen-like place you have to get into to write effectively. Is this true for you?

DMZ: After so many years of writing, I find my inspiration from life, from my children, and by just writing, writing, and writing. I've always kind of thought that an actual, physical inspirational place, at least for me, was way too contrived.

WCBFD: Do you have a special place where you do your writing? How is it set up?

DMZ: I have an office set up in my home — a computer, desk, fax, and phone. And, oh, my two dogs lie at my feet, something which really makes me feel like a writer. The space around my computer must be neat or else I get too distracted and look for reasons to procrastinate. Also, I have learned to turn off my instant messenger so as not to get interrupted. I have to write on the computer since longhand does not work for me anymore.

WCBFD: Do you have a set schedule for writing? What is it?

DMZ: I try to write in the late morning/early afternoon — while my kids are at school. However, if I'm in the middle of writing something that I'm totally into, then I go back to my computer in the late evening, after my kids and husband have gone to bed.

WCBFD: Is your schedule strict or flexible? How do you enforce it?

DMZ: If my schedule were strict, I feel that I wouldn't be a "creative" person. I have to be flexible with my time. I try so hard to be strict, but old habits of procrastination are hard to break. If I miss a writing appointment, I try to make it up later that day or the next day.

WCBFD: How do you keep your writing life from intruding into your family life and vice versa?

DMZ: My family is my priority, and I work my writing into my family life. Writing is my creative outlet, time just for me, my escape. I try to make sure the two do not collide by setting times for writing that are inviolate, but knowing that if my family needs me, I'll just have to try again tomorrow.

WCBFD: What advice do you have for new authors who are just getting set up?

DMZ: Join or start a writer's group. The feedback you will receive will be invaluable. Also, take writing classes, as they will really help you with structure. Most importantly, write, write, and write.

WCBFD: What pitfalls should new authors watch out for?

DMZ: Feeling frustrated over writer's block and rejection. Just keep on going. Creativity is ongoing and full of change.

Chapter 5

Starting with a Great Idea

In This Chapter
▶ Looking around for inspiration
▶ Brainstorming new ideas
▶ Combating writer's block

*E*very spellbinding story begins as an idea. Sometimes you have the idea from the start of the writing process. Sometimes you have to conjure it out of thin air. The act of writing itself can generate ideas, and ideas that strike your imagination can generate writing; the two go hand in hand.

What are some good ideas for children's books and how do you come up with them? This chapter is about generating ideas and starting writing. We help you come up with ideas through activities and by trying to look at the world in a different way. We also help you figure out how to use brainstorming to create additional ideas. And if you get that dreaded disease — writer's block — we help you work through that, too.

Once Upon a Time: Coming Up with an Idea

If you're like most aspiring children's book writers, you may already have an idea that you've always wanted to write about. On the other hand, maybe you have no specific ideas and are looking for a way to address your deep-seated yearning to communicate with children. Or perhaps you've always wanted to be a published writer and you have this curious notion that because children's books are relatively short (how hard can 5 spreads or 32 pages be to write?), writing for children must be the easiest way to get published.

Settling on whether your story is true

You have to decide whether your story is going to be fiction or nonfiction. Fiction is writing that comes from your imagination; it's made up. Nonfiction is writing that is based on a true event or real-life person and verifiable facts. We cover the elements of writing nonfiction in Chapter 12, but be aware that nonfiction writing can certainly benefit from the basics we go into in this chapter. If you're writing fiction, you next need to choose what the basics of the book will be.

Whatever brought you to plunk down your hard-earned money to buy this book, having an idea starts you off on the process of actually writing your story. But guess what? Even if you don't have an idea, you can still start writing because ideas and writing go together. Ideas lead to writing, and writing can generate ideas. But we have to start somewhere in this book, so we start with ideas.

An idea is like a seed ready to be planted. With the right soil and fertilizers, it can develop into a strong plant that can survive many seasons and many generations. In other words, the right idea can lead to a masterpiece of a story — one that brings joy to children for years to come.

A children's book idea is just a seed, a kernel, a morsel. It doesn't need to be complicated or long or even developed. It just has to be a notion of something relating to children that you think you can spend a lot of time and effort working on. (And even if you love an idea at first and find out you don't later, don't fret; you never have to stay married to any idea you don't adore. You can just chuck it and move on to a better one.) Coming up with ideas is supposed to be fun.

But how do you come up with an idea that really moves you? One that fills you with the passion you need to skip through the writing process with anticipation and glee? We give you a few tips in this section.

Relying on the tried and true

Many new writers figure that they have to have a *big* idea to get started writing a children's book. Big ideas are the ones you remember from high school English that involve such grand, overarching concepts as *good versus evil* and *man (or woman) versus nature* — the concepts your teacher assured you were in Shakespeare's mind when he tackled each and every one of his plays. Although most ideas in the universe can indeed be broken down and made as simple as *man versus himself,* where's the fun in those concepts? How many children's books do you think are sold based on the pitch "I've written a sweeping epic poem of child versus nature in iambic pentameter"? None, we hope.

So now that you've dumped the big ideas, focus on ideas that are more specific and less grand. More specific ideas don't involve the entire universe, but a narrower subset of the world. They're carefully defined and can be nailed down in one descriptive sentence, such as

- ✔ Six-year-old anteaters are having a hard time adjusting to life in anteater kindergarten.
- ✔ Eight-year-old princesses can't imagine kissing a frog, much less pledging their lives to one.

You may cry, "But that subject/concept/idea has been written about so many times before! Why bother doing it again?" Good question. Nearly every idea you generate has already been written about at least once by someone else. So why bother indeed?

Here's why: You can probably name dozens of books about a young boy's adventures in a magical world filled with witches and warlocks and animals that talk. But are any of them quite like J. K. Rowling's *Harry Potter* series? We don't think so, either. The way to make an "old" idea yours is to research the competition, make sure you don't copy, and write from the heart.

Starting off with a more specific idea makes the writing process more manageable right from the start, and more manageable is always better. Maybe very few ideas are truly new, but there's a big difference between taking a well-worn idea and writing about it in a boring, repetitive manner that lacks soul and conviction, and taking that same idea and making it fresh again by writing a story with passion, heart, and humor. (See Chapter 20 for lots of classic storylines you can mine for great ideas.)

Tapping into your own experiences

You have had experiences in your life that could make great stories. It's all in the way you look at those experiences and memories. Many successful children's book authors rely on personal experiences to provide them with ideas that they can develop into fun and compelling books. Dig deep into your childhood and try to recall the events and moments that were so intense that the memory can still bring the feelings you had then to the forefront. For example, remember

- ✔ When your mom told you the family was moving to another part of the city — the day after you finally found a best friend and pinkie swore to be pals forever?

- ✔ When you went to preschool and discovered that you had forgotten to wear your underwear?

- ✔ The night your dad came home from a trip to a foreign land carrying twin babies that were now your new brothers?

- ✔ Feeling small and scared as you hid under the sheet, convinced that the monsters hiding in the closet were going to get you?

- ✔ Feeling like you owned the world as you zoomed across the finish line in first place?

- ✔ Feeling overwhelmed and excited as you stepped on the ice in front of a girl you really liked — and promptly fell on your backside?

Children have very strong feelings about the events of their daily lives. Although an event may seem trivial to an adult, a child — who has little sense of time — can't really reassure himself that "it will be over soon" or "this too shall pass." Children are the center of their universes and live very much in the moment. Everything that happens to them is cause for a reaction, positive or negative — rarely ever neutral, unless they aren't paying attention. If you have an idea based on an experience you had as a child that elicits powerful feelings, you can develop that idea into a story that other children can relate to and appreciate.

The heart of your story: theme

The theme is the subject of the story, its central core, its heart. Most themes can be expressed in a phrase or sentence at most. Common themes for children's books include the old standby, *love*, plus themes of *overcoming problems*, *dealing with change*, *getting reassurance*, *reaching achievements and developmental milestones*, and *becoming independent*. The best themes are simple, easy to understand, and applicable to most children at some time or another in their lives.

When choosing a theme, you need to keep in mind where your target audience is developmentally. To be appropriate, themes for young children have to take into account their emotional growth, their interests, their ability to comprehend increasingly complex issues, and, to a certain extent, their limited reading ability (depending on format, more on that in Chapter 2). Themes for older children can still embrace the same issues, but they are fleshed out with more depth and complexity.

Be sure to choose a theme that really excites you, one that you can feel passionate about — no matter how many rewrites you have to go through. It's all well and good to write a story whose theme is *reassurance*, but if you're really more interested in writing about *a child dealing with change*, do it! Don't ever write only to please your audience; you also have to please yourself, because you are the one who has to be dedicated to your manuscript for each of the steps in the writing process for the foreseeable future.

Dig through childhood mementos

Got an old diary from when you were little? What about a box of old school papers? Maybe a trunk or dusty suitcase packed with art and class projects? If you can find any one of these, we guarantee that you will get ideas for stories as the memories come flooding back. Jot down whatever comes to your mind: bits of information, names of classmates or special friends, field trips or projects you found, trouble you got in — whatever flows into your mind could be developed into a book now or at a later date.

Look at a photo album

A good activity that can help you get ideas by remembering childhood experiences requires a photo album. Your own baby or childhood photo album is best, but anyone's will do. Peruse the childhood photographs until you find one that strikes you as compelling. Then ask yourself some of these questions about the child in the photo, writing down the answers as you go:

- ✔ Who is the child? (If you don't know her name, give her one that seems to fit.)
- ✔ When and where do you suppose the photo was taken?
- ✔ What is she doing at that moment? (If the surroundings in the photo don't give you any clues, make up something.)
- ✔ How does she feel about what's going on? (Does her body language or her facial expression suggest anything right away?)
- ✔ Why is she feeling that way? (Is she scared? Happy? Put off? Proud? Unsure?) What could have caused her reaction?
- ✔ Is there someone else in the photo who is affecting her? What did they do that may have caused the child's expression?

You are either reviving memories from your own childhood if you're the child in the photo, or you see if your answers help you remember a similar event in your own life if you aren't in the photo. Looking at an old picture of herself, Lisa came up with these answers to the preceding questions:

> That's me! I look to be about three years old. I'm sitting on a blanket at the beach. I'm holding a bucket up to the camera as if to say, "Look at this!" I seem to be very excited. I don't recall what was in the bucket, but perhaps something alive was in there, like a sand crab. The only other person with me is the one who is taking the picture, and that must have been my dad because my mom detests the beach.

What idea did that photo generate? Lisa can recall feeling very strongly about protecting all animals, no matter how small, when she was young, and feeling that it was a very important job that only she could be trusted to do. So perhaps she could use that recalled emotion to write about a child who goes to the beach and discovers a bunch of sea creatures who can speak. They tell her that their world is endangered and that they need her to save it. They try to get her to follow them to an undersea kingdom that only children can see. When she follows them and her feet touch the water, the entire world changes and she finds herself breathing underwater, like a fish. Having this new talent allows her to explore where children have never been before — and the story goes on from there. It may not be the most original idea in the world, but it's a totally viable story idea.

Drawing from other children's experiences

Perhaps your memories of childhood are so fuzzy they're practically nonexistent — or you just wish they were. You certainly don't have to limit yourself to *your* childhood experiences. If, as an adult, you've had experiences with children that you think are important and interesting, you can use those experiences for ideas as well. Maybe you're acquainted with a child who's dealing with a particular issue such as the death of a sibling or a divorce, and you're unable to find a book that addresses her problem in a way you like — what a great idea for a book. Maybe you know a child who is a fascinating character and simply must have adventures written around his unique personality.

Pulling ideas from the world around you

Open your eyes. Look around you. Really pay attention to your life. What do you see? What's going on with children today that you find interesting? What have you read or seen about children that grabs your attention?

When you read magazines or newspapers, read with the intent of finding ideas for children's books in the content. When you watch TV, search for stories that have kid appeal. In Chapter 6, we take you into a child's world and help you figure out what may appeal to children. Start looking at the world with writer's eyes: eyes that see everything as an idea or a possible subject.

For example, just the other day Lisa read an article about how researchers believe the teen brain grows and develops. As Lisa read, a thought popped into her head: What if a teenager re-created Mary Shelley's *Frankenstein* monster in robot form from used computer parts? Lisa understands the impulse that many teenagers have to gain control of their lives in one way or another, so she likes the idea of a teenage scientist attempting to create a robot monster to wreak havoc on his world. You may say that Lisa's idea has nothing to do with the article and that her idea has been done before, but that doesn't matter. One day Lisa may be able to use the idea and write a story based on it. And even if she doesn't, at least she's generating ideas, which is one of the first critical steps in the writing process.

Stumped? Break Through with Brainstorming

Brainstorming is a creative technique in which you freely express random thoughts and ideas on a subject in the hopes of coming up with a creative solution. It's a process of taking your brain's inventive energy, focusing it on a subject, and then opening up and letting ideas flow out of you.

You can brainstorm by yourself or with others, but whatever you do, never say never. The key to brainstorming is to get as many ideas together as you possibly can in a relatively short amount of time, withholding judgment about whether an idea is good until later. You should worry about the quantity of ideas, not the quality. Children aren't bound by the constraints that adults live by, and their imaginations are free. You want your imagination to be as free as theirs.

The purpose of a brainstorming session is to amass a pile of information that you can then cull down into usable ideas at a later time. The best brainstorming sessions are ones in which you allow yourself to think thoughts that are as crazy, outlandish, far-fetched, and miraculous as possible. When you don't constrain your thinking by what you know or think is plausible and instead allow yourself to go wild, cross boundaries, and turn the world upside-down, you're using brainstorming for what it can truly offer: interesting information that can be turned into great ideas somewhere down the road.

All by yourself

Do you have a ritual that you follow when you want to come up with new ideas? For Peter, the best solo brainstorming occurs when he's in the shower. That's where his very best ideas come to him. Something about hot water pouring over his head — the sound, the heat, the steady pulsing — simultaneously focuses and frees his thoughts, allowing his brain to roam and generate ideas like crazy. Lisa gets ideas while trolling huge gift shows and toy fairs. All those knickknacks somehow get her brain going, and she always fills up a notebook with lots of notes about what she sees and what she imagines creating.

Here's a simple approach to brainstorming by yourself (don't try this in the shower; the paper gets really soggy):

1. **Find a quiet place where you can be free of distractions for at least 15 minutes.**

2. **Get a big pad of paper, a timer, and a couple of pencils or pens.**

3. **Set your timer for 15 minutes and start writing down every idea for a story that you can think of.**

   If you have trouble getting started, picture a child in your head and try to take that child on a trip to experience as many different things as you can think of.

   Your ideas may be similar to stories you're already familiar with, or they may be totally new. Don't judge the experience as you write it; just write it down and move on to the next one.

4. **When your 15 minutes are up, stop writing and look at your ideas.**

   Although many of your ideas may not prove usable for stories in the long run, chances are you have a gem or two hidden in the (hopefully) many pages that are the result of your brainstorming session. Pull out these ideas and hold onto them.

When you go back to your lists (we hope you make time to engage in brainstorming every so often and have multiple lists), you may find that one of the ideas has potential. You will know an idea is worth pursuing if reviewing it makes you think of lots of ways to expand it, or if you can't stop thinking about it, or if it incites some sort of passion in you. That's when you know you can write about that idea in a heartfelt and sincere manner.

You have to care about an idea to make expanding it into a story fun. No matter how uniquely fabulous an idea may seem, if you don't care about it, it isn't a workable idea for you. It may work for the writer next door, but not for you. At least not at the moment.

Free association

Another way to brainstorm about a particular subject is to *free associate,* meaning write down all the words you can think of that are even randomly associated with a starting word or phrase. Free association works great when you have a *very* vague idea that you would like to solidify a bit more. Say that you want to write about a bunny rabbit. To free associate, you write down all the words you can think of that are related to *bunny rabbit*. You can write them in a column or write *bunny rabbit* in the center of a piece of paper and use arrows to point to the encircled words radiating out from it.

Off the top of our heads, we can free associate the following from *bunny rabbit:* toothy, furry, fluffy tail, fast, lots of sisters and brothers, jumpy, hoppy, long ears, twitchy nose, timid, whiskers, long paws, jackrabbit, hare, white, brown, lop ears, claws. We also find that it's helpful to list as many opposites to those words as you can think of, because a lot of the drama of a story later comes from conflict, which is often generated from opposites clashing in some way (more on that in Chapter 8). Some opposites we might list would be toothless, bald, tailless, slow, only child (well, only bunny).

The more free associating you do, the more your vague idea forms into a solid idea. Later, when you're ready to write, come back to your lists and see whether any of these words help you with character development (more on that in Chapter 7).

Structured and free-form journaling

Not all solo brainstorming is done in one session. Sometimes, idea brainstorming is done over time. A very popular and common way to record your ideas as they come to you is to engage in journal writing. Brainstorming in journals falls into two primary categories: free-form and structured.

Journaling is an a great way to free up your mind and create a living record of your life that you can go back to again and again for ideas.

- ✔ **Free-form journaling:** Some like to begin journaling by writing about whatever prevailing emotion drives them at the moment. Others like to record dreams and use them as problem-solving devices — attempting to decipher hidden meanings and possible connections to waking life. Others like to use a journal as a listening post. Whatever you decide to write about, free journaling helps you develop ideas and get used to writing on a regular basis.

  Regardless of your approach or topic, you must follow one rule about free-form journaling: *Thou must not judge thyself, nor even reread what thou writes, until thou art done for the day.* This writing is intended only for your eyes, to help you come up with ideas for your children's books, so feel free to simply let yourself go. Writing in a journal can be a joyful experience. And before you can discipline yourself as a writer, you need to feel the freedom of what writing for the joy of writing is like.

✔ **Structured journaling:** Are you the type of person who prefers structured activities? Some writers like to take a formal approach to journaling. They keep a journal that is restricted to one set of ideas. For example, they may keep a food journal, a dream journal, a journal written only when it's raining, or a journal of ideas.

Consider buying a bunch of journals and keep them all going at once, each with a different purpose. Or, if you're really brave and have a trustworthy colleague or writing partner, share a journal, leaving a space after each of your entries for commentary or companion entries by your writing partner. If you want to make it really easy, you can keep an online shared journal. With the idea that two heads are better than one, companion journaling is a good way to brainstorm with a friend. At the very least, you may be surprised at what you read.

Aside from helping you get into the habit of writing, structured journaling leaves you with a potential treasure trove of ideas to draw from during your long career in writing children's books. Who knows? One day, a children's book starring a reptile hatched from an egg found buried in a desert may bear your name on its cover.

Your journals don't have to involve "good writing;" simple one-liners can later prove immensely inspiring. Your writing can be as straightforward as this: *No rain today. Feeling parched and dry, much like a reptile bone buried in the sand.*

The buddy system

Brainstorming with writing buddies is a fun way to generate ideas. You and your buddies agree to come to a meeting prepared to discuss current events, trends, changes in the world — whatever you choose to start yourselves off — with the understanding that these issues should all revolve around the lives of children. Then steer the conversation toward coming up with ideas that may lead to stories or books for children.

In a round-robin fashion, each person gets to bring up his first topic of interest and present it to the group for discussion. So if Peter and Lisa were playing the brainstorming game, it would go something like this:

LISA: I really want to write something about fairies, but I can't think of anything new about them.

PETER: Will your fairies fly? Will they have magical powers? Will they speak?

LISA: Hmmm. Maybe they have forgotten how to fly. Maybe they are like children who have lost the ability to have fun. Or maybe they are just uncoordinated and can't get their wings to work. Maybe they are like fairy immigrants who have had to adjust to a new culture and in the process have forgotten about their old, magical lives.

PETER: If they're immigrants, where do they hail from? And how exactly are they magical? How are they different in terms of the magic they can do versus the magic that trolls, gnomes, elves, and other creatures of that ilk can do?

LISA: I don't really know. I should find out about all that.

PETER: Maybe there's a battle going on between magical creatures of all sorts.

LISA: Yeah, maybe fairies aren't the only ones who have forgotten their magic. Maybe the entire world of these creatures is in crisis. Okay. I have to do more research about this before we come up with more ideas. But I really like something about getting their magic back, and maybe bringing in other creatures. I like gargoyles. I'll add those to my list.

PETER: Now I had a particular idea in mind. I wanted to write about children who stay in after-school programs. I wanted to start with a group of kids who are sort of abandoned between the time school closes and the time their parents pick them up and they go on all sorts of adventures related to learning.

LISA: Maybe the adventures involve magic in the sense that they can travel to space or to foreign countries or inside an acorn or whatever. But I wonder what they have to do to get there? Is there science involved in the travel part or do they just magically arrive there and then the particular adventure begins?

PETER: I dunno yet. I'll write that down. And maybe they have to solve problems that are set way back in time, going all the way back to the dinosaurs. Like they could explore age-old questions that we all wonder about, like how the dinosaurs disappeared and what made the ice age occur.

LISA: I really like those ideas. Time travel is always intriguing. And maybe you have kids who aren't necessarily the usual stereotypes like the Brain or the Loser or whatever. Maybe these kids each have special powers that help them look at things differently, like scientists do.

PETER: Yeah. I like that. Okay, that's enough for me to start with.

Brainstorming by going back and forth between you and your writing buddies can generate and hone ideas, helping you develop them much faster than most writers can accomplish alone. Also if your writing partners are as brutal as ours are, they tell you when your ideas are lame and underdeveloped and encourage you (or bully you) into going back to the drawing board. After you get an idea that you feel strongly about and your partners think rocks, you can get started writing your children's story — or at least you can go to Chapter 6 and discover what to do next.

Finding new brainstorming partners

Writing classes are great for many reasons, one of which is that you have access to an expert in the field who can tell you if, idea-wise, you're headed off into a place you'd best not go. Writing teachers are great resources.

You can also brainstorm with your classmates to get ideas and then go over them with your teacher, who can help you figure out which ones work better for you than other ones. Or you can brainstorm alone with your teacher and have her help you work out which ones have the most promise in terms of uniqueness and interest to you (you're the one investing a lot of energy to make the idea come alive as a story, after all).

You can also get into online forums and chats for writers, which we cover in Chapter 15, and you may be able to engage someone to help you brainstorm on one of them if you don't have other sources of feedback, which we also discuss in Chapter 15. (But don't expect people in chats and forums to be experts.) Online children's book writing courses that are attached to major universities can also be a boon, offering individual interaction with a teacher without ever having to leave the comfort of your ergonomic desk chair. But we suggest that you check out these resources before investing any time or effort in them to make sure they offer what you need and involve experts who can really help you reach your goals as a writer.

If you're not taking a class that gives you easy access to a writing teacher, see whether you can pay a professional writing teacher for an hour of her time. Just make sure she knows the specific purpose of the session and come prepared so that you get the most for your money. Oh, and bring cash, because your Visa card probably doesn't do the trick.

Getting help from your audience

Children themselves are a wonderful resource when it comes to ideas. Brainstorming with them, however, needs to be directed, because many kids love every idea you present to them (bless their hearts).

If you're visiting a classroom, consider bringing a list of ideas and generating discussion based on these topics. Brief the teacher beforehand by sharing your list and reiterating the purpose of your brainstorming session. We guarantee that if the children are verbal enough to carry on a conversation, and if you can get the teacher to facilitate based on your list of topics, you'll find out stuff about your topics you never even considered.

A typical session of brainstorming picture book ideas with a group of 4-year-olds may sound something like this:

LISA: So I was thinking about writing about little sisters and brothers and how you get along.

CHILDREN: (Silence; no response.)

LISA: Like, if you have a little brother, how you manage to get along with him.

CHILDREN: (Silence; no response.)

LISA: (Getting a little desperate, trying not to let it show.) Like, what would you think if I wrote a story about a little brother who disappeared and had to be found by his older brother?

CHILD 1: You mean his big brother would save him?

CHILD 2: Like a hero?

LISA: (Relieved.) Yes! Exactly. Would save him . . .

CHILD 1: (Interrupting.) . . . from a mean fire-breathing dragon? Who would melt the little brother because he took toys from you and broke them?

CHILD 2: And you didn't have enough time to save him before he got scared some by the dragon. So he would drop the toys he stole from your room?

LISA: Yes . . . and maybe there would be a princess . . .

CHILD 3: I like princesses!

CHILD 1: As long as they aren't wearing dresses. Because you can trip on dresses when you are climbing the tower to save your little brother.

LISA: Then maybe the princess could be a brave one who can help you find your brother. But first you have to find the magic key.

CHILD 3: The key to the castle? Or to mom's car? Because sometimes my little brother takes the car keys and drools all over them.

CHILDREN: Eeeeew!

Cross our hearts and hope to die, you'll never leave a classroom without at least one great idea that makes your fingers itch to write.

Interview with Barney Saltzberg

Whatever exercises you choose to help you generate ideas and get writing, you need to put pen to paper or fingers to keyboard and just go. Take it from Barney Saltzberg, acclaimed musician as well as successful children's book writer and illustrator, who tells it like it is about ideas and writing.

WCBFD: You have written and illustrated over 25 books for children, not to mention the tons of songs you've written and performed on your CDs. How do you get your best book ideas?

BS: There's no formula. If I had one, every book I write would be a hit! Ideas come to me in many different ways. *Crazy Hair Day* (Candlewick Press) came from seeing a student show up at my son's school, a day early, for Crazy Hair Day. My brain took over from there. Sometimes I'll hear something and say, "That's a great title for a book or a song," and that's how it begins.

WCBFD: Do you think that brainstorming with others is a good way to come up with ideas? Why or why not?

BS: I try to brainstorm with other people from time to time, but personally, I find that I need to sit with whatever I'm working on and brainstorm by myself. It works the best. It's not a bad idea to get someone else's viewpoint, but you really have to trust them to have the same way of thinking as you do, and that's nearly impossible in my case!

WCBFD: Do you use any particular idea-generating exercises to come up with ideas?

BS: No.

WCBFD: Do you start with a format idea that you fit a book idea into, or do you begin with a book idea that you fit to a format?

BS: I begin with an idea and see which format it fits into later.

WCBFD: When an idea comes to you, how do you record it? And how can you tell if it is a good one?

BS: Sometimes I find myself making notes on scraps of papers, napkins, or on my computer. It depends where I am when the idea hits me. I always think they're good ideas. It's only when I've worked on them for a long time that I know if they will truly work or not.

WCBFD: How do you proceed to develop an idea that you feel really good about?

BS: Since I'm a writer and an illustrator, my working habits are different from writers who only write. Sometimes I'll be writing and then find a piece of paper and start drawing the characters I'm writing about. The body language and facial expressions of those characters sometimes color how the written story develops. Mostly, I just force myself to sit with my computer and write and write and write.

WCBFD: Is there such a thing as writer's block?

BS: Unless you're talking about a neighborhood full of writers and that's where you live, "on the writers' block," no, there is no such thing as writer's block. Only a writer who's avoiding writing. I guarantee that if you sit down and just write, things will happen for you! Will everything you write be great? Absolutely not. But you're writing.

WCBFD: Any advice you can offer to new writers trying to come up with great ideas for children's books?

BS: You have to start writing. Write from within yourself, as a child. It sounds corny to say, "Write from your inner child," but that's where the voice is. Don't set out to write an entire book. Just make short sentences, blurting out anything and everything. Eventually, something will pop out. Recess. Homework. Walking home from school. Playing in the yard. The neighbor next door. Something will trigger a flood of memories from which to start a story.

Going back to school for ideas

Another way to open up creative outlets is to teach a class, especially if it's been a while since you spent any time around children. How about coaching children at a community center or a nearby school? Ever try teaching children at your local church or synagogue? Many volunteers give their time and expertise for altruistic reasons, and you can *say* you do, too, while secretly gathering material from children by hanging out with them in a way that benefits both of you. They get an adult to oversee and guide activities, and you get to observe them on the sly, mercilessly using them for the material and ideas they contribute to your notebook.

REMEMBER

The more time you spend around children, the more your ideas reflect their world, and the more your writing speaks to them.

Or instead of signing up for a writing class, take a class in painting, pottery, drawing, woodwork, beading, gardening — any art or craft class that may interest you. Using your hands and eyes in creative activities other than writing can actually help your creativity, which in turn helps you think of good ideas, which in turn helps your writing — even if you can't make the connection right away. This is the *backdoor approach,* meaning that if purposefully trying to generate ideas instantly freeze-dries your brain, some other unrelated but enjoyable creative endeavor may melt down your resistance. Working with your hands to make actual, physical objects also relaxes you enough to help you come up with new ideas.

At this point you should have a bunch of simple ideas. You may or may not have developed them or added a lot of detail, but you ought to have at least a one-sentence idea to start with, much like the anteater or frog princess ideas we describe earlier in this chapter. (You may also want to jump ahead to Chapter 20 to take a peek at a bunch of storylines that are up for grabs.) If not, don't worry; you may simply be one of those writers who needs to actually practice writing in order to come up with an idea you can fall in love with. And if that's the case, don't fret about your one sentence; simply delve into the upcoming writing exercises. At least one of them ought to leave you with an idea you can use to write your children's story.

Fighting Writer's Block

Picture this: You have a great story idea that has kept you writing for days. On the fifth day, you're happily writing when the door bell rings. You answer it to discover a package delivery. You sign for the package and return to your desk and realize that you've completely lost your train of thought. Minutes pass. Then a half hour. Then you notice dust in the corner of the room that you hadn't seen before, so you grab the broom. Next you're at the kitchen sink washing dishes. Finally, you return to the computer, but you realize your writing has come to a crashing halt. You're paralyzed in front of a computer monitor that seems to mock you. And no matter how many times you straighten up your desktop and change the pretty background pictures, you can't seem to write a word.

Getting stuck is something that all writers — no matter how skilled they are or how much practice they've had — experience from time to time. The writer's brain is like a mighty river — usually it flows along smoothly, but sometimes a 40-foot barge sinks right in the middle, causing the river to back up and the words to stop flowing.

If you get stuck long enough, you can experience those two little words that are guaranteed to strike fear in the heart of anyone who has ever faced a deadline or had to earn a living from his words: *writer's block.*

Based on some research, we found out that not everyone believes in the existence of writer's block. (See "The psychology of writer's block" in the nearby sidebar for the counterargument.) Some blame shiftless Americans who created the so-called phenomenon because they were too lazy to power through the tough times when writing got the best of them. Other people even think that writer's block is a creation of psychologists who want to take advantage of writers' insecurities and make piles of dough from them. (Hmmm . . . do we sense a lucrative new career path here?)

We think writer's block does exist and is simply a condition that requires one of two remedies:

- ✔ Giving yourself permission to get away from the pressure of writing for a while until the urge to write strikes again
- ✔ Using writing exercises to get your writing juices flowing again

If writer's block seems to be plaguing you, flip to the writing exercises at the ends of Chapters 7, 9, 10, and 11.

You do writing exercises for fun. For laughs. For the sake of doing them. Why is this important? Because the first half of the problem with writer's block is losing the urge to write, and the second half involves being stuck about what to write. So exercise your imagination — a very important muscle in getting over writer's block and finding out how to master the process of writing.

The psychology of writer's block

Ever wonder why your brain gets stuck? We have (more than once or twice), so we did some research on writer's block. Much to our surprise, writer's block is not the result of watching soap operas on TV (which is *very* good news for Peter) or eating too many carbs, or sticking pins into twin voodoo dolls crudely designed in our images (though we're still a bit suspicious about that one).

According to the folks in white lab coats who spend their working days and nights researching this phenomenon, writers actually get stuck when a temporary disconnect between the frontal (located behind your forehead) and temporal (located behind your ears) lobes of the brain occurs. Among other things, your frontal lobes act as your writing organizer and editor, while your temporal lobes control your understanding of words and come up with those fabulous ideas that are sure to capture the interest of your publisher.

When your frontal lobes take charge — pushing aside the ideas set forth by your temporal lobes — you quickly find yourself stuck (bad). When your temporal lobes take charge, the words flow unimpeded, fast, and furious (good). So can you do anything to help your brain move through the occasional slow spots?

Bang your head against the closet door really hard. (Just kidding.)

Pay attention to what kinds of things in your life or environment seem to lead to writer's block, and what kinds of things make it go away. Then do less of the former and more of the latter. (Yeah, yeah, we know that solution sounds facile, but remember: Not everyone believes in writer's block anyway. And how much do you want to bet that those who don't believe in it don't suffer from it either? Ten bucks? You're on.)

Chapter 6

Researching Your Audience and Subject

*I*n Chapter 5, we discuss generating ideas; in this chapter we talk about going out into the world to explore and learn about what children like and do. Before you research and write about the subject you are writing on, you need to understand your audience. By going on a field trip into the places children spend their time as well as into the places of people who market to children, you may find yourself fleshing out your original ideas, taking them to the next stage by connecting them to a child's world.

The best children's books have some grounding in a child's reality. In this chapter, we take a look at some of the best places to find out more about kids and about the people standing between your manuscript and the children you are trying to reach: how they think, how they act, what they like, what they think is gross versus what they think is cool, and what is popular. By the time you've finished, you'll know everything you've ever wanted to know about kids and books and maybe a little bit more.

We also touch a bit on researching your topic itself. If your subject happens to be nonfiction, you have a lot of facts to get straight. But even if your subject is fictional, you may choose to ground certain aspects of it in reality — a reality about which you are unfamiliar, such as Victorian England — or perhaps one of your characters is a beaver and you have no idea what beavers eat or where they live. Using some of the same strategies you use to delve into the secret lives of children, you must go even further when it comes to presenting the facts. The facts have to be right on target, and this chapter helps you get ready, aim, and fire.

Hanging Out with Kids

If you're writing about kids and the issues that they deal with in everyday life, you want to make sure to write from their perspective. Many new writers make the mistake of writing from a grown-up perspective. As a children's book writer, you need to keep in mind that the children you're writing for are looking for entertainment, not parenting. Your job is to capture their imaginations and bring them into your world, not teach them lessons about right and wrong. No one likes a lecture — especially not children, who are probably already getting more than their share of those at home and school.

But writing a good children's book involves more than just perspective. Writers have to remember that children aren't only their target audience, but are often the subjects of the book they're writing, and so the information, the descriptions, and the language have to be accurate. Every detail matters.

But what if the only thing you can remember from your childhood is that you wore smaller clothing or that you used to love peanut butter and jelly sandwiches? If you're going to write about and for kids, your characters need to be believable. You need to know how they talk, what they wear, what they do, and how they go about doing it. And guess what? We have a suggestion on how to figure all this out: Hang out with kids.

Go back to school

For nine months of the year, from 8:00 a.m. to 3:00 p.m., children are captives (some may claim to be prisoners) in school, which therefore happens to be a great place to go to do your research. Lucky for you, many teachers are open to having writers come into the classroom.

Being around children at school is the perfect research venue. You can make the experience active by leading a project or volunteering for an activity or game, or you can simply lurk passively in a corner and watch and listen. How do the kids dress? How do they interact with one another? What do they say to one another? How do they handle conflict? What toys or games do they prefer and is there a difference between how the boys play act and how the girls do? What about during lunchtime? Is there a time set aside for art? What kind of art do kids create at different ages?

With older children, do they seem to roam in packs? How are those packs differentiated from one another? Is dress a big deal? How can you tell? What do kids have in their lockers? How do they speak to one another or to their teachers?

Get by with a little help from your little friends

Want to observe thinking, busy, creative children in action inside a classroom? Don't just visit a school empty-handed. Take along all the fixins for a book-making session! All you need are:

✔ White construction paper: Five sheets of white per child. (You will fold these width-wise, so that you have ten interior pages or five spreads of a portrait-oriented book.)

✔ Colored construction paper: One sheet of colored construction paper (not too dark of a color that art won't show up on it) per child for the cover of the book

✔ Crayons or markers, one complete set per five children or per table

✔ A ball of yarn

✔ A single-hole punch

If you already have a story completed that you want to use for this activity, bring yours in. But if you are still at the beginning stages, bring in someone else's book. (A few caveats: Bring in a book whose subject matter is at least similar to your own; and find a more obscure book or one that is less popular because it's best if the children aren't totally familiar with every word). Read it aloud to the children. Then tell them you need their help to figure out what happens to the characters next or the next day. (Some writers like to leave out the ending in order to fire up their listeners' imaginations.)

Before you get to reading your story, you are going to help the children make up their own book. Have each child fold the five white sheets of construction paper width-wise. This consti-tutes the interior of their book. Then have them take the colored sheet of construction paper and wrap it around the interior pages. To tie the sheets together (the binding), you are going to punch holes on the left side of the book. Punch the first hole about an inch from the top and ¼ inch in from the outside folded edge, and the second hole about an inch from the bottom and ¼ inch in from the same outside folded edge. Take two pieces of yarn about 8 inches long each and loop one piece through each hole, tying the ends. Voila! You have a blank book.

Together, as a classroom, each child writes the next five spreads of the book to create the ending or the "sequel" to the story. Every child gets to pick a number out of a hat and those numbers will be used to solicit answers to the questions you will ask of them to get the story going (the numbers help keep the chaos of many willing participants in check by giving each a turn in order). Tell the kids not to worry about the words, they are just going to draw the pictures for what happens next to the characters.

If you want to go even further: Use the numbers again to get the kids answering questions about what the illustrations should look like and what should go on the front and back covers.

All this information and more gives you a peek into the lives of real children — the ones you hope will be reading your book after it gets published. And if you are privileged enough to end up in their hands, you best make sure you haven't misrepresented or miscast them. So, grab your backpack and your pencil case, your iPod or MP3 player, and head back to class, where you are the student and the students are your teachers.

Become a storyteller

A great way to understand how children in your target age group think is to read a book to them and then have a question and answer session. You can do this with children who are as young as 2 or 3 years of age, depending on how verbal they are and how accustomed they are to speaking in front of other kids (preschoolers are ideal for this kind of exercise because they love to raise their hands, give their opinions — often in great and meandering detail — and listen to themselves speak to an adult who actually cares to hear what they have to say). Or you can pick older children, such as tweens or teenagers — whoever you think your target audience is, the actual bodies that fall into these age ranges are the ones you need to be getting information from.

Regardless of where you go to get the attention of children, it's important to make sure you're prepared to have a good read. Don't just read any random old book — make sure it's one that's similar in subject matter or topic to the book you want to write — maybe it's the competition or an out-of-print version of a topic you want to handle. And make sure you know the book pretty well so that you can ask some really good questions afterward.

Here's another idea: Don't do the actual reading. Bring someone else to do it. Writers who really want to get the most of the time spent with children turn the time into a partnership of sleuthing. When you read out loud, chances are you are so engaged in the act of reading and turning pages and trying to sound interesting to a child that you can't make adequate observations. This is where your partner comes in:

1. **Seat yourself next to your partner, but off to the side a bit so that you can see the faces and bodies of most of the children listening.**

2. **Have your partner read the book aloud.** While he or she is doing that, you will be taking notes.

   > What you want to note is how the children respond to the story. At what point in the story do they lean forward in anticipation? Do their faces ever show fear or amazement or sadness? Take note.

   > When do the children start fidgeting? Perhaps the timing or pacing of the story is lagging, or something about it is not appropriate for your audience.

   > Where in the story are they interrupting or asking questions? Maybe something isn't clear.

   > Watch their bodies — do they seem interested or bored? Maybe the story is not as great as you thought it was.

After you're written down everything you can, and the book has been read, start asking questions. What did the children think about the main character? Did they like or dislike him or his friends? What did the children think about the chosen subject? What do they wish they could have heard more of? Was there anything in the book they did not like? Was there anything they would have changed about the book? Why? The answers to these questions will tell you a lot about how children of that age approach the subject you are interested in and what issues are relevant to them — as well as those that are less so.

 To make the most out of any question-and-answer session with children, you want to formulate good questions that will yield the kind of detail you need to use as a writer. For that you use the reporter's Trusty Six, detailing them to your particular needs and concerns:

- **Who:** Ask questions that focus on the main character. Can the children tell you more about this character? Who is he exactly? What kind of person (animal or object) is he? Is he a good person? A bad person? Does he have any problems? What are they? Does he solve them? How? How would they suggest he solve his problem? What about the secondary characters? What are they like? Are they appealing or not? Why?

- **What:** What is the story really about (that is, what is its core or central theme)? What is the main problem that had to be solved? Does the main character have good ideas about how to handle himself in every situation? Why or why not? What happens to make the story interesting or boring? What do they think happened to the main character or his friends after the story ended? For nonfiction: What did they learn about the subject that they didn't know before? What is most interesting to them about that? What do they want to learn more about?

- **When:** When does the story take place? If in the past, can that story have happened today? Why or why not?

- **Where:** Where does the story take place? Is the place a real place or a pretend place? How can they tell? Can that story have happened where they live? Why or why not?

- **Why:** Why is the story interesting? Why is the story important for children to read or hear? For nonfiction: Why is the main character or subject important for children to know about?

- **How:** How does the main character solve his problem? Can the children use the same solution to solve a similar problem? Why or why not? How do the issues brought up in the story or nonfiction account affect children today?

The answers to these questions help you as a writer in so many ways. You get to see how children process information. You get an inkling into what they focus on and the issues that are of paramount importance to them (you may be very surprised). You get to hear about the way they deal with fears or excitement. And, if you're very lucky, certain audience members may veer completely off subject and give you some very valuable insider information that you can then use in your writing.

Borrow a friend's child for a day

Think you know how your subject matter really thinks? Consider yourself an expert in children's speech patterns and interests? Unless you work with children on a daily basis or live with some of your own, you probably don't know how their sinister little minds really work and you may not be as good at picking up on how they talk as you could be.

Do your writing a favor and make some grateful parent (very) happy at the same time: Borrow a child for the day to test your theories. Don't just take the kid to a movie, where conversation will be minimal, take him to a museum, a park, a meal — or all of the above. Engage the child's senses. Then observe and listen.

Getting children to open up isn't always easy. But it shouldn't require hair-pulling on your part. Make your queries seem to be about your needing some information, such as, "I was wondering . . . do you know how a bee makes honey? Want to go to the bookstore and try to find out?" The goal is to engender discussion, getting children to talk about their lives and their feelings, which will give you more information to write about in your book. In order for you to write children's characters who grab your readers, you need to have some familiarity about how kids think, feel, and express themselves.

A good trick is to build a comparison between your ridiculous childhood and theirs. For example, "When I was a child, we had to wear orange ties and purple top-hats to school every single day. Isn't that silly? What happens at your school that you think is silly?"

Monsters don't touch

Lisa learned one of her most valuable lessons about writing for children of picture book age during a reading. Early on in her career, she had written a story about monsters. These were your run-of-the-mill kind: the ones hanging out under the bed, outside a darkened window, and in the closet. The story's protagonist had to figure out a way to make them all go away so he could get a good night's sleep. The story had been edited by a professional editor friend, vetted by a teacher, and was all ready to submit. But Lisa wanted to see and hear what the children might think about monsters in general. So she brought two stories about monsters with her on the train. One was written by a famous author. The other was hers. While reading her story aloud to a small trio of children on the way from Providence to Boston one morning, Lisa learned that monsters can be scary, mean, smelly, and generally odious, but *they must never, ever actually touch the child protagonist* or someone he loves, because then the story is too scary and makes children cry — and worse, that children crying on a train somehow seems to echo in a loud and disturbingly public fashion. Now whose story do you suppose made that horrible faux pas? (Clue: It wasn't the famous author's.) As you can imagine, Lisa never forgot that particular lesson, and it has helped guide her writing ever since.

A good story is a good story

Barney Saltzberg is a successful author, illustrator, and children's music performer. Through his varied careers, he's spent plenty of time with children and he continues to discover more about them with each encounter.

WCBFD: As a writer/illustrator/performer who has had success in both books and music, can you tell us what kinds of things you learn from children when you visit them at schools or other venues that help you as a writer?

BS: That life as a child isn't always as fun as I sometimes remember. Traveling around the country, I've seen children going to school hungry and who don't have any books at home. I find that no matter where they come from and how they live, when we sit down together, they want to sing and draw and laugh and that they all have stories they long to tell.

WCBF: Do you use the Web for researching subject matter for your books? Any clues as to how to start?

BS: I Google a lot. Sometimes for images, when I need to draw something. Other times, I'll Google a title I think up to see if it's out there already. If it is, I'll look up the book or song and make sure I'm not stepping on someone else's toes. If it's not out there, then I run with it. I just finished a book called *Cornelius P. Mud, Are You Ready for Bed?* (Grosset & Dunlap). And I found tons of Web sites where parents talked about all the things they do in order to put their children to bed at night. It was very helpful in developing my story.

WCBFD: Your children are in high school, and you write mostly for younger children. With the advent of video games and other media that conflict with books, how do you make sure the topics you choose are still relevant?

BS: People are still people. A good story is a good story. You may be blasting aliens on a handheld device, but if a story has soul and speaks truth, readers will be captivated.

WCBFD: You teach writing and illustrating children's picture books at UCLA Extension Writer's Program. How do you guide your students when it comes to their own research of their subject matter?

BS: I suggest they go to children's bookstores and libraries, find the picture books, and read and read and read. When they're done reading, read some more!

WCBFD: What do you think about conferences and book conventions for learning about a chosen topic or for researching ideas? Why?

BS: I think any place you can go to gather information is great. You'll never use everything you hear and see, but any way you can get information about publishing and about the writing process can be invaluable. Also, it helps to meet other people who are doing what you are doing so you can learn from the authors and illustrators who have made it. It's also helpful to meet your peers, people at your particular level of writing. People like yourself, who are trying to find their way in this field. You'll have plenty of stories to share.

WCBFD: Have you ever gone to an expert in the field to get some help on any aspect of your writing, illustrating, or performing? What was your experience?

BS: As far as performing for children, the only way I've improved over the years is to continually put myself in front of an audience. I learn something every time I perform. Watching videos of my concerts has helped me improve as well. I see things I like, some things I don't and I try to make adjustments. In terms of my writing, I've read books from other writers on the process of writing, and I have always found some nugget that set off angels singing, "AHA!" and "YES!" I guess that's why they call them experts!

When you come home from what we are sure will be an interesting — albeit exhausting — day of research, try to write down everything you can recall about what happened. Then when you go back to developing your idea, you can see how what you learned adds to or changes the direction of your story.

Dipping into Popular Culture

Whatever the latest trend, whether it's related to food, fashion, music, toys, games, cartoon characters — you name it — you can bet that kids and their friends will be the first to know about it, if not actually the ones who create it themselves. Why? Two reasons: First of all, children have an insatiable curiosity and desire to know what the latest and greatest is; second, advertisers that produce products for children target them mercilessly through television advertising, programming, and movies that are thinly veiled infomercials for some toy.

Kids are on the cutting edge. By taking a dip into their world — and the popular culture that pervades it — you'll have a much better understanding of what kinds of things need to go into your story.

Watch cartoons

If there's one quick way to dip your toes into the prevailing popular culture, it's by watching children's cartoons. And some cartoons — in recent years, for example, Japanese cartoons like *Pokemon, Yu-Gi-Oh!, Sailor Moon, Hamtaro,* and so forth — have created their own popular culture (and generated millions of dollars in spin-off toy and DVD sales in the process). You can gather all sorts of information about what to write about by watching cartoons.

Although long-running cartoons like *Scooby-Doo, Tom & Jerry,* and *Looney Tunes* (originally developed decades ago) always draw an audience, the more recent cartoons are most reflective of current popular culture. You can find those by scouring entertainment magazines such as *Entertainment Weekly,* perusing *TV Guide,* reading reviews of new children's movies, videos, and books in parenting magazines, or simply turning on the TV on Saturday morning, or anytime if you have cable channels that run cartoons 24/7.

When you watch these cartoons, pay attention to the way the characters speak, what they wear, what they spend their time doing, and what their attitudes are about each other, grown-ups, school, home, and all the other commonalities they and real children share. Even if they come from a newly discovered planet, have one big eye, and wear no clothing but overalls made of supersonic gel, they were still fashioned with real children in mind, and, thus, have concerns and issues (perhaps disguised) that real children also share.

Read parenting and family magazines

Parenting and family magazines are another great way to take a dip into the popular culture. Within their pages, you'll find all sorts of articles tackling topics of concern to parents — many of which reference the current popular culture for kids. Whether it's how to deal with a teenager who idolizes pop singers (and who wants to bare her belly button at school just like they do) or which licensed character piñatas are hot (and which are not), you'll find plenty of references to pop culture here.

Major parenting and family magazines include *Family Circle, Parenting, Family Fun, Parents, Working Mother, Today's Parent,* and *Child.* While flipping through these, note the advertisers and the types of products they're selling. Often, you can get good ideas for stories this way, as we discuss in Chapter 5.

But in terms of research, you can glean details about what parents are really talking about, the issues that concern them, the new things children are introducing their parents to, and the like. Kids torture their parents daily with all the new information and gadgets they bring home, and if you want to know what those are, reading about parents trying to wrap their brains around all this stuff is pretty interesting — and often hilarious. And then when you go to write your story, the details you choose to include can help you create a more realistic world. Conversely, the details you choose to leave out can also make a big statement about the world you are trying to create, be it reality- or fantasy-based.

Read pop culture magazines

Of course, what better place to get instantly steeped in popular culture than by buying and reading a stack of magazines that worship at the altar of all things celebrity and pop? If you want to get a quick course on pop culture, you can't go wrong with *Entertainment Weekly, People, Teen People, Us Weekly, Blender, Jane, Star, Teen Vogue,* or *In Touch.* Children are the early adopters of most new technologies, trends, attitudes, and patterns of speech. If you want to see what they are wearing, read about the music they are listening to, see the celebrities they are obsessed about, get familiar with the TV shows and movies they are raving or ranting about, get inundated by the same advertisers that are after their dollars — these magazines are the way to go to get information about your tween and teen audience.

Look for items that have relevance to your topic. Are you writing about a main character who is a girl? Research what girls of that age are playing with, wearing, and talking about. Thinking of writing a relationship story for teens? Look for articles that focus on what relationship issues between teens really involve today. Those personality and love quizzes in teen magazines are great for clues into this arena, by the way!

Surf the Web

Whether it's the massive Web site of *Entertainment Weekly* magazine or a one-page online sales brochure for an obscure cartoonist who is soon to become a household name, the Web is loaded with pop culture.

Most of the pop culture magazines listed in the previous section maintain their own Web sites. And there are many more Web sites specifically devoted to the study and understanding of popular culture in all its glory:

- ✔ Center for the Study of Popular Culture (www.cspc.org)
- ✔ PopCultures.com (www.popcultures.com)
- ✔ PopMatters (www.popmatters.com)

Pop culture often defines a great deal of what children care about. From the TV shows and movies they watch, to the music they listen to, to the books they read — pop culture envelopes a child's world and provides the context that most children today are immersed in. If you don't know what kids are into, how can you hope to relate to them? Keeping up with pop culture can keep your writing current and on the ball. Research like this does not have to be directly included in your story. Sometimes, just knowing about what is going on in pop culture can make you feel more in touch with a generation that may have left you behind years ago.

And although some issues for children are universal and ageless and never change (such as finding acceptance, being appreciated for who you are, and so on), a lot of issues do change as a result of pop culture. For example, 20 years ago, most children would not have aspired to achieve fame as rappers, because rappers were not as popular as they are now. Now that rappers are part of what defines popular culture for many children, it helps to know just what rap music is, the effect is has on clothing and material desires, and the messages it sends to children.

No one can spot a faker faster than a child. There's a big difference between being aware and trying to pretend you are one of them. As such, we strongly discourage you from taking your pop culture familiarity too far. For example, referring to current music or fashions or trends in your book can quickly date it. Using the latest slang is a no-no for the same reason — besides the fact that it sounds absurd when penned by an adult, trust us. On the other hand, knowing about the issues children face and at what ages they face them these days (compared to when you were a kid) is important. So is embracing their lives and their issues and taking them seriously as people. Just don't fake it, whatever you do.

Browse bookstores

Browsing bookstores — particularly independent bookstores devoted to children's books, such as A Whale of a Tale in Irvine, California, (www.awhale ofatale.com), Children's Book World in Los Angeles (www.childrensbook world.com), and Books of Wonder in New York City (www.booksofwonder. net), or in the often huge and inviting children's book departments in the big chains like Barnes & Noble and Borders — is a great way to find out what's new and exciting in popular culture. Amazon.com (www.amazon.com) and Powell's (www.powells.com) are other great places to browse, but it's far better to be able to hold a children's book in your hand, especially books that are heavy on illustrations or are uniquely packaged.

If you want to know what children are reading, sit down and read. Read books from every section and every shelf — at least a few pages or a chapter. And haunt the section that features the format you are concentrating on so you can know intimately what is out there. A lot has changed in publishing in the last ten years, and you should be aware of what the formats described in Chapter 2 really look, feel, and read like. After you are truly immersed in these formats, you'll find yourself further honing your idea as you come across approaches you like and those you don't.

For instance, if your idea is to write a picture book about pirates, are you going to take the pseudo-real-life approach like the one taken by Melinda Long in *How I Became a Pirate?* (Harcourt Children's Books)? Or are you going to teach children about pirate life in a whimsical, rhymed fashion like Kathy Tucker in *Do Pirates Take Baths?* (Albert Whitman & Company)? Perhaps you prefer to answer questions about pirates in a more encyclopedic (and purposely ridiculous fashion) the way Tom Lichtenheld does in *Everything I Know About Pirates* (Simon & Schuster Children's Publishing). The point is that all of these are fictional picture books about pirates targeting the same audience and all approach the subject in a unique manner. The hope is that by studying them, you can invent yet another different and exciting approach.

Just be careful not to clone your idea directly from the latest smash-hit bestseller — you can bet that as a result of the popularity of that particular book, every publisher has been swamped with hundreds of manuscripts for knockoffs. Be different and stand out from the crowd, regardless of what's currently popular.

Visit children's stores online or in person

Toymakers are always ready, willing, and able to leverage the latest kids' trends by designing and selling products that are hardwired into them. If it's hot, there's bound to be a doll, action figure, video game, costume, playset, or some other toy devoted to it. Again, although there's nothing quite like wandering the aisles of your local Toys 'R Us or other toy purveyor to steep yourself in a world that is uniquely oriented toward children and their tastes and desires, let your fingers do the walking and visit some of these popular online toy sites:

- Toys 'R Us (www.toysrus.com)
- Silly Goose (www.usillygoose.com)
- Hamleys (www.hamleys.com)
- Geodonka (www.geodonka.com)

And, although much slower to respond to fast-moving trends in the popular culture, children's furniture stores can sometimes be fertile fields to explore in your research — especially when it comes to licensed or classic children's products. Be sure to include one or two on your list of places to visit.

Visiting toy stores and places that cater to children's lives and activities can help you get in the *kid zone*. By that we mean that when you are surrounded by what kids are surrounded by and get to see what kids like and don't — when you stand in their shoes — it helps you approach your story more from their perspective. For example, maybe your idea involves writing about a kid who loves to build things. You go to the toy store to see what kinds of building sets are popular today. Surprise! Tons of new building toys and materials have been invented since you were a kid. Does that change what your character does? Maybe!

Study kids' fashion trends

Clothing and fashion are reflections of the prevailing pop culture. What did today's pop idol wear on last night's MTV Video Music Awards show? You can bet that clothing manufacturers around the world are gearing up production of whatever fashion is hot within hours after the show hits the airwaves. Whatever the trend — from surfing, to hip-hop, to goth, to nerd gear — clothing stores can show you what's hot.

If you can't find any dedicated children's clothing boutiques in your area, be sure to check out the children's clothing departments in large retailers, like Target, Macy's, Kohl's, Nordstrom, and Dillard's.

Again, standing in children's shoes (or their clothes, for that matter) helps you get a feel for what children appreciate and what they don't. Fashion and clothing trends especially affect tweens and teens, so if they are your target audience, it behooves your writing to develop a familiarity with this part of their world, too.

For instance, if you are writing about a tween girl who wants to be just like her bigger sister, who happens to be a completely different type of person than she is, when you have her steal her sister's clothing, what is she going to steal? Chances are it's not the saddle shoes, cashmere pullover, and pleated skirt from some people's childhoods.

Researching Your Nonfiction Topic

Although you can play fast and loose with some facts in a fictional work, you don't have that luxury when you're working on a nonfiction book. To do so not only potentially risks your reputation with publishers and book buyers, but it can lead to disillusioned children who discover that their favorite nonfiction author is a fraud. And you wouldn't want to disappoint all those children, would you?

Also, many educational publishers and publishers of nonfiction require that all information be verifiable and that all attributed dialogue be documented. Your audience is not as savvy and discerning as an adult audience and thus your responsibility for verifying your facts is acute.

So how do you make sure that your "facts" are really true and not just the latest urban legend being passed around the Internet? You research, you research some more, and then you research your research.

Trebling up on your research is known as *The Rule of Three.* If you can find three trustworthy references or resources (go for hardcopy published sources you can hold in your hands and that have been deemed trustworthy by three separate publishers), chances are good that your research is accurate.

The research process

The amount of research you're going to need to do, where you're going to do it, and the depth of your efforts will be very much determined by the exact genre of nonfiction children's book you're planning to write, how deeply you're going to cover the topic, and the sophistication of your audience. A board book on fire trucks — with less than 100 words — will require far less extensive research than will a nonfiction middle-grade reader on the life and times of Rosa Parks.

So how do you go about the process of researching your nonfiction children's book?

1. **Choose a topic.**

   The topic you select will have a great impact on where and how you will do your research.

2. **Outline your book.**

   How will you know what research to do if you don't know what topics you'll cover in your book? Here's the short answer: You won't.

3. **Create a research plan.**

   The plan should include the sources you intend to look up (newspaper and magazine articles and books), places you intend to visit (libraries, museums, research institutions, historical sites), and people you intend to interview (experts, researchers, celebrities). If, for example, you are writing a nonfiction book on farm animals, your plan might include visits to a local library, some time on the Internet, time at a 4-H club meeting, interviews with children who live on farms with animals and, of course, a number of visits to real working farms. And don't forget to include in your plan the images you might need to create or acquire permission to use along the way.

4. **Put your plan into effect.**

   Get out there and start researching your topic. For many writers, researching is almost as fun (and in some cases, more fun) than the actual writing process. Peter once wrote a book on New York City's Orpheus Chamber Orchestra which required him to accompany the orchestra on an all-expenses-paid concert tour through Germany, Italy, Spain, and the Czech Republic to do his research. It was a tough job, but someone had to do it.

5. **Organize your results.**

   Interviews should be transcribed, articles organized, facts compiled, and sources credited. Be sure to triple-check your facts — when in doubt, check it out again and then once more.

To make sure you note all the information you need from each source or reference book — before you place it back in the stacks and forget where you found it — avail your self of copies of two of the best guides for writers of nonfiction: *The MLA Handbook* by Joseph Gibaldi and Walter S. Achert (Modern Language Association) and Kate L. Turabian's *A Manual for Writers* (University of Chicago Press). Both of these tiny (but mighty) books can guide you on how to attribute and credit sources properly and completely.

Get around locally

Depending on the topic you're researching, plenty of local resources can help with your research. Some of these resources include

- Local newspapers
- Libraries
- Government offices
- Company headquarters
- University research labs
- Planetariums
- Museums
- Long-time residents

Go far afield

You're not limited to doing your research locally: You also have the option of doing your research long distance. Check out these additional resources for doing your research:

- Library of Congress
- Smithsonian Institution
- The National Archives
- National Geographic Society
- National magazines
- Out-of-town newspapers
- Associations and societies
- National experts
- Research institutes
- Universities and colleges
- Government offices
- Foreign embassies
- Businesses

Using the power of long-distance telephone directories and the Internet, it's pretty easy to track down a phone number for even the most remote resource. Don't be shy — most of these organizations are accustomed to fielding questions like yours. And most experts are happy to help, either by guiding you to the next step, foisting you off on someone else, or stepping up and sharing some expertise.

Visit cyberspace

The Internet is a great thing — it's entertaining, it's informative, it's immediate, and it's plain fun. But although much of what shows up on the Net is presented as fact, too often these facts are actually fiction.

Sadly, the Internet is chock full of falsehoods, half-truths, and outright lies. When you're using the Internet to do your research, be particularly careful about so-called experts who really aren't. Anyone can put up a Web site promoting himself as an expert on any topic.

You need a plan for separating Internet reality from Internet fantasy. Consider these tips for doing just that:

- ✔ If it sounds too good to be true, suspect that it probably *isn't* true.

- ✔ Establish trusted online sources of information on the Internet, such as online encyclopedias or national newspapers and magazines or other long-established, reliable media.

- ✔ Remember that blogs (Web logs) are particularly notorious for playing fast and loose with the truth. Consider them sources of opinion, not necessarily fact.

- ✔ Confirm your information. Use other sources to confirm what you may have found on a site.

- ✔ Challenge the information mongers by e-mailing them and asking for links to their sources. If they can provide them, great. If not, suspect that they're not telling the truth.

Have an expert look over your work

If you're writing nonfiction and you're incorporating lots of obscure facts that are hard to verify, consider having an expert take a look at your manuscript. There are a number of benefits of taking this approach:

- ✔ If your expert is plugged in and up to date, you'll have the latest and greatest information available anywhere.

- ✔ You'll increase the chances of avoiding a potentially embarrassing factual faux pas.

- ✔ You'll be able to sleep better at night knowing that the facts you cited in your book really are facts.

- ✔ Your editors will sleep better at night for the same reason.

- ✔ You may establish an ongoing relationship with your expert that can be beneficial in your future projects.

- ✔ It's fun hanging out with people who know what the heck they're talking about.

Experts are everywhere. After you decide on a specific topic, do some research to find out who the experts are in the field. Get their names and e-mail addresses and don't hesitate to pop the question when it comes time. Quite often, experts are happy to review short manuscripts for little or no money. It gives them something fun to do while contributing to their communities.

Just ask. The worst that can happen is that your expert may say no. And if you can credit your expert on or in the book, chances are that she may just give you a break on the cost of her services, because she, like you, may be able to use the added credibility.

But be careful: Not every expert is truly an expert, and some experts may have been top dog 20 years ago, but today are lagging well behind the pack. Choose your experts carefully — check out their current publications and their reputations within their industry or the academic community before you commit. A little bit of research on your part when selecting experts to work with can save you much heartache down the road.

Part III

Creating a Spellbinding Story

The 5th Wave   By Rich Tennant

WORKING DECKSIDE, FREELANCER JANINE
WALKER MISTAKENLY COATS HERSELF
WITH WRITERS BLOCK INSTEAD OF SUN BLOCK

@RICHTENNANT

Dang!

WRITE NO MORE

SUN BLOCK

In this part . . .

Getting started is both exciting and daunting. You have a basic idea and all these thoughts about it and now you get to put it all together. But how do you start? You need to decide on a few simple but crucial basics as you start writing your story. If you're writing fiction, you need to create and develop characters, figure out the plot, establish the setting, and work on dialogue, point of view, and voice. If you're into nonfiction, you need to do some research and find a way to make the material interesting to young readers. We tackle these issues one at a time, helping you get the connections as you move along in this part.

Chapter 7

Creating Compelling Characters

. . . .

In This Chapter

▶ Creating memorable characters

▶ Building supporting characters

▶ Keeping your characters real

▶ Climbing up (and down!) a character arc

▶ Doing character-building exercises

. . . .

Your main character is the soul of your story. Flawed or perfect, full of love or temper tantrums, your protagonist must be memorable and must grow. Think of all those great characters you remember from stories of your childhood — they're great for the very fact that you can recall them so many years after reading about them. There must have been something special about them. What exactly is this magic potion that you add to a name and a face that makes a character come out so well?

It's not magic at all, actually. In this chapter, we tell you how to create memorable characters. We advise you on how to keep those characters real and not stereotyped or boring and we show you how a character arc can help you check up on your character to make sure that she does the growing and changing she needs to do within the course of your story. At the end, we add in a few character-building exercises for practice.

What makes a character great is the way he sees the world and interacts with it. Not just the way he talks (although that is very important), but also the way he walks, the look on his face, the ticks he shows when nervous — in other words, the manner in which he does everything he does. His actions tell your reader who your main character really is.

Creating Your Exceptional Main Character

Kids read children's fiction to encounter characters who are exceptional, not mundane. They want their main characters to be prettier or uglier, more evil or sweeter, nobler or meaner, braver or more fearful than real people are. Even if the characters are boring, kids want them to be exceptionally, hilariously more boring than the average bear. That doesn't mean that the characters should be unrecognizable as human — but they should embody just a tad bit *more* of everything than a child or an adult would in real life — more doses of the curious, silly, funny, awkward stuff. Adding a *little extra* highlights the personality quirks that are important to the story and that make the character more memorable.

So how do you go about creating a character who is three-dimensional and real? You get to know him, that's how.

Recognize your main character's core

Sometime at the beginning of the writing process, or perhaps after you have finished your first draft and right before you start your first major edit, ask yourself just what makes your main character groove. What is he really about? What drives him to act the way he does and do what he does when other characters come into his life? What is his central defining attribute, the one that sets him apart?

Every main character needs to have a goal or something he wants very badly. We call this the *character's core;* just as an apple without a core would collapse in on itself, a character without a discernible core is hollow and forgettable.

A character's core needs to be realistic so that many children can relate to it. Although you can spell out these desires in a straightforward manner in children's books, such as, "Harley wanted to be the best dancer in the entire world," you don't have to. You can opt for a subtler approach in which the reader discerns the protagonist's core by observing how he acts. In longer stories for older children, it is more interesting for your readers to figure out the core for themselves. But in order for readers to do this, you, the writer, must make sure to adequately flesh out the character.

Flesh out your main character

Giving your main character a set of physical attributes is important, but what makes a great character are all the quirks and desires and emotions that comprise a human being. *Fleshing out,* as this process is known, involves making your character real, just like the Blue Fairy made Pinocchio a real boy with his own little boy's agenda. You make a character real by planting clues throughout your story about how the character thinks and feels, by showing him reacting to other characters, by demonstrating his powerful desires as he takes steps to make them come true. It's all about nuance and what your character does. The old adage holds true here more than ever: What you *do* shows more about who you are than what you *say.* Readers need to see your characters *doing.*

In order to flesh out a character well, you need to work him through the basic plot or the action of your story, which we cover in Chapter 8. But if you don't know him well enough to do that yet, you can do one of two things: You can practice having him talk to another character (see the following section and Chapter 9) or you can make a character bible (see the "Making a Character Bible" section).

Using Dialogue to Define Characters

Using dialogue to get to know your main character better is not the same as having your character talk and talk in your story. Instead, you're practicing having your characters speak to each other in dialogue form in order to flesh them out. Chapter 9 discusses the ins and outs of getting your characters to talk to each other, so we give you only a short preview here of how developing a dialogue between two characters defines them much more clearly.

Here is a sample of an exercise from Chapter 9 that you can use to get your characters talking to each other:

Take two characters (ones you're thinking of using in your story) and write a dialogue between them. This can help jump-start the story and develop the main character. Don't worry about how good your dialogue is right now, just let the characters talk to one another. A good place to have them start is to give flesh to your *theme* (the subject of your story; see Chapter 5) and have the characters argue about it. For example, if you're writing about love, perhaps you can have a supporting character challenge your main character on that topic. Like this:

BUNNY RABBIT: I think my mom is going to return me for a new bunny.

MOUSE: What do you mean? Are you broken? Sometimes my mom returns broken stuff.

BUNNY RABBIT: No, I don't think I'm broken, but the other day I heard her say that the new bunnies were on their way.

MOUSE: Oh. . . .

BUNNY RABBIT: And when new bunnies come, what happens to old bunnies?

MOUSE: Oh. I see what you mean. What will she need old bunnies for if she has new ones? Like shoes. When you grow out of the old ones you give them away.

BUNNY RABBIT: Yeah. I guess I better get ready to live in a store. But what does the store do with returned things? Do you think I will end up in the trash?

MOUSE: No. At least I don't think so. We better come up with a plan to show your mom you're not really broken. And quick.

Keep going in this manner until you get a real feeling for who these characters are. Already, you can see here that Bunny is a sweet, sensitive, and naïve little tyke. And also, with the help of his friend, he will become a take-charge sort of bunny. Plot-wise (more on that in Chapter 8), this dialogue shows you that Bunny has misunderstood what he overheard and is in for a big change in his life (although not the one he expects), and that Mouse is going to help him try to solve his problem. This dialogue fleshes out Bunny, Mouse, and their problem. It helps the writer understand more the role of each character, their particular personality, and how they will participate in the plot development so far.

Other writing exercises, such as writing about people you know or imagining yourself in an animal's paws for a while can also help you further flesh out your characters. You can find those kinds of writing exercises in the "Developing Characters through Writing Exercises" section later in this chapter.

Making a Character Bible

A great way to really build a character, attribute by attribute, is to create a blueprint of him, which we refer to as a *character bible*. A character bible is a type of character outline, in which everything about your character is laid out in one place so one can find answers to many questions about the character's personality and desires. We suggest starting a separate document from your story, in list or prose form, so that you can refer back to it and amend it as you get more into your writing. It can even include visuals, if you are a doodler or illustrator. Some really good questions your character bible can answer include the following:

- What is his name? Whom was he named after and why?
- How old is he?
- What color are his hair, eyes, skin?
- What is his ethnicity?

- What does he look like (tall, thin, short, round, gangly)?

- Where does he live? Where was he born? (If not the same place, when did he move and did it affect him in any way?)

- How would you describe his personality?

- What are your character's physical quirks (bites nails, blinks when nervous, brushes hand through his hair, sniffles a lot)?

- What does he wish for more than anything?

- What are his character weaknesses or flaws?

- Does he behave the same way around his friends as he does around adults? Why or why not?

- Is he smart? Not so bright? In what does he excel? In what does he fail?

- Is he talkative or more introverted?

- Is he athletic? If yes, what are his favorite sports? If no, why not?

- What small details set him apart from others? (Does he wear a special totem hidden under his shirt? Does he speak only in a whisper? Does he always have a headset on in one ear?)

- Does he have brothers and sisters? What are their names and ages?

- Does he have a best friend? Name and age, please.

- What's his big secret that he keeps from everyone?

These questions incorporate the emotional, social, and physical — all aspects that contribute to making each one of us who we are. And because people can answer these questions about every child in the world, you should be able to do so for your main character.

So what would a character bible look like using these very questions? Here's an example of a character bible from a middle-grade novel in progress:

- **What is his name? Who was he named after and why?** Barnaby H. Lee. He was named after his granddad, Barnaby Hollis Lee, the man who invented a time machine, performed one public exhibition of how his technology worked, then disappeared three weeks later on the day Barnaby was born. Sometimes, Barnaby's mother looks at him funny, explaining hastily that he reminds her of her dad in many uncanny ways (which is explored later on in the story when Barnaby finds his granddad's hidden time-machine blueprints).

- **How old is he?** Barnaby is 9 years old, but he seems wiser than his years. Not in a geeky way, but in the way he expresses himself and how he speculates about complicated social and emotional issues.

✔ **What color are his hair, eyes, skin?** Barnaby has platinum blond hair, big green eyes, and translucent skin. He looks a little other-worldly.

✔ **What is his ethnicity?** Barnaby's parents are both olive-skinned, of Mediterranean descent. Barnaby looks like no one else in his family — except that he resembles his granddad in a way that is not physical.

✔ **What does he look like?** He is tall for his age, slender, almost jelly-like in his flexibility — it seems as if his limbs kind of flop around when he walks, as if they are attached, but barely.

✔ **Where does he live? Where was he born?** Barnaby lives in Dead Oak Village, a suburb of a big American city, where he was born and where his family has lived for five generations or more.

✔ **How would you describe his personality?** Barnaby is a dreamer, but he is also very smart. Unlike most boys his age, he is very sensitive and aware of emotions and feelings. He often has premonitions that turn out to be true, but he has not articulated this to anyone. He likes to be around people, but often seems not present when he is, as if he is listening to a conversation happening in another room. Barnaby is the first to comfort you if you're hurt, he is also the first to defend you if you need it. He has only one enemy: Shark Kittridge, a boy down the street who has been losing first place in the Invention Fair to Barnaby for two years.

✔ **What are your character's physical quirks?** Barnaby's eyes are weird: Even when they focus on you, you can't really get a fix on what's in them and what Barnaby's expression is. Barnaby's most noticeable characteristic is that he looks up to the left often, as if he is listening to a conversation you can't hear.

✔ **What does he wish for more than anything?** Barnaby wishes he could talk to his granddad. There's something about the old man that niggles at him. He has never met him, of course, but he feels as if there's something important the old man has to say to him, and Barnaby has no idea how he's going to figure out what that is. It is unusual for a boy his age to care about a dead relative this way, so his interest spooks his mom and creeps out everyone else in his family.

✔ **What are his character weaknesses or flaws?** Barnaby has the courage of his convictions. He won't ever shove them down your throat, but he won't back down, either. This makes him a great friend to have, and an exasperating one, too. It's as if Barnaby came into this world fully formed, not precocious, but not needing much improvement. For example, his mother never spends time lecturing Barnaby on how to behave; Barnaby came out of the womb knowing right from wrong, it seems. However, when Barnaby gets an idea in his head, he will do whatever necessary to go where he wants, get what he wants. He never means to hurt anyone, but someone always seems to get hurt by accident. This determination of his will imperils his best friend, Phoebe, in a way that he may not be able to resolve alone — she is going to disappear, and people are going to assume she is abducted and dead, and Barnaby will have to answer for it. But Barnaby does not like to ask for help, and so he will make the situation worse for himself and for her.

✔ **Does he behave the same way around his friends as he does around adults? Why or why not?** Barnaby is interested in everyone — from the smallest baby to the oldest elderly person. Strangely, Barnaby likes to sit with old people and get them to tell him stories. He even volunteers at an old-age home. And he seems to be able to communicate with infants, who are practically hypnotized by his bulgy green eyes. Barnaby acts the same around everyone (polite, well-mannered, not at all hyperactive or pushy), it's just that he's more interested in some people than others.

✔ **Is he smart? Not so bright? In what does he excel? In what does he fail?** Barnaby is smart and excels at school. He's not so good at group activities, as he tends to "disappear" in them, because he is not that outgoing.

✔ **Is he talkative or more introverted?** Barnaby can talk up a storm on issues he's interested in, but he's generally more introverted. He's not shy, he just doesn't offer up of himself.

✔ **Is he athletic? If yes, what are his favorite sports? If no, why not?** Barnaby is a great wrestler. Even though he weighs next to nothing, his flexibility allows him to outmaneuver everyone in his weight class, and some even heavier wrestlers. He's good at track and other solo outdoor pursuits, but he has to be careful in the sun, due to his paleness. He's not good at team sports, because he doesn't seem to be able to pay attention for a long period of time to only one thing.

✔ **What small details set him apart from others?** Barnaby is set off from others by the way he looks, the way he's so ethereal-seeming, and his maturity. It's not that he's adult-like or precocious, or obnoxious, it's just that he seems to already have been wherever you are going: In a conversation, in a car, Barnaby is ahead of himself somehow. But he's wistful about it, not a know-it-all, so you don't hate him for it, you're just perplexed by it.

✔ **Does he have brothers and sisters? What are their names and ages?** Barnaby has a sister and a brother. His sister Tracy is older, age 16, already driving, and moving on into adulthood pretty quickly. She adores Barnaby, but rarely has time for him. His brother Gil is 14 and also has little time for Barnaby, but he's not mean to him like many older brothers would be.

✔ **Does he have a best friend? Name and age, please.** Barnaby's best friend is a girl named Phoebe. She lives next door. Phoebe is also a quiet, strange child who shares with Barnaby an affinity for the paranormal and the ability to stay happily by herself for hours. Barnaby and Phoebe have been best friends since they were three months old.

> ✔ **What's his big secret that he keeps from everyone?** At the end of the first chapter, Barnaby is going to have found the map of his own house, which will lead him to the blueprints for his granddad's time machine. But he knows he can't tell anyone about it because his granddad died making time travel a reality. Besides that, his mother would completely freak out.

Now not every character will be developed to this extent for every story in every format. But even in a picture book, where your word count is limited, it can never hurt for you to know lots of details about your characters. Character enrichment is all about adding layers of complexity with bits of text, phone calls, dialogue, and action. The more you have fleshed out a character, the more real you will make him or her (or it) seem to your reader. And the more memorable he or she will be in your story.

Whether a story is real or not, the characters must always be believable and consistent. When you figure out who they are and flesh them out — and be sure to give them enough interesting traits so as not to make them one-dimensional or boring — make sure they stick to who they are. So if you have a character who is afraid of heights and all of a sudden decides to go mountain climbing, you have a little problem. That does not mean that your characters can't have qualities that make them seem odd or bizarre — bring them on! — but they need to be consistently odd or bizarre.

When you come to a point in your story when you have to make a decision about something your character is about to do to make your plot work, or vice versa, ask yourself this: Would he really do that? If you know your character well enough, you'll have your answer.

Beware dumping tons of background information in successive paragraphs. Character development must be more subtle and oblique, not hitting the reader over the head with gobs of information all at once. Dumping tons of info at one time is also known as *telling instead of showing*. Add character development bit by bit throughout your story.

How do you know when you have made someone real? If you find yourself referring to him as you would your children, your spouse, your best friend, or your partner, he has become real for you. The challenge is making sure he is just as real to your readers.

Stories with Two or More Main Characters

Many beginning children's book writers are told never to try to write a story with two or more main characters unless they have a lot of experience doing so. While we think that is sound advice for some writers, we don't think every new writer needs to be constrained by this dictate. However, we do suggest the following to make sure that your characters stay distinct and different from one another:

- ✔ Create a character bible for each main character, making sure to flesh out attitudes, manner of speaking, and any other small details that set each character apart from the others.

- ✔ Write out how each of your characters would behave when faced with a crisis that requires a choice that compromises the character no matter what he or she chooses — then use this example to inform the rest of your fleshing out. For example, what if Main Character #1 is caught with a forbidden item in her locker that is not hers, but she knows whose it is. What does she do? If she tells, she will lose her best friend. If she doesn't, she will get expelled. Whichever she chooses, she suffers, but we know more about her. Use the same situation to help define each main character's core.

- ✔ Consider limiting your main characters to two; one of each gender. That helps you to draw differentiations and flesh them out while lessening the chance that they will start sounding or acting alike.

- ✔ Consider making the background of one of your main characters very different from the others. For example, if Main Character #2 is a recent immigrant from India, his cultural background and experiences will inform not only his actions, but also the way he speaks. Or what if one of your characters is a foster child, raised by many different families, attached to no one? Something to make him or her really different will help you differentiate this character in your writing.

- ✔ Tape up a picture of each character so that you can really picture him or her in your mind. If you aren't the best artist, try cutting out photos from magazines or other sources that really inspire you. Perhaps assign an actor or a celebrity to each of your characters.

- ✔ Use people from real life as inspiration. Your best friend, a close relative, a coworker, someone you really like or dislike — use that person as the framework for your character as a child. You may even want to use their name in the manuscript until your very last editing, when you change it to protect the innocent — or not so innocent.

- ✔ Make sure that when each character speaks, he doesn't sound like every other character. For example, if you have one character who is garrulous, never coming up for air, make sure that your others do not possess this particular attribute.

Choosing Supporting Characters

In deciding who else to add to your cast of characters, ask yourself who you need in addition to your main character to tell your story. "Who does my main character need around her to make her believable as well as to help her carry out her destiny?" For example, in 99 percent of stories, the main character needs at least one other character to speak to and interact with no matter what your story is or how long it is.

Supporting characters

✔ **Help to convey the context of the story:** If your story takes place 150 years ago, supporting characters could show how life was back then: blacksmiths, butchers, street cops on horseback, one-room school-houses filled with children of all ages, and the like.

✔ **Can also be catalysts in the plot, causing events to occur or information to be shared:** If your story is about a boy like Barnaby (whom we developed a bit in the "Making a Character Bible" section earlier in this chapter) who is looking for some hidden information, perhaps your supporting character tells him a story about her grandmother, showing Barnaby a photo album that gives him a clue as to its whereabouts. Or maybe your supporting character unwittingly leads the enemy right to your main character's secret hideout.

✔ **Can be so dissimilar to the main character so as to highlight the main character's assets or flaws:** Perhaps your main character is an introvert and his best friend, your supporting character, is an extrovert who puts your main character into a situation that causes him extreme discomfort and leads to his doing something that completely messes up his life (as your main character sees it). Or maybe your supporting character chooses an honorable way to address a situation, a way that would not have occurred to your main character, who is too impulsive or too self-involved to realize the effect his preferred choice will have on others.

Unlike main characters who have to push the story and plot further (more on plot in Chapter 8), supporting characters don't have that limitation and thus can often be colorful, silly, super-brave, or even magical. Literally, they support the main character's journey, whatever that is. Think Tink (Tinkerbell) in the movie *Peter Pan* and Donkey in the movie *Shrek*. Whomever you choose for your supporting cast, be sure to make them three-dimensional and avoid stereotypes unless you're consciously using a particular stereotype for a specific purpose.

You develop supporting characters as you need them in your story, and that becomes apparent as your plot calls for someone for the main character to interact with at various points in your plot to pull the story forward. You can ask many of the same questions about the supporting character to develop him, but you needn't go into quite as much detail.

Chapter 7: Creating Compelling Characters

Great supporting characters

We think the following supporting characters are really notable. Go to the library or a local bookstore and read the books they are found in. We think you will see that the authors of these books managed to draw characters who are interesting and contribute to the development and resolution of the main character and his story, without overshadowing him or her.

The fish in *The Cat in the Hat* by Dr. Seuss (Random House)

Charlotte in *Charlotte's Web* by E. B. White (HarperCollins)

Clara Peggotty, Betsey Trotwood, Uriah Heep, and Wilkins Micawber in *David Copperfield* by Charles Dickens (Penguin Books)

Sport and Ole Golly in *Harriet the Spy* by Louise Fitzhugh (Yearling)

Hagrid in *Harry Potter and the Sorcerer's Stone* by J. K. Rowling (Scholastic)

Centipede in *James and the Giant Peach* by Roald Dahl (Puffin)

Aslan the Lion in *The Lion, the Witch and the Wardrobe* by C. S. Lewis (HarperTrophy)

Samwise Gamgee in *The Lord of the Rings* by J.R.R. Tolkien (Houghton Mifflin Company)

Monster Mama in *Monster Mama* by Liz Rosenberg (Philomel Books)

Falkor in *The Neverending Story* by Michael Ende (Puffin)

Dickon in *The Secret Garden* by Frances Hodgson Burnett (Dell Yearling)

Monkey in *Sign of the Qin* by L.G. Bass (Hyperion)

Sam in *Stella, Fairy of the Forest* by Marie-Louise Gay (Groundwood Books/Douglas & McIntyre Ltd.)

Jesse in *Tuck Everlasting* by Natalie Babbitt (Farrar, Straus and Giroux)

The Tinman, Scarecrow, and Cowardly Lion in *The Wonderful Wizard of Oz* by L. Frank Baum (Tor)

Charles Wallace in *A Wrinkle in Time* by Madeleine L'Engle (Yearling)

Here are some steps to help you develop supporting characters:

1. **Decide the function of the supporting character in your story.** For example, is the primary reason for including this character so that you have someone who can serve as a foil between your main character and his goal? Or is the supporting character one whose job it will be to serve as the conscience of the group, reminding them of the correct path to take, while they insist on going the other way?

2. **Figure out what the function of the supporting character is in relation to your main character.** In other words, how does this supporting character support the development of the main character? Children need parents or adults around them to highlight their uniquely childlike perspectives. Is the supporting character a grown-up who clarifies the child's role as a child?

3. **Flesh out the supporting character by adding in details.** Create a character bible just as you would for your main character.

4. **After you create the character, figure out how his differences from the other characters help him fulfill that function**. If you have an introverted main character like Barnaby in the "Making a Character Bible" section, perhaps the function of his best friend Phoebe is to serve as the one who reaches out to others, who gets things done in the real world while Barnaby is living inside his head.

5. **Step into their shoes.** And when you're writing this supporting character, imagine yourself inside that person's head: What is she thinking right now? What is she seeing? What impulses or emotions is she showing or suppressing? What does she notice while another person is talking? What is her mood? All these markers will help you make her real — which is important, no matter how minor a character she is.

No matter how minor a role a supporting character has, she is critical enough to warrant your attention. She will have a point of view, an attitude, particular behaviors, a personality — even if we only glimpse a bit of these attributes. Whether she is there to help convey the theme of your story (more on themes in Chapter 5) or move the action forward at a crucial point, your supporting characters are there to add to your story's flesh and bones.

Avoiding Character Don'ts

Just as important as what you do with your characters is what you shouldn't do. This section gives you some of the most important no-no's.

Avoid stereotypes

Stereotyped characters are ones who are too familiar and thus wooden: the smart geek, the airhead cheerleader, the mean beauty queen. When every expectation a reader has about how a character will end up is met, you've created a stereotyped character. When your reader finds no contradictions or surprises related to him throughout the story, your character is in trouble.

One way to avoid stereotyping your characters is to combine traits that the reader would not expect to encounter in one character. So if that mean beauty queen turns out to be moonlighting as a janitor at a homeless shelter to pay for her uniforms while conjuring up spells to cure ailing pets at the local animal shelter, then you have a character who is potentially very interesting.

Another way to avoid stereotyping is using a character bible (see the "Making a Character Bible" section earlier in this chapter) to spell out interesting traits and combinations of traits. What exactly makes people interesting? Here are steps to creating interesting characters.

1. **List the people you've known in your life who are memorable.**

   Don't just list the ones you know really well who made a difference in your life, but the ones who were so quirky and enigmatic that you just had to learn more about them, that you would have been willing to tag along with doing ordinary things like errands all day long, just because they were so different.

2. **Try to identify what makes them so memorable.**

   Is it the way they act around others, constantly pointing out things about the world and other people that no one else seems to see or care about? Is it the way they rarely offer anything up unless they are asked — and then whoa! Is it the paradoxes within their own personality that sets them apart (such as one who is compassionate about the plight of all animals and insects great and small but who would not share his afternoon snack with another human even if you threatened to rip out his fingernails out one by one)? What is it that identifies this person as truly unique in the world?

3. **Consider whether your character(s) can include one or several of these characteristics.**

   Instead of labeling a character as smart or dumb, athletic or not, get deeper into these labels and decide what they really mean to you. For example, instead of a character who is smart, how about one whose abilities allow him access to secret and special information or events that others might miss? Instead of a character who is beautiful, how about one who is so attractive that she constantly finds herself feeling very alone and wishing she could have a companion who saw her soul instead of her lovely face.

When you think of memorable people, think about the ones who:

- **Really moved you:** The coach who came to a neighbor child's house every day for a week after school to make sure the child mastered skills in a sport, thus allowing him to compete in that week's game.

- **Made you laugh:** The child in the classroom who had to add her two cents to absolutely everything the teacher said, regardless of what it was, and always had something interesting to add (believe it or not) because of the strange way she looked at the world.

- **Perplexed you:** The miserable grandma who smiled only when the grandchildren left and she could play with her cats.

The list can be endless if you just mine your own life. Every person has some aspects that are shared by many people, so it is the combination of those characteristics that makes them interesting. Try to take some of the characteristics you have described in these exercises and see whether you can use any of them to build your main character.

 If you need an exercise to help you develop interesting, nonstereotypical characters, check out the "Developing Characters through Writing Exercises" section at the end of this chapter.

Show your character in action

Don't underestimate the power of motion. As a matter of fact, it is referred to by a phrase you hear a lot in writing classes and writer's groups: *Show, don't tell.* But what exactly does that mean? *Showing* involves

- ✔ Getting the character involved with another character.
- ✔ Going from one place to another.
- ✔ Interacting in some active way with the universe.

Telling is describing all of the above but never actually demonstrating the character in the act.

Showing (and not telling) is so important that it merits an example. Here is telling:

> Chloe felt bad. She wished she could call up her best friend and tell her how much she wanted to take back what she had said, but by the time she actually did it, it proved too late. The friend had already left. So Chloe sat and pondered what she could do. In the end she called up another friend.

This passage tells us Chloe feels bad, when it should show you by dramatizing Chloe expressing her feelings instead. Then it tells you about a phone call to a best friend instead of showing Chloe making the phone call so you can see how she goes about it.

> Chloe wiped the tears from her eyes and picked up the phone. "Is Genevieve there?" she blurted. "No, she's already gone home for the summer." "But-but-I never got to tell her that . . ." "Sorry, hun. She'll be back in September." A dial tone filled Chloe's ear. Chloe stared at the phone. She punched in a different number. "Hello, Olivia? It's me. I have an idea . . ."

We discuss dialogue more in Chapter 9, but suffice it to say here that writing out what a character says instead of telling us about it in prose is a lot more compelling. It also reveals a lot about a character for us to see exactly how she expresses herself verbally, whether she is wordy or terse, respectful or mean, confident or shy — all of these details contribute toward thorough character development.

When your main character appears in your story, and you do not see him engaged in dialogue or some action within a paragraph or so of his appearance, then you know that you are probably telling, not showing.

Toss out passivity and indefinites

Don't overuse the *passive voice* ("to be" verbs). If you want to keep your characters interesting, your plots active (more on plots in Chapter 8), and your writing strong, avoid overusing the passive voice.

- **Cut out "to be" verbs.** Strong, direct writing eliminates passivity and "to be" verbs. For example, instead of writing, *The sound could be heard from Annabella's house a mile away*. You could write, *Annabella heard the shot from a mile away*.

- **Get rid of the passive voice whenever possible.** Passive voice makes characters and plot boring:

    Passive: *There were a lot of people in the square.*

    Active: *Tons of people packed the square.*

    Passive: *The reason she felt so bad is that she had a bothersome pain in her leg.*

    Active: *A sharp pain shot up her leg. "Ouch!"*

Search for the phrases *there is*, *there are*, and *it is* (or their past tenses) in your story. When you find these phrases, cut them out completely and rewrite the sentences.

In the same way, *indefinite prose* (writing that ultimately says nothing and adds nothing useful because it is so nondescript) is colorless, tame, and ultimately timid. Write like you mean it. Instead of meandering into your what you want to say, jump right in.

> **Indefinite:** *She was not sure that going to that school really made any sense for her life.*
>
> **Definite:** *Going to school was a total waste of time.*

Indefinite: That story is really not defined in spots. The plot does not have any real climax, the main character seems listless, and the writing could use a little spicing up.

Definite: How mushy can you get? Could the plot get any more lifeless? Does the main character feel anything? Is the writer of this piece even breathing?

It's hard to stress enough how important positive, strong, direct writing is in character development — as well as in every other aspect of your writing. For more on writing style, see William Strunk Jr. and E. B. White's classic *The Elements of Style* (MacMillan Publishing).

Don't rely on backstory or flashbacks

Backstory is the account of your character's birth to the day before your story begins. Backstory may include historical references, family connections, allusions to other parts of your story, psychological set-up — you name it, but it's basically all the information about how your character came to be the person he is in your story before the action begins. In longer works, dropping in hints of backstory here and there is okay. Even in picture books, allusions to the past are acceptable if they're definitely relevant. But most backstory doesn't belong in your book.

What makes backstory relevant? Backstory should be used only as an immediate development tool for the character or the plot of your story. If it is important to know that your character has lived in foster homes before she gets the scholarship to the boarding school, let your readers know, but only if doing so moves the action forward. If mentioning her backstory causes you to spend a lot of successive paragraphs explaining the character's past, chances are that we don't need to know all that, especially because it's holding up the story. The best way to let out details in a character's backstory is to show it in her character and the way she acts. So if the effect of living in foster homes causes her to act unusually skittish around adults, that skittishness is all the reflection of the backstory that we need to know.

A *flashback* is a literary device used to reveal information about some past event by having the character, in her mind, literally flash back to the past, recalling some event so the reader can experience it as well. Flashbacks can be interruptive of the flow of most stories. If you must use a flashback, do so judiciously (meaning briefly and only once in a while) and only if you absolutely have to (meaning that if you did not, the reader would be truly lost and would not be able to comprehend what happens next).

Yes, we know that *The Catcher in the Rye* by J. D. Salinger (Little, Brown), arguably one of the most successful children's books in history, is found on every high school reading list, and is told almost entirely in flashback. However, this book, like many classics, is an *exception* to the rule. That means that it's something a new writer should almost certainly not attempt. Why? Because a flashback happens entirely in the past and is often referential only, meaning it is told only to explicate something in the present that the story is really about. Most child readers do not care to read about a character who admits he's going to tell you about everything that happened to him prior to his ending up where he is when you find him, because that implies that you are going to have to wait to read about what is going to happen next in the real story. In other words, by using a flashback or a series of flashbacks, you're telling your reader, "Hold your breath while I tell you about what happened to me from birth to age sixteen, and now that I am seventeen I can tell you my story today." You're better off not turning your readers blue and just telling your story in the time it is set.

Calling All Character Arcs

A *character arc* is a fancy visual tool that can help you chart out your character's development. The changes your main character makes in her life can actually be drawn into this arc so that you can see how she is a part of the action as the story starts, then she has an event happen that requires action, then her plight reaches a climax, and finally she heads toward resolution. You use a character arc by assigning different points of your character's development to the different dots; this helps ensure that your character goes through enough changes and struggles to make her and her story compelling. Here's a summary of the steps that characters tend to face:

> When you first meet your main character (ascent begins), she has something happen to rock her world/challenge her reality (steeply ascending), she has to deal with it (ascending higher), she fails (peak), she tries some more and fails (dips, then peaks even further), she hits a seeming stalemate (flatline, but not too long), she figures it out (begins descending), she hits a bump but instead of reverting back to old way tries out new one (further descending), and she ends a changed and better (you hope) person after all (fully descended).

So take the old-fashioned story of Cinderella and apply it to the arc in Figure 7-1:

1. **You first meet your main character (ascent begins):** Cinderella is a happy, well-adjusted girl living a privileged life when her father remarries and brings a stepmother and two sisters into her life — all three of whom detest her. Show Cinderella as sweet and trying to cope, a girl who is confused but still has her father watching her back.

2. **She has something happen to rock her world/challenge her reality (steeply ascending):** Cinderella's father dies, leaving the poor girl to the mercy of the merciless stepmother and stepsisters. Cinderella tries to stay the same, but fails to move these women whose abuse of her escalates.

3. **She has to deal with it (ascending further):** Cinderella still uses her same old way of coping (being sweet and working hard to avoid the reality of her situation), but the abuse gets worse.

4. **She fails (peak):** Cinderella fails to stand up for herself, and she ends up a scullery maid in her own home. Time for a change, but is she strong enough?

5. **She tries some more and fails (dips, and then peaks even higher):** Cinderella and everyone else in the household is all excited over the upcoming ball and is getting ready to attend. Cinderella again resolves to put a happy face on her situation, but she is thwarted and is unable to attend the ball.

6. **She hits a seeming stalemate (flatline, but not too long):** The fairy godmother helps her to attend. Cinderella rises to the occasion, dazzling all attendees including the prince, but has to run out of the ball at the last minute, leaving a slipper. So she's back to where she started: in rags, with no prospects.

7. **She figures it out (begins descending):** Cinderella decides that she is going to get a chance to try on that slipper no matter what her stepsisters, who may suspect her involvement with the prince, say or do.

8. **She hits a bump but instead of reverting back to old way tries out new one (further descending):** Cinderella gets locked in the cellar when the prince arrives, but instead of accepting her fate with a smile and cleaning even harder, Cinderella gets wise and fashions a way to break out in time. Eventually, she gets hitched. Wiser and back to her old position and privilege, we have to see how she uses her power.

9. **She ends a changed and better (you hope) person after all (fully descended):** Although she could have her stepmother and stepsisters thrown into a dungeon from where they would never ascend (or worse), Cinderella opts to take the higher road and allows them to live.

A character arc is just a fancy way of making sure your character goes through enough changes and struggles to make her compelling to your readers. You can replace each point above with one in your story, no matter how short (like a picture book) or how long (like a novel). It's your arc, and you get to decide what goes where. All we ask is that you make sure your character has done some growing throughout the course of the story.

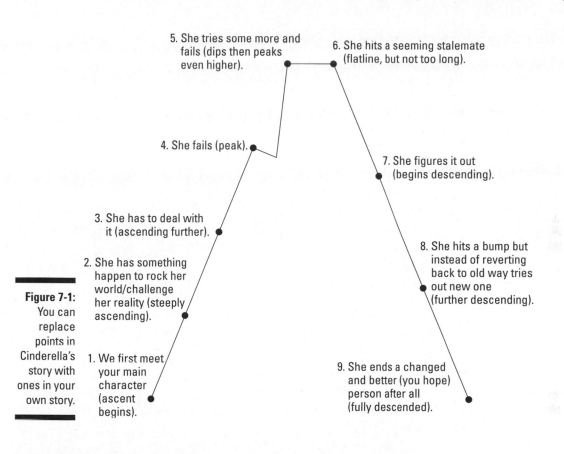

5. She tries some more and fails (dips then peaks even higher).

6. She hits a seeming stalemate (flatline, but not too long).

4. She fails (peak).

7. She figures it out (begins descending).

3. She has to deal with it (ascending further).

8. She hits a bump but instead of reverting back to old way tries out new one (further descending).

2. She has something happen to rock her world/challenge her reality (steeply ascending).

Figure 7-1:
You can replace points in Cinderella's story with ones in your own story.

1. We first meet your main character (ascent begins).

9. She ends a changed and better (you hope) person after all (fully descended).

Developing Characters through Writing Exercises

Children are wild creatures at heart. If they didn't have adults around them to teach them, discipline them, and rein them in, they would naturally grow into wild animals, experiencing whatever they wanted to and never holding back. That tendency to revel unrestrained in their lives is what allows children to experience events and emotions very deeply. That kind of open emotionality is a good thing to incorporate into children's books.

But we, as adults, have usually forgotten what it means to have emotions right at the surface; to care about someone so deeply and unselfconsciously that you notice everything about them and take it all in.

Exercises are great ways to exercise general and specific writing muscles. Each exercise we introduce here (and in the following chapters) can be used not only to get you writing, but also to come up with ideas if you have still not found one you want to write about. Writing memorable characters is of the utmost importance, and you can't write memorable characters unless you know them really well. So, the exercises here not only get you writing, but also get you working on knowing how to write good characters, because you will be writing about someone you know very well.

Describe your first best friend

As a children's book writer, writing memorable characters is the single most important skill for you to master. (See the "Creating Your Exceptional Main Character" section for all you ever wanted to know about character development.) But sometimes you may have trouble coming up with a good idea for a character. You can get a head start on this skill by writing about your first best friend.

Devote an entire single-spaced page to everything you can remember about your first best friend. Use each of these descriptions to paint her as the substantive character she was:

- What she looked like

- What she liked to wear

- Her favorite color

- What her family was like

- Her favorite food or treat

- What you two did together

- Her favorite activities

- The secrets you shared

- The things about her you envied or tried to emulate

- Her way of walking or talking or eating that set her apart

Writing about someone you knew well as a child is the perfect way to develop your ability to create good child characters. Ultimately, you'll change a lot of attributes about a character to fit your story (and to protect the innocent), but knowing how to build a unique person out of words on paper is the most important skill you can have as a children's book writer. Long after you forget exactly what happened in Louise Fitzhugh's *Harriet the Spy* (Yearling), you still remember Harriet. Years after reading Roald Dahl's *Charlie and the Chocolate Factory* (Puffin Books), you may not recall the plot, but you do recall Charlie, the Oompa-Loompas, and the inimitable Mr. Wonka (a better childlike adult character has never been written!).

Describe the love of your life

When you're done writing about your first best friend (see preceding section), practice writing characters again by writing about someone you know intimately in your current life, say your wife, partner, husband, significant other — even someone you may be pining after. Try not to write about that person as a grown-up would; instead, cover all the details you can think of about him or her that a child might focus on:

- ✔ What he (or she) looks like
- ✔ What he smells like
- ✔ What his hair does when he runs
- ✔ What his favorite possessions are
- ✔ What he likes to eat
- ✔ What he does that seems illogical or eccentric
- ✔ What his favorite pastimes are
- ✔ Whether he's a fast runner or a good ball thrower

You can't get too much practice writing about people. If you can, sit in a busy coffee shop and write a mini character bible about every person sitting near you. Try to create a unique personality, a real character — all based on what you see, overhear, or sneakily peek at when they are not looking. It's fun and it's really good practice for character development in your children's story writing.

Steal from your favorite children's book author

Pick up one of your favorite books and write down the names of the main characters, the ones who made you fall in love with the book in the first place. Now take those characters and write them a new adventure in your own voice.

This exercise allows you to write using someone else's ideas and characters that you know well (so you don't have to come up with your own), while allowing you to take those characters on a totally different adventure written in your own voice.

Exercises like these may seem unrelated to the task at hand (writing your children's book) but they are *directly* related. They help you hone skills that you will need to put to use in your writing, allowing you to practice before you commit to the real thing.

Chapter 8

The Plot Thickens: Conflict, Climax, and Resolution

In This Chapter

▶ Creating a compelling story
▶ Beginning, ending, and everything in between
▶ Building conflict
▶ Designing your plot
▶ Writing your first draft

Most writers aren't exactly sure what a *plot* is. Is it the storyline itself? Is it the action within the story? Is it the steps the main character takes as he progresses from beginning, to middle, and through to the end? The answer is yes — to all of the above.

The plot is *what happens*. It's a bunch of events that tie in together and lead up to a climax. In order to be convincing, a plot has to unfold in a believable way, regardless of the fact that the characters may be animals or the story may take place in the future.

In children's books, plot is king, and stories that children like are always filled with lots of action and a satisfactory resolution.

Your plot should begin with your main character (see Chapter 7) in opposition to something: In other words, he has a problem or a challenge to overcome that becomes apparent right away. Then your story details that problem and adds to its complexity. It then moves on to your climax, where the situation gets worse or more acute, and then you need to resolve the issue.

Make sure not to go on and on after the climax, dragging out the resolution or introducing new ideas. Just end it, making the benefits of the ending obvious. And try to end on a positive note.

Consider the example of J. R. R. Tolkien's *The Lord of the Rings* novel in three volumes (DelRey). The climax of the story is when (spoiler alert!) Gollum bites the ring off Frodo's finger (finger included) and then proceeds to fall into the fiery depths of Mount Doom, destroying the ring and causing the downfall of mighty Sauron and his nasty armies of evil. The story could have easily ended right there — the hobbits are heroes, evil is defeated, and everyone lives happily ever after. But no. Instead, Tolkien decided to drag out the story for another 85-plus pages, including the oft-complained-about ending, "The Scouring of the Shire." Believe us: Sometimes shorter can be sweeter.

Because the main character is the one that drives the plot — and vice versa — in this chapter, we concentrate on showing you how the events and acts involving the main character make up a plot.

Centering on the Story

The plot and your main character are closely intertwined in a successful story. That means that the way you flesh out your protagonist is by showing readers how he reacts and what he does at each point in your story. However, there is a big difference between a plot, which is a narrative of events, and a narrative of *meaningful* events involving characters who change as a result of their actions. That's a *story*.

A plot that only narrates a sequence of actions one after another is not meaningful, even if the main character is involved at every step. Consider this basic plot:

> A spoiled young girl's wealthy father remarries a woman with two daughters. The father dies. The stepmother enslaves the girl, treating her badly. The girl grows up as a maid in her own house. A prince holds a ball to find a bride. With a bit of magic, the girl is able to attend, but must leave at midnight. The prince falls in love with the girl. The girl runs from the ball right before she would have been reduced to rags. The prince searches all over the kingdom for her, but can't find her. Many would-be wives scheme to get his attention. He devises a way of ascertaining the girl's true identity. She figures out how to get noticed. At last they are reunited. They marry, and the girl no longer has to be a maid. The princess employs her stepmother and her stepsister in the house, but does not mistreat them as they did her. The prince and the princess live happily ever after.

Even though this is a narration of events, you know instinctively that it isn't a story because you don't care about these characters. You don't see the main characters, the prince and Cinderella, in action. You don't see Cinderella getting ready for the ball and sneaking out. You don't see the prince's agitation at her disappearance. As a result, you don't care about them or what happens to them.

But if you were to show the emotions the characters feel, as revealed through their actions and reactions to events, you would have the beginnings of a real story. And if you were to show the main characters being shaped and changed and molded by the events they encounter throughout the story, going through conflict and struggling to get to the other side, you would have a chance of snagging your readers' attention.

A good story is one in which at least one main character participates in a series of meaningful events, facing and actively overcoming the conflicts that shape him, changing him from the person he was at the beginning.

By taking the basic plot just discussed and adding all the necessary ingredients of character development, conflict, action, and change, you can center in on the *story* of Cinderella.

Beginning, Middle, and End

Every good story has a beginning, a middle, and an end. The beginning reels you in, the climactic middle keeps you going, and the end satisfies you with resolution.

1. **Your plot must have a beginning in which you introduce your main characters and hook readers into the action by introducing conflict right away.**

   Cinderella's dad dies, leaving her at the mercy of a cruel stepmother.

2. **The conflict must then build to a point where the main character is really in trouble and the story could go either way. This is your middle, where the conflict reaches a climax.**

   Cinderella has met a partner who can help her escape her terrible life, but he cannot seem to find her.

3. **You must begin to shape your ending by providing an opportunity for your main character to face the conflict and overcome the worst of it, becoming a different, perhaps better person, as a result of all she has gone through by the end of the story.**

   Cinderella decides to escape her situation and tries on the slipper, thus ensuring she lives a better life.

Conflict: Using Pacing and Drama

After you have a beginning, middle, and end down, you need make sure you have incorporated enough drama into your story, using pacing to keep the reader interested. *Drama* is struggle and conflict, emotionality and turbulence. *Pacing* is keeping the drama at a more heightened note than you would find in real life. If your character experiences strong emotions due to the events of the story, you have drama. Likewise, if your character is tossed about by the turbulence of those events, such that his life is changed or his way of life is threatened, you have drama.

The best way to make sure you have enough drama is to ask yourself whether your character is struggling at each major plot point. Is Cinderella suffering? Is she challenged? If not, show her confronting her miserable life, hopefully determined to do more than just make the best of it. Are the events in her life turbulent enough to keep us interested? If not, you have work to do.

Pacing is the force that keeps the reader turning the pages, wanting — no, *needing* — to find out what happens next. In your story, each major plot point has to keep us guessing as to what may happen next. In a picture book, you can keep the story going at a good clip by drawing out conflict evenly throughout the story and writing tightly and well. (For a practical tip on how to check picture book pacing during the editing phase, check out Chapter 13.)

Pacing for novels, especially chapter books for younger readers, tends to have chapters end on a high note, in the middle of a scene, at a tense moment. This keeps the reader turning the pages. Action is quicker and chapters shorter than in the past. Your audience has grown up on television, so stories are paced more like TV shows, with a hook right before the commercial break to keep the audience from turning the channel. The same practice applies to young adult novels, but it's just not as heavy-handed.

In younger children's chapter books and middle-grade books, you can end the chapters with cliffhangers that leave the reader with a question (literally, you can end with a question: Would Amanda figure out a way to get enough oxygen before the flooding waters completely engulfed her?) or figuratively (Amanda watched the flood waters rise, wondering when she would be forced to take her last breath.).

Even if you have a good story, well-fleshed-out characters, and a beginning, middle, and end, if you don't have adequate drama incorporated into the action or if your plot plods along from one event to the next, you will lose your readers.

Outlining Tools to Structure Your Plot

The primary goal of *outlining* is to plot out the story in terms of what the main character does and then keep adding additional information. If other characters become important, you want to see what they do. Your outline becomes a repository for the who, what, when, where, why, and how of each of the three parts (beginning, middle, end) of your story. From there, you can easily flesh out your story.

Satisfying readers with plot structure

You hear a lot of talk about *structure* in writing circles, and it's true that structure is the key to a good story. To give a story structure simply means that you tie in your story's beginning, middle, and end with information about your characters and with your plot development. The structure is the skeleton of the story, while the skin and organs are the other elements such as drama, pacing, effective transitions, and strong point of view (discussed in Chapter 11). That skeleton or plot structure can be pretty easily turned into an outline.

Sometimes, it is hard to visualize just how plot structure looks. Flip to Chapter 7 to read about character arcs, and when you're looking at Figure 7-1, of Cinderella's character arc, you're also looking at a plot structure. Notice how the beginning is illustrated at the bottom left of the arc, the middle/climax is at the top, and the resolution moves on the down slope. If you can take apart your own story and plot it out on an arc like that one, chances are you have your basic plot laid out.

Plot and character are closely intertwined. Character and plot are so connected that they proceed neck and neck on the same schedule. When the plot hits a bump, so does the main character. When the conflict in the plot approaches resolution, so does the main character's desire. And when the ending results in a changed character and a wrapped-up plot, the reader feels like the journey was worth it.

Creating a step sheet

A *step sheet* can help you keep track of plot points, beginning/middle/end, and pacing — and character development. You can make your step sheet be as detailed or as thinly written as you feel is necessary.

Here's what the beginning of a step sheet may look like, using the story of Cinderella as an example. We've cut out a lot of the steps in the plot and left just a few key examples for you to look at. Your step sheet, on the other hand, should have a bullet point for every single action that takes place.

✔ **The beginning:**

- **Plot point:** A spoiled young girl's wealthy father remarries a woman with two daughters.

- **Character development:** Show Cinderella in action trying to befriend mean stepsisters.

- **Pacing:** Show emotion behind the growing dejection she feels.

✔ **Also at the beginning:**

- **Plot point:** The father dies.

- **Character development:** Show Cinderella's grief.

- **Pacing:** Show stepmother and stepsisters plotting to take over house and grounds.

✔ **The middle:**

- **Plot point:** A prince holds a ball to find a bride.

- **Character development:** Show entire town excited over event, Cinderella low at not being able to participate.

- **Pacing:** Show Prince in action as adventurer, romantic — a definite catch.

✔ **The end:**

- **Plot point:** The prince and the princess live happily ever after.

- **Character development:** Show the rightness of the good guys winning.

- **Pacing:** Slow down into final ending and wrap it up.

A step sheet is also referred to as an *action outline,* because it always notes the action in the plot. Notice how your main character is always the focal point. Secondary characters who affect the main plotline can also be added, and their fates also need to be satisfactorily wrapped up at the conclusion of the story.

Step sheets can be used to plot out everything from a picture book to a chapter book to a novel. They're great tools for a new writer trying to figure out what comes next and how to organize all the parts of a story that make for a wonderful whole.

Fleshing out your outline

Consider the many plot points of Cinderella's story and suppose you have chosen to write a short chapter book. Now you can create a full outline of the story, starting with the journalist's trusty six questions:

- **Who:** Character development
- **What:** Plot point
- **When:** Time
- **Where:** Setting
- **Why:** Drama, pacing, and character motivation
- **How:** Plot point

So the start of the outline may look like this:

- **Chapter 1:**
    - **Setting:** A castle and its grounds.
    - **Time:** Medieval Europe.
    - **Plot point:** A spoiled young girl's wealthy father remarries a woman with two daughters.
    - **Character development:** Show Cinderella in action trying to befriend mean stepsisters.
    - **Supporting characters:** Father, stepmother, stepsisters, house staff.
    - **Pacing:** Show foreshadowing of Cinderella's efforts failing entirely.
- **Chapter 2:**
    - **Setting:** Same but widens to include the town and church and burial ceremony.
    - **Time:** A few months later.
    - **Plot point:** The father dies.
    - **Character development:** Show Cinderella's grief.
    - **Supporting characters:** Introduce Cinderella's best friend, Jude.
    - **Pacing:** At end of chapter, show stepmother and sisters plotting to take over house and grounds.

✓ **Chapter 3:**

- **Setting:** Same castle, but show Cinderella going to town.

- **Time:** A week later.

- **Plot point:** The stepmother enslaves the girl, treating her badly.

- **Character development:** Show Cinderella facing up to her tasks with good cheer, determined to survive despite the conditions.

- **Supporting characters:** Further develop relationship between Cinderella and Jude. Show townspeople watching her demise from upper-class to working class.

- **Pacing:** Show how stepmother begins plundering Cinderella's father's assets to feed her own vanity and greed.

Knowing when to circumvent an outline

When the issue of an outline seems absurd or overkill, chances are it is — for you. For example, it is doubtful that you will need an outline for a board book. Most picture books don't get written with an outline unless the writer gets stuck and needs help figuring out why. And some writers simply can't work with an outline at all, preferring to just get writing and work on (and rework) the written pages without an organizational tool to fall back on.

Outlines are organizing tools. They are not holy words carved in stone. If, in the course of writing fiction, you find yourself veering away into some interesting but unforeseen place, you're allowed to follow your characters to see where they lead you. But make sure to either re-create your outline later accordingly or recheck using a step sheet to make sure you have all your character, plot, and pacing issues covered from start to finish.

Michael Green tells it like it is

For the real scoop on plotting, pacing, and drama and what they all mean after you get your manuscript to a real-live children's literary publisher, check out what Michael Green has to say. He's the Associate Publisher and Editorial Director of Philomel Books, a division of Penguin Young Readers Group.

WCBFD: You have been working in children's publishing for 14 years and have become an expert in what makes a good story work. What is usually the first thing that captures your attention when you pick up a new manuscript and begin to read?

MG: I take an uncommon interest in someone's opening sentence. A weak one doesn't necessarily signal a weak manuscript, but a strong one does tend to bode well for what lies ahead. I also listen for a writer's voice. Before plot or characterization has the chance to take root, voice can blossom.

WCBFD: In a similar vein, what is the one thing that when reading a manuscript can cause you to pitch it immediately into your round file?

MG: Nothing earns a rejection slip faster than an overwritten first paragraph. It *never* bodes well.

WCBFD: How can a new writer tell whether his main character is working? What should he be looking for?

MG: His main character should take life unto itself. It should speak, breathe, and react on its own — that is when an author knows the character comes across as real.

WCBFD: As far as plots are concerned, what are the most important elements in a well-constructed one?

MG: A well-constructed plot is a bit like an open umbrella. It forms an arc that envelopes and reaches out toward all characters and plot points. It unifies and gives purpose to everything that touches that arc.

WCBFD: How important is dramatic pacing to a picture book? A novel?

MG: Picture books and novels are separate beasts. A picture book will always have a sense of pacing, a sense of movement. A good part of that movement is owed to the artwork, though, which needs to move along the story on its own terms. Within the spacious boundaries of a novel, dramatic pacing and characterization are vital. An author needs to be careful, however, of not forcing the issue. Quiet, subtle moments in Chapter 2 might very well be setting up an earthquake in Chapter 5; the contrast between the two will help the tension pop when it finally arrives.

WCBFD: What are some tricks a new writer could use to help him figure out how to accomplish sufficient drama and adequate pacing?

MG: Watch for the unusual when reading other writers' books. Different writers play different games with pacing and drama — be attentive to what works for you as a reader. Also, pay attention to how chapters close. Chapter closing lines should be tiny jewels that close a door on one scene while tempting a reader to tear open that door and burst through the other side to see what happens next.

Writing Your First Draft

Don't expect to sit down and craft a perfect children's book from start to finish, even if you've fully outlined your characters and plot. Unfortunately, writing is not just about putting your first thoughts on paper and being ready to publish. Instead, writing is about writing, rewriting, and rewriting some more.

The only way you're going to be able to write freely is to turn off your inner critic and just get going. Your first draft can be written without any concern about character arcs (see Chapter 7), plot steps, pacing, drama — or any of the elements you just learned about. Go ahead and describe in as much detail every little aspect of everything that you want to include in your story. Get in all the settings (see Chapter 10), dialogue (see Chapter 9), supporting characters (see Chapter 7), and such as you like. Find yourself blathering on and on?

No problem. Just keep going until you've reached the end. When you do get to the end, pat yourself on the back! You have an official first draft done — which no one is ever going to see.

Then you have two choices. You can either go back and work on your second draft using everything you're reading in this chapter and the preceding one, or wait till you have finished reading all the chapters in Part III — and then go back and start work on your second draft.

We suggest that in between each draft (or every few drafts, if you're writing a chapter book or longer work), you print out your story and reread it with a pencil, just like many editors do. There is something about reading printed matter on paper that makes it read more "real" than reading it on screen. And save each of your drafts until you really are ready to submit it to a publisher — you never know what you may discover when you look back at all the progress you have made.

No one can tell you how many drafts it will take till you are done writing, but you will know. Then you will be ready to edit, which we cover in Chapter 13.

Chapter 9

Can We Talk? Writing Dialogue

Writing good dialogue isn't the same as writing realistic dialogue. Realistic dialogue is actually pretty boring if you write it out as it actually occurs — and boring as all heck to read. To write good dialogue, you must develop a good ear and be able to translate what you hear into a wittier, smarter, more meaningful version of itself. Which is to say, in order for your characters to sound good, you need to write the way people actually talk — and then make it better.

In this chapter, we help you figure out when to use dialogue and discuss the functions it must serve within the story and character development to make it worth including. We discuss how good dialogue requires drama and tension and how to get in the groove of putting words into children's mouths by listening and paying attention to some actual, living owners of those mouths. We show you how your character bible can help you define each of your characters to make them sound different from one another, and how dialogue exercises can help you hone your skills. Then we take you step-by-step through some of the most common dialogue writing mistakes. We even help you check your dialogue by listening to it read aloud.

When to Use Dialogue

Writers are like jugglers, having to keep many elements of writing going at the same time: characterization, plot development, setting, and more. Dialogue can be used to develop all of the above: your characters, your plot, and your setting. Dialogue increases a book's readability by transmitting necessary information and breaking up passages of narration and description.

Dialogue needs a function

The first step in writing good dialogue is to figure out when to use it at all. While we cannot give you a rule of thumb about when to use dialogue (mostly because there is no such thing as a rule of thumb and also because each format differs as does each writer's style) we can tell you that you can use it whenever it seems like you have a lot of descriptive or narrative paragraphs, or if you find yourself telling us about a character or characters to develop them in your reader's mind, instead of showing the characters interacting in order to reveal who they really are. Using dialogue also helps when the plot needs to move forward and you need a character to take the reader to that next part of the story.

Although it's a great tool for enriching your fiction (and your nonfiction), dialogue is not the same as talking. Talking is two or more people exchanging words, meaningful or not, boring or not. Dialogue has a function. It has a job to do. You use dialogue in your story only if it performs at least one of the functions discussed in the following sections.

Gives information

Consider the following example of how dialogue gives information:

> JANE: Didja call him?
>
> NELLY: Yeah. But he wasn't home. Let it ring and ring. Called a bunch of times, too. I think he never came home last night.
>
> JANE: C'mon. I bet I know where he is!

In this exchange, we find out that the person the girls are discussing is missing and that they are going to go find him. The narrator could have revealed this information in prose, but it's not as interesting:

> Jane called Nelly to find out if Nelly had contacted James. Nelly revealed that she had tried, but that James had not answered despite repeated tries throughout the night. Jane then dragged Nelly off to go in search of the missing boy.

Develops characters

In the following example, the dialogue develops characters:

> "Do you mean that you think you can find out the answer to it?" said the March Hare.
>
> "Exactly so," said Alice.
>
> "Then you should say what you mean," the March Hare went on.

"I do," Alice hastily replied; "at least — at least I mean what I say — that's the same thing, you know."

"Not the same thing a bit!" said the Hatter. "You might just as well say that 'I see what I eat' is the same thing as 'I eat what I see.'!"

"You might just as well say," added the March Hare, "that 'I like what I get' is the same thing as 'I get what I like'!"

"You might just as well say," added the Dormouse, which seemed to be talking in its sleep, "that 'I breathe when I sleep' is the same thing as 'I sleep when I breathe'!"

"It *is* the same thing with you," said the Hatter, and here the conversation dropped, . . .

In this exchange from Lewis Carroll's *Alice's Adventures in Wonderland* (PD), we learn that the March Hare and his cohorts are a bunch of semanticists, picky regarding specificity, especially when it comes to their beloved pastime of talking in riddles to Alice, whom they accuse of fast and loose treatment of the language. As the dialogue continues, we also learn that Alice is quite easily puzzled by her companions, by which we take to mean that Alice, as a character, is not as smart or as quick-witted as the others.

We could have accomplished the same character development in prose, but chances are it would not have been half as fun to read, or half as revealing of the characters.

Moves the story forward

Check out this example of how dialogue moves the story forward:

"What's the matter, Mother?" he said.

"Oh, Diamond, my darling! you have been so ill!" she sobbed.

"No, Mother dear. I've only been at the back of the north wind," returned Diamond.

"I thought you were dead," said his mother.

But that moment, the doctor came in.

"Oh! there!" said the doctor with gentle cheerfulness; "we're better to-day, I see."

In this exchange from George MacDonald's *At the Back of the North Wind* (PD) between the main character, a boy named Diamond, and his mother, we learn that Diamond does not realize that his journeys with his friend, the North Wind, leave him sicker and sicker. We realize also that Diamond has no idea how long he has been gone or that he leaves his body behind when he travels with her. This dialogue not only moves the story forward to Diamond's recovery in the world inhabited by his family, it also adds information, characterizing the journeys he goes on as somewhat otherworldly.

Again, this dialogue could easily have been put into straight prose narrative, but it would not have contained the same drama. Which brings us to our next important point.

Dialogue needs drama

Dialogue should also be dramatic. It should create arguments, strong emotions, or conflict between your characters. That conflict should lead to some new action on the character's part (and move the story along). Good dialogue is short, potent, and meaningful.

Let's say you are at a point in your story where you need to move the plot forward. You could do it in narration or you can accomplish it in dialogue. Often, dialogue conveys more drama and much more emotion, while revealing more about the characters' personalities.

> Jane nearly tripped over Nelly as she approached the train door. There he was. "I don't believe it," she muttered to herself, feeling her heart start to race. He saw her and stopped, causing those behind him to grumble and shove in their hurry to get past him. "I was sure you wouldn't be here," she whispered.
>
> He grinned, raising an eyebrow. "I just lost a bet, too."
>
> "With who?" Jane demanded.

In this short exchange, in which we move the plot forward by discovering James's whereabouts, we also glean important information: that the boy James that Jane and Nelly sought to find has just come back from a trip somewhere. We learn about Jane that she feels more for James than just platonic concern, based on the depth of her emotion, her heart racing, her speaking in whispered tones, and her instant jealousy at his mention of a bet with an unnamed person, perhaps a rival for his affections. And we also learn that James, a funny, confident boy, shares some of her feelings, because of his happy-go-lucky grin and his raised eyebrow.

This exchange could have proceeded completely differently. James could have stuttered and blushed, indicating that he is not as confident or happy-go-lucky. Jane could have attacked him verbally, demanding to know where he was and why he had not contacted her or Nelly. Written that way, the dialogue would have told us different things about the characters themselves, would have moved the plot forward differently, and would have given us different information about the relationship between Jane and James.

Another way to work in dialogue is at the beginning of a scene. Try writing the entire scene in dialogue, and then just in narrative. Then take the best of the prose parts, those that add to the setting, the actions, the indicators of tone of voice or body language, the expression, the characters' movements, the short descriptions. Between the two versions, you should come up with a scene that is fleshed out, actively moving the plot forward and sustained by characters that are making it all come alive by what and how they speak.

If you can't spell out exactly why a piece of dialogue exists, chances are it doesn't belong in your story. For example, small talk or simple greetings between characters don't pass muster if they don't add anything concrete to your story. The dialogue needs to accomplish one of the functions described above and it needs to be interesting to read.

Listening to the Kids

Training yourself to listen and really hear is the first step. Go to any park or classroom with children the age of your audience, and listen. Chances are you will encounter the following:

- Contractions (*it's* and *can't* versus *it is* and *cannot*)

- Lots of stuttering and hemming (*uh, yeah, um, well, hmm,* and all their incoherent relatives)

- Incomplete sentences (*If you wanna . . .* versus *If you want to go, you can go*)

- Nonverbal communication taking the place of actual words (a nod or a shake of the head in reply)

- Body language contradicting words (crossed arms signaling a specific attitude even if the words contradict that attitude — just ask the parent of a teenager what we mean by this if you don't understand)

- Communication shortcuts, such as slang

There's no way you can write dialogue exactly the way it's heard in real life, because it will come out sounding as tedious and wooden as a court transcript. This is how an actual conversation between two teenagers may sound. Notice the shortcuts and the incomplete sentences. Pay attention to how body language must be saying a lot because not much information is actually conveyed here, despite the number of exchanges.

KID A: Didja hear what happened to Sarina?

KID B: No. What?

KID A: She got narced on.

KID B: By who?

KID A: Dunno. Maybe her sister. Maybe that other . . . you know.

KID B: Dawg.

KID A: Yeah, and now she's grounded

KID B: Wonder who . . . ?

KID A: You gotta watch it. Grown-ups. . . .

To make this dialogue really work for you, by developing a character and moving plot forward (see Chapters 8 and 9, respectively), you'd have to rewrite it to make it better.

KID A: Didja hear what happened to Sarina, the new girl who was trying to hang with the popular crowd?

KID B: No. What?

KID A: She got narced on. Someone told about her shoplifting. You know how they make you steal to prove you're cool.

KID B: Yeah. But who told?

KID A: I dunno. Maybe her sister; you know she's gotta be jealous since she's kinda brainy and all. Maybe it was that other kid, you know, the red-headed one.

KID B: Yeah . . . I wonder if that means she won't be driving the homecoming car.

KID A: No way. She's grounded.

KID B: What about the homecoming race then?

KID A: If we don't have that race, then the contest is over. They lose!

KID B: That'd be good for us.

This version tells us a lot more about who the players are, what happened and what is really at stake in terms of the plot. It's not much changed, only blown out to make it better than it was, while still retaining the tone of the teenagers' original speech.

Dialogue and Your Character Bible

In Chapter 7 we discuss creating a character bible that really lays out who your character is in terms of personality, looks, history, family, quirks — all the elements that contribute to making a person who he or she really is. A character bible functions to help you get to know who your character is and to help you differentiate between characters.

A great addition to a character bible is a speech section where you identify how your character speaks. Consider the following characteristics of speech and lay out where each of your characters falls where these attributes are concerned:

- How articulate is she? (We're referring to characters who are old enough to be articulate here.) Is she educated and is it reflected in her speech?

- Is she not a native speaker? What is her native tongue? Does her English sound like she got it from a book? Or is your character a younger child apt to make grammatical mistakes such as mistaking one word for another?

- What is the quality of her voice? Is it hoarse? loud? soft? squeaky? high? low?

- Does she have any verbal anomalies such as lisping or stuttering?

- Is she direct in her speech or shyer, more obtuse?

- Does she use swear words or slang, jargon or street talk?

- Is she loquacious or terse? abrupt or apt to talk your head off?

- Does she answer every question with another question?

Though not all of the preceding questions can be answered (nor would be appropriate) where every character is concerned, they can be very helpful in finding your character's particular voice and keeping that voice consistent and differentiated from the other characters in your book.

Common Dialogue Mistakes

People really do speak in fits and starts, but that doesn't mean your characters should — it simply takes up too much valuable space to include all those hems and haws and pauses and incomplete sentences — unless you can fill them with meaning, and that takes practice. A big difference between speech that you hear and speech that you read is that all the nonverbal communication, nuance, and inflection of real dialogue is lost when it's written down, so your words have to work extra hard.

It takes practice listening, writing, and editing to become a good writer of dialogue. But there are some common mistakes that we list here to help you figure out when something isn't working.

Dialogue without conflict or tension

Dialogue that just delivers information or develops a character without, in itself, containing any hint of drama or tension is not very interesting. That doesn't mean your characters have to get into a fight or speak meanly to one another. For example, here's our short scene with Jane, James, and Nelly without any tension:

> Jane and Nelly approached the train door. James appeared a moment later. "There he is," she said. He saw her and stopped, causing those behind him to mutter and shove in their hurry to get past him. "Good, you're here," she said.
>
> James hefted his backpack over his shoulder. "Yep, I'm here."
>
> "OK, let's go then," Jane said.

Repeated information in your dialogue

If you've just written a dialogue exchange between James and Jane that reveals that James had taken the train that afternoon to see his uncle in prison and had returned the following evening, why on earth would you want to say the exact same thing right before it in narrative?

> As they made their way out of the train station, Nelly wanted to find out where James had been, so she asked him. He told her he had been to visit his uncle, the murderer. She was so shocked, she could hardly let him finish his sentences. Jane had to get her to quiet down so they could hear James speak.
>
> "Where'd you go?" Nelly asked, trying to act casual now that they had left the bustle of the station.
>
> "I went to see my uncle," James replied. "And he told me . . ."
>
> Nelly interrupted him in a rush. "The one in prison? The-the murderer?"
>
> "Yep. And boy did I find out . . ."
>
> "You went to visit a murderer? Are you crazy?" Nelly nearly shouted.
>
> "Will you please shut it?" demanded Jane. "I want to hear what he found out."
>
> Nelly sniffed, looking at the ground. "Fine. But I still think it was dumb of him."

Many beginning writers feel they have to introduce the dialogue with an explanation of what is to follow, essentially causing the dialogue to repeat the information in dialogue form. Don't waste the reader's time. Choose one or the other, not both.

Describing dialogue

Some beginning writers forget that dialogue is an option and describe verbal exchanges between characters instead of just giving us the exchange in dialogue:

> Once they had steered clear of the train station, Nelly casually asked James where he had gone. He told her that he had gone to see his uncle. Nelly, shocked, interrupted him, demanding to know if he was talking about his uncle the murderer. James admitted that that was indeed the uncle that he saw and tried to explain, but Nelly interrupted him again. Finally, Jane had to tell Nelly to be quiet so James could tell them all about what he found out.

Putting this exchange into dialogue instead of reporting about it would have been so much more interesting.

Too many speaker references and attributions

Believe it or not, you do not need to have your characters use each other's names in each leg of your dialogue. Nor do you need to identify each speaker by name each time with an attribution *(he said, she replied, he asked),* though when there are three or more speakers in one exchange, you might choose to for clarity.

> "Hi, Nelly," said James.
>
> "Hi, James," replied Nelly.
>
> "How are you, Nelly?" asked James.
>
> "Oh, doing fine, doing fine, James," said Nelly.
>
> "Hey, Nelly, how is Jane?" asked James.
>
> "Jane is fine, James," replied Nelly. "How is your Uncle Bob?"

People just don't talk that way, whether they know each other or not. Notice also the lack of contractions (*How is* instead of *How's*), which is also unrealistic.

Heavy-handed and unrealistic dialogue

Speaking of how people talk, people talk in shorthand, using contractions and body language to convey meaning. Don't load up your dialogue with a lot of information that would not ordinarily be found in dialogue. For example,

> "Your uncle is in prison for a reason. He stole all that money from your grandfather with that no-good best friend of his in 2004, killing that poor nurse from Kentucky in the process. The bullet went straight through her heart, which we all considered symbolic, considering he broke your grandmother's heart, not to mention ruining the family name when your family history was dragged through the papers, revealing your illegitimate birth and your grandfather's sketchy past," said Jane.

> "Yes," agreed James, "he is in prison for a reason. But that reason is not what you think. That reason is wrong. He was wrongly convicted because he was not holding the gun when it went off and he did not even want to go into that bank in the first place! And . . ."

As you can see, this is narrative disguised as dialogue. These words do not belong in young people's mouths, especially the way they are written. The amount of detail is unrealistic for the context in which it is given. There is too much information packed into each speaker's turn. Dialogue needs to be simple and to the point, not encumbered by tons of background information and backstory or flashback (more on those in Chapter 7).

Unnecessary dialogue

Dialogue shouldn't be used to fill up space on the page or accomplish things that are best left up to a sentence of narrative. For example, when characters are being introduced to one another, chances are you do not need to do it in dialogue, not unless something else important happens during the introduction that gives it a clear function in the story.

> "Hello, Mr. Sloan," said Nelly.

> "Hello, Nelly," said Mr. Sloan. "And who have we here?"

> "Mr. Sloan, I'd like to introduce you to my friends, Jane and James," said Nelly.

> "Hello," said James, extending his hand.

> "Hi, nice to meet you," said Jane, smiling.

This exchange is much better off in narrative, where it is short and to the point:

> Nelly walked into the office of Mr. Sloan, her father's lawyer, and introduced her friends.

Here are some more common dialogue mistakes:

- ✔ Writing long speeches, lectures, or monologues. These are passages where one character goes on and on, uninterrupted, for paragraphs. Yaaaaaaaawn.

- ✔ Making all the characters sound alike (when your teenage protagonist sounds the same as his mother and his coach, then you have a problem).

- ✔ Having children sound like small adults. When a toddler speaks in complete sentences and finishes every thought neatly, then you have an adult, not a kid.

- ✔ Using lots of adjectives and adverbs (happily, sadly, tearfully, angrily). The words of dialogue that you put in the character's mouth should be specific and well-chosen enough to convey the emotion without requiring clarifying adverbs or phrases.

- ✔ Phonetic spellings of dialects, such as "*Yah, mon*" to represent a Jamaican speaker, or "*Chee say for you no to go,*" to represent a Hispanic speaker attempting English. The use of dialect or regional accents in dialogue should only occur if the writer is *very* familiar with the dialects — for example, if you have lived in a region where it is spoken, or if you have done a lot of research and can accurately and consistently write it in dialogue each time the character speaks.

  Think of how annoying it is in movies where American actors try in vain to speak in a British accent, succeeding sometimes and failing at other times, or mixing up Americanisms with a bad British accent. It so abruptly destroys the moviegoer's ability to suspend disbelief that it's almost better if the actor were to simply speak in her normal accent so that we couldn't be constantly reminded that she isn't. The same goes for writing accents or using dialects — unless you can do it flawlessly and consistently, don't do it.

Reading It Out Loud

The best test of whether your dialogue is working is to listen to someone else reading your story back to you. When you hear your story read aloud, pay attention to the dialogue and ask yourself:

- ✔ **Do the child characters sound like children?** If they consistently speak in complete sentences or use strings of huge words, you probably have your English professor in mind and not a child. Shorten sentences. Add a lisp or a stutter. Fill in some blanks between speech with brief descriptions of telling body language and facial expressions.

- ✔ **Do the characters sound different from one another?** If not, you need to listen to how different people speak and try to capture those differences. And revisit that character's speech section in her character bible to see if you are remaining true to your original idea of how she actually speaks.

- ✔ **Is the speech wordy or to the point?** If wordy, chances are you have too many adjectives and are describing too much. Shorten. Hone. Tighten. Make better, more precise word choices.

- ✔ **Is the emotion clear from the words chosen?** If not, try to be more precise with your choice of words, making each one count; keep your thesaurus within reach. Go back to your character bible. Between important speaker's lines, add occasional, brief descriptions of their revealing facial expressions or body movements.

- ✔ **Does your main character have a strong voice? Does he sound interesting and unique?** If not, you may want to reexamine his personality and see what special speech patterns or tone of voice may make him more compelling. Perhaps you do not know him well enough? Try some of the exercises described at the end of this chapter.

- ✔ **How does each piece of dialogue move the story forward or further embellish a character?** If it doesn't, *sayonara*, baby!

Dialogue is never easy for a new writer. But you can write much better dialogue with practice and determination. And when in doubt about a particular piece, leave it out.

The great thing about writing dialogue is that on paper you have time to craft the ultimate witty comebacks, astute questions, and on-target answers (unlike in real life). On paper, you can make your characters sound better than the rest of us lugheads. So, for all those times you went home cursing yourself for failing to deliver that perfect retort — the one that came to you on your way home — consider writing books as your revenge and make those characters talk pretty.

Improving Dialogue through Writing Exercises

Writing dialogue well takes developing a good ear and practicing a lot. But you may be better at it than you think, even if you have never written dialogue before. These writing exercises are part of the process of getting in the practice of regular writing and can help you practice writing dialogue without the pressure of having to make the dialogue good. Besides, they can be a lot of fun.

Talk on paper

One of the freeing aspects of letter writing (or e-mail writing) is that it can be as free-form as you want. You can write like you speak — about what interests you at the moment. You can be trivial and funny and even use bad words. And you can write ungrammatically, in truncated sentences, using shorthand and even smiley faces to get your meaning across. This exercise provides a no-pressure outlet for self-expression that can help get you in the groove of writing every day — with the added benefit of giving you practice writing dialogue.

So sit down and open up that e-mail or word processing program or grab some gorgeous stationery and start *talking on paper*. Write letters to anyone, about anything. Got a friend you owe a call to? Surprise her instead with a handwritten page or two about what has been going on in your life the last few weeks. Haven't been in touch with that friend from college for months? Pretend she's on the phone and carry on a one-way conversation with her on your computer, print out the pages, and then snail mail them before you have a chance to change your mind. Got an overseas buddy who could use some entertainment from an old pal (you)? E-mail a message that requires him to scroll down at least a few times. And to get some practice with dialogue, instead of writing it all in narrative, relay some conversations you've had recently with others (or overheard others having) — and feel free to make your replies more witty and to the point than they really were.

And if you really want to increase the usefulness of this exercise, write a letter or an e-mail or even a long instant message to a child that you know: your niece or nephew, your own child, your best friend's child. Keep the subject matter appropriate, but just write whatever comes into your head and keep it flowing. The recipient will be delighted because kids love to get letters and messages.

Being yourself and being relaxed on paper, not worrying too much about how you sound, is a good way to get comfortable with writing. Then when it comes to writing the "real thing," you won't feel as if you are embarking on a scary journey.

Introduce your first best friend to the love of your life

Try a tactic that can really bring characters to life through dialogue. Simply choose two people you know (such as your first best friend and your significant other — see the exercises at the end of Chapter 7) and begin a dialogue between them on paper, just as you'd imagine them talking with one another face-to-face.

A famous writing teacher, who guided many aspiring novelists to fame and fortune, always had her writers begin her workshops with this exercise. Now that Lisa runs her own workshops, she also has new writers try this exercise. She always tells them that if nothing else happens, they are holding in their hands some interesting character studies to auction off on eBay when they become rich and famous writers. At the very least they have accomplished a first attempt at writing dialogue.

Pretend to be someone you aren't

Here's a fun exercise. Is there an accent you think is hilarious? Or one that you have always tried to imitate, such as Porky Pig's or John Wayne's or some revered (or hated) public figure whose patterns of speech just cry out for imitation? Well here's your chance to make fun to your heart's content. Take a familiar story such as Little Red Riding Hood or any of the classic storylines we list in Chapter 20 and rewrite it entirely in dialogue, as if you were recounting the story out loud to someone else, using the silly accent you have chosen. It's really fun and gives you practice writing dialogue (here, with Little Red Riding Hood): "Whah, oh whah, Grandmama, has you got sech big ole ears?" "The better so's ah kin hear y'all wif!" and will make you laugh as you go.

Chapter 10

Setting the Scene

- -

In This Chapter

▶ Establishing setting and context

▶ Understanding the whens and whys

▶ Including the right amount of setting and context

▶ Incorporating sensory elements

▶ Using writing exercises

- -

Many books about writing don't talk about setting, and maybe that's why we've read so many children's books with stories that seem to lack a satisfying sense of place. Whether you are writing fiction or nonfiction, your characters need to do whatever they do *somewhere,* right? And that particular somewhere needs to be set up for the reader almost the same way you would set up a character, only much more subtly and much more briefly, so that the reader gets a picture in their heads about the places all the action in the story occurs.

In this chapter, we show you how to set up scenery to give your stories and characters context, creating a much more interesting and believable children's book in the process. We find out exactly when to include scenery and context and how much of it to include. Next, we dip into the use of sensory elements — tastes, smells, sounds, and more — to engage your readers. We wrap up this chapter with a demonstration of how to use writing exercises to set the scene in your story.

Giving Context to Your Story and Its Characters

The most important reason for setting up scenery is to give your story and characters a context. For example, when your adventurous main character comes from a house in a city, it's not enough to just name a city, real or imagined, and leave it at that. You need to give that city *character,* to imbue it with a sense of uniqueness so that it adds to who your protagonist is. Why? Because the places you live in shape you, positively or negatively. They contribute to who you are and form some of who you want to become.

How many times do you hear about people who left home and never looked back? That's indeed interesting, but we need to know more: What's the character's hometown like that made him want to never return? Describe the things about the town that created such a strong emotion in your character. It follows that our characters are also shaped by these contexts. In addition, a well-established context gives us a starting point from which to begin the action.

Often, you read books starring characters that come from real cities. The author drops the name of the city and leaves it at that. What a rip off. Chances are, the reader doesn't even know what he is missing.

Lisa comes from Los Angeles, California, which isn't just a huge city, but also a huge county with many different cities within it, each with its own character. People who live in each of these cities are assumed to share in the character of the place they have chosen to live. For example, people who live in Venice, California, have chosen to inhabit a beach community that is artsy, packed with pedestrians, culturally mixed, and impossible to drive through on sunny summer weekends. There are lots of restaurants and funky shops, with the decrepit right next door to the brand-spanking new. If you're familiar with Venice, you know that people who choose to live there accept and even embrace what Venice has to offer — both good and bad. So a character who comes from Venice will be assumed to possess an artistic and accepting attitude or to enjoy being surrounded by others who do — but only if you're familiar with that area can you know enough to assume that about the character. If you're not familiar with that area, you need the writer to let you in on its secrets so that you can better understand your main character.

When to Include Scenery and Context

A reader who is not getting enough information about a main character's whereabouts won't necessarily be able to tell you that's the reason he's not enjoying your book. But he will feel a certain lack of interest in the character itself — which is the kiss of death. If a main character isn't engaging (see Chapter 7), the book is put down and never picked up again.

How do you make sure you are providing enough context and scenery? Every time you start a story, it needs to take place somewhere. That somewhere should be given at least one fabulously descriptive sentence within the first few paragraphs of the book. Then as the book progresses, and the character moves from place to place in each scene, you need to make sure you have at least one descriptive sentence about each new place that matters.

Establishing scenery and context is not as important in books that are illustrated if the images do the work for you. What that means is that board books, picture books, and other formats for the youngest readers don't necessarily require descriptive sentences establishing context. In these cases, identifying home or school or the park as such is sufficient. You can include scene-building sentences or phrases, but what you don't need to do is go into great detail. If you go into great detail regarding scenery when writing a shorter format book, two things happen:

✔ You use up your word count.

✔ A lot of it should be cut when you get a good illustrator.

So, although you can establish your context in picture books, don't go on and on about what the reader sees — it's the illustrator's job to do that. It's really with middle-grade novels and longer books that involve many different scenes and chapters in which the main character moves from place to place that you need to make sure we know something about where we are.

Here's an example of a picture book setting that works:

> Barden Woods was haunted. Everyone knew the story about Barden, the famous wood carver. He had spent his days among the giant redwoods, surrounded by children, whittling toys, tiny furniture, even tree houses. One day, not long after The Great Fire destroyed part of the woods, Barden disappeared. The villagers whispered that he had been carried off by wood spirits. Barden Woods became a place forbidden to children. It still was.

How do you know when a scene needs scenery description or contextual establishment? The next sections help you out.

If there are no pictures to tell us about where we are, and if you can say yes to any of the seven examples in the following section, you need to describe the scenery.

When place figures prominently in the story

Every story needs living, breathing characters — people, animals, or anthropomorphized objects such as the dancing teapot and candelabra in Disney's *Beauty and the Beast* — to create reader interest and move the action forward. But sometimes, the place in which a story occurs can be almost as important as the characters that inhabit it — and therefore deserving of a level of description sufficient to provide complete context and scenery.

For example, a mystery story involving the inhabitants of a haunted house requires the description of the house. In the same way, a story involving a character who is an explorer means you need a brief description of each place explored. Consider the important role that context and scenery plays in historical fiction, such as the American Girls Collection series of books (Scholastic) which are set in specific years and places, for example, *Meet Kirsten: An American Girl* by Janet Shaw, which opens with Kirsten's first view of the United States from the vantage point of a ship in the ocean, moving — along with the main character — to New York City and finally Minnesota. Or the elaborate descriptions of Master Stevens's plantation in *Meet Addy: An American Girl* by Connie Porter, which is about a girl who moves from slavery to freedom in 19th-century America.

When the place isn't just incidental

What we mean is that the place isn't just a starting place for the character or an ending place in the action. For example:

> Nina left for school every morning at seven o'clock. And she returned home promptly at three in the afternoon. At noon sharp, she sat down for lunch and after school she allowed herself a snack at 3:15 on the button. Nina was a very punctual person. So when Nina did not show up for her first class right on time, Ms. Greenberg knew something was wrong.

In this passage, school is not a place that needs describing because it is not important to the plot. It is incidental. Nina's punctual personality is the subject of the passage, and to describe her school would both interrupt the flow of the prose and fail to add anything interesting that we readers need to know. If however, the passage reads like the following, a description of the school is merited:

> Nina left for school every morning at seven o'clock, dragging her feet the entire way. With each step, she thought of recess at ten, lunch at noon, and, best of all, the end of classes at three. With her shoulders slumped, Nina barely managed to get to her first class on time, no matter how hard she tried. Today was no exception. As she heard the first bell, signaling three minutes left to get to class, Nina lifted her eyes and increased her pace. The tall, red-brick façade soon came into view, its disheveled eaves and broken windows looking like a face that had barely survived a bad accident. She slipped into Ms. Greenberg's room just as the last bell rang.

Here, the main character's reluctance to go to school is the subject of the passage and since she is reluctant about a place, we are interested in the reason and would like to be able to see it in our minds.

When description of place doesn't interrupt flow of action

Sometimes, tossing in a description of the place where the action is occurring can interrupt the flow of the story that you have been so meticulously crafting. When that happens, your reader may become momentarily confused or disoriented or may simply lose interest in the story — outcomes that are not ones you want as an author.

Suppose your main character is plummeting down a mineshaft, mere seconds away from certain disaster. This is probably not a good time to describe what California in the year 1849 looked like. It is, however, a good time to describe the thoughts going through your character's head as the bottom of the shaft fast approaches.

Or suppose a giant squirrel is chasing your knight in shining armor through the woods, teeth bared and saliva dripping from its furry mouth. Stopping the action to describe the verdant soil, the softly swaying flowers, and the gentle pollen-filled breeze would certainly interrupt the story — distracting the reader and ruining the moment.

How do you know whether your description of a place interrupts the flow of your story? A sure sign is if you feel like putting it in parentheses — or if you find yourself moving it around because you are not sure where it really should go.

When in doubt, leave it out.

When description of context adds something measurable

Sometimes, adding a description of place or context in a story isn't absolutely essential in and of itself, but it adds something measurable to the mood or power of the scene or to the main character. In cases such as this, you may very well want to include the description.

What do we mean by measurable? If it moves the plot forward by providing information causing the character to move his feet. Or if the description creates the mood you want to set for the scene. Or if it adds flavor and spice that really sets the tone for the scene.

Consider the example of a witch's house deep in an ancient, dark wood, with a huge, black, bubbling cauldron over a raging fire in the center of the kitchen. The tendrils of steam flowing from the cauldron add to the foreboding mood of the setting, and the character is moved forward and given power as she reaches for ingredients — an eye of newt here, a lock of a young child's hair there — to add to her evil soup.

When you must mention an exotic locale

We don't mean to sound America-centric or xenophobic, but the great preponderance of readers of books written in English do come from North America, Great Britain, Ireland, Australia, and New Zealand. It's important to consider your probable audience when dropping in a reference to an exotic locale. If, for example, you're writing in English and you mention a place like Borneo or Tierra del Fuego, consider it exotic to most of your readership and let us in on what it's like there. If you're writing in French, and your character goes to Belize, describe it a bit.

For an example of a children's picture book that does a great job of describing a foreign country — in this case, Kenya — for an English-speaking audience, see *Ndito Runs* by Laurie Halse Anderson and Anita Van Der Merwe (Henry Holt & Company).

When beginning a novel and a specific place is mentioned

You have read a zillion books that start off with a lovely description of a place in the first paragraph or two and then plunge right into the action. There's a couple of good reasons for that. First, when your reader encounters your reference to a specific place, his curiosity will be piqued — he'll want to know more about it. Second, setting the scenery and context at the very beginning of the story quickly transports the reader out of the day-to-day reality of his current environment and into the fantasy world created by the book's author. Indeed, this is part of the magic of any well-written book — to transport readers to new places, to meet new people and see new things.

Consider the first words of L. Frank Baum's book *The Wonderful Wizard of Oz* (PD):

> Dorothy lived in the midst of the great Kansas prairies, with Uncle Henry, who was a farmer, and Aunt Em, who was the farmer's wife. Their house was small, for the lumber to build it had to be carried by wagon many miles. There were four walls, a floor and a roof, which made one room; and this room contained a rusty looking cookstove, a cupboard for the dishes, a table, three or four chairs, and the beds. Uncle Henry and Aunt Em had a big bed in one corner, and Dorothy a little bed in another corner. There was no garret at all, and no cellar — except a small hole dug in the ground, called a cyclone cellar, where the family could go in

case one of those great whirlwinds arose, mighty enough to crush any building in its path. It was reached by a trap door in the middle of the floor, from which a ladder led down into the small, dark hole.

Can you picture Dorothy's home in your mind? Did you forget where you are right now because you moved to a different place? Although it isn't always going to be the case that your book will begin with a description of the scenery or context (your book may, for example, focus on a detailed description of your main character), it's an approach that merits your serious consideration.

In a new scene where place is used to transition

Not every story stays in the same place for the duration of a children's book. In fact, more than a few stories start in one place and then move to one or more other places during the course of the action.

When you end a chapter or scene in one place and start the next one in a new place, you need to tell readers where we have gone, because if you don't, they'll soon get lost.

The following description from Lewis Carroll's *Alice's Adventures in Wonderland* (PD) ends a chapter and marks Alice's arrival at a new scene — at the March Hare's house (which happens to be the location of the Mad Tea Party, which commences at the beginning of this new chapter):

> She had not gone much farther before she came in sight of the house of the March Hare: she thought it must be the right house, because the chimneys were shaped like ears and the roof was thatched with fur. It was so large a house, that she did not like to go nearer till she had nibbled some more of the left-hand bit of mushroom, and raised herself to about two feet high: even then she walked up towards it rather timidly, saying to herself "Suppose it should be raving mad after all! I almost wish I'd gone to see the Hatter instead!"

Be sure to describe new scenes as your characters encounter them — your readers will appreciate it.

How Much Setting and How Often

Knowing how much to write and how often to set a scene by describing scenery or context is a skill that you develop as you become a more experienced writer. Here's a simple rule for how long or involved a description should be in a children's book without pictures:

One sentence per new place is enough, except where to write more adds significantly to plot or character development.

When writing chapter books, middle-grade readers, and novels, don't think that just because you have more space and larger word count, you should feel free to devote entire pages to scenery or place descriptions. Keep it short. Make your words work hard for you. More than a paragraph for the most important place/context in your novel should be considered too long.

Consider the description of the workhouse that opens Charles Dickens's classic story *Oliver Twist* (PD — public domain). It manages to provide enough information in one sentence — albeit a *long* sentence — for the reader to develop a picture of the building in her mind, but not so much as to begin to distract from the overall flow of the story:

> Among other public buildings in a certain town, which for many reasons it will be prudent to refrain from mentioning, and to which I will assign no fictitious name, there is one anciently common to most towns, great or small: to wit, a workhouse; and in this workhouse was born; on a day and date which I need not trouble myself to repeat, inasmuch as it can be of no possible consequence to the reader, in this stage of the business at all events; the item of mortality whose name is prefixed to the head of this chapter.

Or consider this brief mention of the town of Cardiff Hill early in Mark Twain's *The Adventures of Tom Sawyer* (PD). Is there reason to say any more about Cardiff Hill? (We think not!)

> Cardiff Hill, beyond the village and above it, was green with vegetation and it lay just far enough away to seem a Delectable Land, dreamy, reposeful, and inviting.

Although writing delectable descriptions of scenery and context is one of the very real pleasures that children's book writers get to enjoy, be careful you don't go overboard. It's an all too easy thing to do because writing such descriptions is so enjoyable.

Engaging Your Readers' Senses

What constitutes a good sentence or description of scenery, of place, of context? One that evokes a strong image in the reader's mind. Getting someone to read words and see what you'd like them to see requires careful writing.

One way to help you create a vision for your readers is to engage their senses. You engage their sight when they are reading your words, but to engage the mind's eye, you need to help them see in their imagination. The best contextualizations about a place describe

- ✔ The way it tastes
- ✔ The way it feels on the skin or to the touch
- ✔ The way it sounds
- ✔ The way it smells
- ✔ The way it looks

Most of these make sense, but how can a place taste? Try this on for size:

> The house reminded her of a sour lemon on a hot day, both refreshing and surprising. Flanked by traditional white houses with blue trim, it was light yellow with screaming purple trim and an enormous orange entry door.

Here you are using the reader's sense of taste to evoke an image in their mind's eye. And what about:

> From somewhere deep within the school came screams of fright, groans of pain. Staring at the dark windows and boarded-up doors, Lesleigh couldn't move a muscle.

With this description, you use the reader's sense of sound to convey the terror the main character must feel. For examples of how the senses can be engaged, check out C.S. Lewis's *The Lion, the Witch and the Wardrobe* (Harper Trophy) for the tastes of Turkish delight, the bitter coldness of Narnia, and the sounds of footsteps and carriages approaching. Also read Natalie Babbit's *Tuck Everlasting* (Farrar, Straus and Giroux) for the bristly, itchy grass; the heat of the noontime sun; and the deep, damp mattress of leaves on the ground. Finally, read Frances Hodgson Burnett's *The Secret Garden* (HarperCollins) for the wailing of cholera victims and the sweet taste of wine.

Scene and Setting Writing Exercises

Because writing can be scary to some new writers, here are some exercises and writing activities that are so simple, you won't even feel as if you're writing. Start with something familiar: your life. And start with the most mundane parts of your life, moving on to other sections from there.

Write about the mundane

Believe it or not, even the most mundane daily events in your life can inspire a very productive writing exercise. Dropping the kids off at school, sitting through one more endless staff meeting at work — even your to-do list. Ever heard of "taking the power away from something by voicing it"? This refers to the notion that if you're scared about something (namely, writing), directly addressing it can take the edge off your fear.

So if you still haven't given it a shot, take away the power of having to actually try writing by sitting down and working on tomorrow's to-do list. Give this first exercise a try.

Instead of using bullet points, write your to-do list for tomorrow in complete sentences, including every errand, activity, personal hygiene item, and trip you want to accomplish. For instance:

> I really need to go to the market because my children have nothing but limp broccoli for their lunches for tomorrow, and the only thing I can think of serving for dinner is canned beans. Then I should see my hairdresser because my locks are beginning to look more like those yellow climbing ropes attached to swing sets than hair. And if I could just stop by the waxing salon for two measly little minutes to deal with these polar bear legs, I might feel a lot less friction under my jeans. After I accomplish that, it might behoove me to go to the paint store because you cannot tell whether the walls in the kitchen were designed with greasy little handprints in mind or not.

Classic literature? No. Breathtakingly interesting? Hardly. Writing? Yes!

What? You can't think of anything particularly mundane in your life? Here are a few ideas:

- ✔ Write a half page about cooking, shopping, eating, or even sleeping.
- ✔ Write about boredom and how it makes you feel.
- ✔ Write about wishing you had time to be bored.

If you apply yourself to these exercises in the mundane, you see that, _voilà!_ You've actually been writing.

Before you can write well, you have to write. And you have to start somewhere.

Pretend to live in an extraordinary world

For this exercise, pretend you've been transported to a world exactly like your own neighborhood with one crucial difference: The world is magical. Pretend you go outside to take your first 15-minute walk in the magical world, writing down everything you see, using familiar landmarks as markers. Keep "walking" and writing for 15 minutes.

Here's an example:

> I walked out the door onto Voyage Street and turned toward Washington Blvd. On my way past the boardwalk, I saw a dog chasing a white bunny rabbit. The bunny rabbit leaped onto the blue Cape Cod-style house with the flowers in front and started to wave his paws. As I approached the house, just south of the boulevard, I could hear the bunny muttering something about carrots as the dog took notes in a small green notebook.

Writing from a magical perspective can help you see setting in a way you may not have before. It can spark an idea for a children's story. So get down and get those paws moving.

Write a smellography

One surefire way to write great settings is to engage your other creative senses and muscles. (See the "Engaging Your Readers' Senses" section for details.) You may think these senses have nothing to do with writing, but they have everything to do with firing up nerve endings that may be lying dormant — nerve endings that can get you excited about writing.

Most everyone has the same five senses operating all the time. Those five senses constantly feed information into our brains without our taking much notice. Whenever we experience an event, our senses record it right along with our hearts and our minds. As a result, most people have years and years of stored experiences trapped inside them that can be accessed by reawakening those sense memories.

Why bother getting in touch with your senses, so to speak? Because the best writing gets the reader's senses fired up alongside the heart and mind. And if you can familiarize yourself with your senses again and learn to translate those sensory experiences onto paper, you are well on your way to becoming an evocative, provocative writer. Engaging your senses, your emotions, and your fertile imagination brings you closer to a children's world.

One of your most powerful senses is your sense of smell. Have you ever found an old tub of delicious-smelling cocoa-butter sunscreen or a vial of flowery, fragrant perfume and been instantly transported back to that precise moment where you smelled it before — years or perhaps even decades ago? Smells often lead to memories and emotions that you can translate into great ideas and powerful writing.

To uncover memories you may have forgotten, give the following smell exercise a try:

1. **Start with the first smell you can remember and write a simple** *smellography* **— an autobiographical record of your smell memories.**

   Set aside enough time to really think back deep into your past.

   For example, here are some of the smell memories from the beginning of Lisa's smellography, starting with her very first memories and working toward the present day:

   • My baby sister's scalp

   • My hands after playing with modeling clay

   • Toe jam from tube socks

   • My wet dog at the lake

   • My grandparents' freshly mowed lawn

   • Hot cinnamon rolls and freshly ground coffee for the grown-ups after dinner

   Your smellography doesn't have to be long — a paragraph will do — but the more smells you can write down, the more effective an exercise it will be, because you will be able to cull more ideas from it.

2. **Come up with as many smell memories as you can until you reach the present day.**

3. **Set a timer for 15 minutes.**

4. **Choose one or more of the smell memories and write a short story about it/them until the timer stops.**

Each of these smell memories can be developed into an idea for a children's book if you do three things: 1) Take the memory and recall the emotion behind it; 2) take that emotion and attach it to a character; 3) start writing from that character's point of view (more about point of view in Chapter 11). The exercise is working if it gets you writing. Don't worry right now about the shape the writing takes or how the story is unfolding; simply write.

Touch something

Touch is a very powerful sense — one that connects you very intimately to the world and to those around you. Think about the things you like to touch or run your fingers through: a bag of marbles, a silk scarf, the leaf of an African violet, your child's skin. Uncovering touch memories can help you generate ideas and begin writing.

Because the goal is to start writing, choose an item you like to touch and take it to the next stage in the writing process. Try the following touch exercise:

1. **Choose something that pleases your fingertips and spend a few minutes just touching or caressing it.**

   Think about what touching this item reminds you of.

2. **Imagine that you have lost this item and that some stranger — a child — has just found it.**

3. **Picture that child in your head.**

4. **Write for 15 minutes from the child's point of view.**

   What does he imagine about you? What kind of person does he think you may be? What does the object tell him about you? Does he wish he could meet you? Why or why not?

This exercise can help you access experiences that make you want to write. And the special thing about this exercise is that it forces you to write from a child's perspective, or point of view (POV). We talk a lot more about POV in Chapter 11, but for now, just know that starting to write through a child's eyes can give you important experience you can use when writing your children's book. Nothing is more boring than an adult telling a child's story through grown-up eyes. Remember when your parents tried to "relate" to you by pretending to be young, but both of you knew they didn't really "get it?" That's what happens when adults write children's stories without having any practice being inside a kid's head. So enjoy this exercise for the progress it's helping you make in writing for children.

Create a sensory short-short story or first chapter

If any one activity deeply engages all your senses at once, it's eating. The tastes, smells, textures, visual appeal and — yes — even the sounds of a meal can create memories that are built to last. So, begin working on a short story or first chapter that includes all five senses in just a few pages.

If writing an entire story or first chapter is too much for the moment, try this: Using the five senses, record all the sense images — the salty taste of fresh corn on the cob, the crunch of biting into an apple — that remain from your last meal. Use each sense at least once in your description. This exercise helps train your writing muscles to be aware of all your senses. When you're more aware of writing from your sensory experiences, you can apply this awareness to the characters, places, and situations you write about in your stories.

Or take the sense image exercise closer to home. Pretend that meal you described was eaten by an alien child who has never seen food before, much less eaten it. He understands somehow that you want him to ingest the material on the plate in front of him, but he's just not sure how to go about it. And when the food hits his senses, imagine what his facial expressions might reveal. Have fun with this exercise. Let yourself revel in the potential for humor here.

Chapter 11

Finding Your Voice: Point of View and Tone

*E*very story is told from some vantage point. That vantage point indicates who is telling the story and what limitations he or she has to contend with. Vantage point is also and more commonly known as *point of view,* or POV for short. And when you write, you must do so from a consistent point of view. In this chapter, we talk about how to choose a POV and how to keep it consistent.

Choosing a point of view is just one of the decisions a writer has to make when developing a writing style best suited to the tale at hand. Along the way, you're also choosing which words you'll use to convey your own style and the tone of the story. Words, the basic building blocks of a story, help to draw pictures in the reader's mind, bringing the reader into a make-believe world. Words give a character a voice, develop a point of view, and elaborate on a plot.

But words serve other purposes besides providing a basic foundation; they also give life to your writing. By using words in creative and innovative ways, writers can evoke all kinds of emotions in readers, from wistful nostalgia to wild hilarity to bite-your-fingernails suspense.

In this chapter, we explore the nuances of how to use words to make your prose come alive, to evoke strong emotions in your readers, and to give your writing a tone of its own.

Building a Solid Point of View

Point of view (POV) is the perspective from which a book is narrated. It is the position or vantage point from which the story is presented to the reader (see the following section for examples). Point of view is used to show readers in *whose mind* and through *whose eyes* they are seeing the world of the story.

Reviewing point of view options

The primary POV decision you have to make before you can write even one sentence is *person*. You have three to choose from:

- First person
- Second person
- Third person

Third-person stories are told by a narrator who is not part of the story; first- (and usually second-) person stories are told by a narrator who is also a character.

- **First person:** First-person entails the author outright telling a story, per-haps his own, by being the main character of the story, narrating the book using the pronoun *I*. Your character (usually the protagonist) is telling the story through his own eyes. First-person point of view means that the teller of the story cannot be *omniscient* (all-knowing), because regular people cannot be omniscient; as such, the teller of the story can report only what he or she can realistically know. For example, she can't know some else's private thoughts or what will happen in the future. Here's an example:

> I could not believe my eyes. There she was. Standing there in the outfit that we both admired yesterday at the mall. She hadn't had the money to buy it then, so how had she come to be wearing it now? That was when I remembered the strange bulk in her shop-ping bag after we had left the department store. "My jacket," she had said, noticing my look.
>
> "Hi," she now said, all cheerful and bright. "Like it?" She shimmied a little and laid a big smile on me, oblivious.
>
> It was clear that in this new school, I was clueless about the rules. I'd learn soon enough.

First-person POV is tough for a new writer to tackle, and although it's fun to experiment trying on various voices for size, most writers try to get plenty of experience writing in the third person before moving to first.

✔ **Second person:** This perspective allows the writer to address the reader directly, using the pronoun *you*. Second-person POV is used for instructional books like this one, because it adds an intimacy to the relationship between writer and reader.

Second-person POV is rare in published novels. In fact, Jay MacInerney's *Bright Lights, Big City* (Vintage) is one of the only successful examples we can think of. Many editors are turned off by stories told in second-person because it requires an extremely unique facility with voice and language; it's also a hard sell. You may feel your story warrants it, but we suggest waiting until you've had a lot of practice writing before you tackle this particular beast.

✔ **Third person:** Third-person POV is the author telling the story through one perspective, using the pronouns *he*, *she*, or *they*. One type, known as *third-person limited POV*, is where the author gets to read the thoughts of only one main character.

Third-person POV can also tell the story through multiple characters' viewpoints *(known as third-person multiple POV)*, but most of the main action viewpoint is still reserved for the main character. E. L. Konigsburg's *The View from Saturday* (Aladdin) is told in third-person multiple POV, with quite a few main characters (Noah, Nadia, Ethan, and Julian) all contributing to the telling of the story.

Third-person omniscient POV is writing told from the viewpoint of a narrator who knows all and sees all — kind of like God. As a totally omniscient author, you are God. You can

- Go into the mind of any character.

- Report on *anything* that is happening *anywhere* with *anyone* in the story at *any time,* even in the future.

- Interpret any character's actions or thoughts.

- Reflect, judge, and reveal truths.

The main difference between the three types of third person is the amount of *omniscience,* or all-knowingness, the author chooses. Most children's books use the third-person limited point of view; it is also the easiest to master.

Picking your point of view

There are so many variations of the nuances that go into every story that it would be impossible for us to tell you in which situation you should choose which POV. What goes into the choice is often personal. But here are some general situations in which the choice becomes more transparent.

✔ Are you an in-your-face type of writer? Do you know your main character as well as you know yourself? If so, the first-person POV might be for you. Just know that its limitations are the same facing us real-life characters:

When writing about the other characters besides the *I* character, you can only reveal their motives, thoughts, and feelings through dialogue. You get to play God, but only with half a deck of cards.

When writing in the first person, your main character has to be involved in the story from beginning to end and everything in between — but cannot read other people's minds, nor foretell the future. As well, do not fall prey to writing long, descriptive passages in which your protagonist is mainly an observer; if you do, you may find that writing in the third person might actually work better for you because it allows you to narrate from more than one character's POV.

✔ Do you count Jay MacInterney's *Bright Lights, Big City* (Vintage) as one of your favorite books of all time? Are you an experimental person who likes to put himself to the test when trying new things, such as writing? Do you think you would like to address the reader as *you* in your story, making yourself, the writer/narrator, an actor in the drama? If so, second-person POV may be the ticket for you.

The other case that may make second-person POV just right is if you've chosen to write a nonfiction, instructional, or how-to book, because it allows you to address the reader directly (just as we are doing with you here in this book).

In the days when oral storytelling was all the rage (before books were common household possessions), the storyteller would often interrupt his tale and directly address the listener, asking questions or making personal commentary and then going back to his tale. Unless you're writing an instructional book in the second-person POV, talking directly to the reader isn't something we recommend. It's disruptive to the narrative, not to mention annoying to the reader who gets thrown off track and jolted back to plain old reality.

✔ Writing in the third-person point of view is the most common way of telling a story. You need to determine how much omniscience you need with how many characters in order to choose between third-person limited, third-person multiple, and third-person omniscient, but we can help you with that.

- If your story is about one main character, such as Ian Falconer's *Olivia* and *Olivia Saves the Circus* (Atheneum/Anne Schwartz Books), choose third-person limited, because you need to get into the head of only one character.

- If your story involves two or more main characters, all of whom have a different take on the story and contribute equally to the telling of that story, third-person multiple POV will probably work best for you.

- If you're writing an epic story, in which you cover many generations or many characters over an expanded period of time, and you feel that you may need to be able to read every character's mind (telling the reader everything about everyone), third-person omniscience is the way to go.

The only real way to figure out which POV you feel comfortable writing in is to try them out. The one which best suits you, your writing style, and your story becomes apparent as you write your story. For example, if you try writing in one POV and find yourself straining to write or sounding completely wrong, chances are you're not comfortable writing in that viewpoint.

If you aren't sure which character's viewpoint should rule, ask yourself these questions:

- ✔ Can this character be present at all the main events?
- ✔ Can this character be actively involved and not just an observer?
- ✔ Does this character have a stake in the outcome of the story?

If you can answer yes to all of these, your character is worthy of being the main viewpoint narrator of your story.

Once you choose one viewpoint, you have to stick to it. When writing short books, like board books or picture books, it's especially important to stay with one point of view. If your story is one narrative, such as in a picture book, you need to choose one POV. Changing point of view in books this short is generally a big fat no-no.

If you're writing a longer work with chapter divisions, you may choose to write one chapter from one character's point of view and the next from another's POV. However you choose to organize the narrative, don't change POV within a scene or chapter. And be consistent; if you choose to alternate POV in every other chapter, stick to the rhythm and don't deviate.

Matching tense with point of view

Part of choosing a point of view includes choosing a tense to write in. When writing a kids' book, there are two tenses to choose from:

- ✔ Present tense
- ✔ Past tense

(Actually, there are a lot of variations on these two, but for our purposes, we are going to keep it simple.) Present tense: I write, you write, he writes, they write. Past tense: I wrote, you wrote, he wrote, they wrote.

If you write in the first-person POV, then you will need to write in the present tense to retain maximum impact with your writing. First-person POV is chosen for its immediacy, its intimacy, its now-ness, and putting it in the past tense simply is not emphasizing the now.

If you choose second-person, you will also be writing in the present tense, taking advantage of its immediacy and addressing your reader as you take him through your lesson or story.

If you choose third-person, you will most likely choose to write in the past tense.

Most children's books are written in third-person limited point of view using the past tense.

Whichever tense you choose to write in, stick to it. It is truly disconcerting to be reading along in one tense and suddenly find yourself in another one.

Word Play, Rhyming, and Rhythm

For many writers of children's books, having fun with words is the best part of the writing process. Getting the opportunity to play with words, create word pictures in your reader's mind, and build rhymes out of thin air can be more fun than you can shake a stick at. Or more fun than a barrel of monkeys. Or something like that.

In this section, we take a closer look at each of these fun things to do.

Add fun to what you write

Words are fun. And what better way to have fun with words than to write a children's book. As a writer, you have far more freedom to play with words when writing children's books than you do when writing other kinds of books. The sky is truly the limit.

Use some of these common methods to have fun with words:

- **Alliteration:** The initial consonant sounds of words repeated two or more times in a line or sentence creates a rhythmic component to the writing. "She stewed in her soft and simple shoes."

   Assonance is similar to alliteration, but uses vowel sounds instead of consonant sounds.

- **Parallelism:** Repeating similar thoughts in two different phrasings. There are variations on the theme:

   - **Antithetical:** When the second phrasing is the exact opposite of the first: "The good boy did his homework and cleaned his room; the bad boy threw his homework in the trash and dumped his dinner on the floor."

- • **Synonymous:** When the second phrasing is almost identical to the first. "The warm sun warmed the faces of the children at play; the children's faces glowed with the first rays of the sun."

- ✔ **Refrain:** A line or group of lines are repeated throughout a story. Consider the following lines, repeated throughout Dr. Seuss's *Green Eggs and Ham* (Random House): "I do not like green eggs and ham. I do not like them, Sam I am."

- ✔ **Polyptoton:** The same word is repeated in different forms. "The ogre was strong, and he revealed his full strength as he toppled tree after tree in the forest, headstrong to the very end."

- ✔ **Metaphor:** Comparing two unlike things using any form of the verb *to be*. "The color blue is a cold, winter's day — snow forming drifts on the sides of the road and icicles hanging from the roof of the house."

- ✔ **Simile:** Comparing two unlike things using *like* or *as*. "His anger was like a summer's storm — arriving quickly and without warning, then soon passing without a trace."

- ✔ **Anthropomorphism:** Human motivations, characteristics, or behavior appear in inanimate objects, animals, or natural phenomena. For example, Thomas the Tank Engine (from *The Railway Series* by Rev. W. Awdry) is an anthropomorphized train with a human face, feelings, and emotions. He's always getting into all sorts of trouble.

- ✔ **Personification:** Human qualities appear in an animal or object. "Flowers danced in the field."

When you can't think of the right word — make one up! As a children's book writer, it's not only your right but also your duty to have fun with words. Feel free to have fun, without going totally insane. But remember: made up words should still make sense within the context. Dr. Seuss (whose real name was Theodor Geisel) was a master at this; his created words could still be understood because of what was happening in the story. Lewis Carroll, author of *Alice's Adventures in Wonderland* (PD) and other stories and poems, also ranks up there with the very best.

Take different approaches to rhyming

Rhyming is an essential tool in many children's books, especially those written for younger readers. In general terms, words *rhyme* when the last stressed vowel and the sounds that follow it are the same — for example, *blue* and *zoo,* or *horse* and *Norse*. The effect of rhyming is to introduce a repetition of sound patterns that makes your words more interesting to listen to or read — and easier to remember. Rhyming, when done well, also gives words a rhythm that can approximate music when read aloud. You can choose from many different kinds of rhymes as you write your children's book.

Rhyming sounds

When playing with rhymes, sounds are the usual place to start. Look at these different rhyming schemes based on sound:

- **Perfect rhyme:** When the vowel and final consonant match exactly, as in *mute* and *pursuit*.

- **Partial rhyme:** When a rhyme is close, but not perfect, as in *fought* and *fault*. Also known as *near* rhyme or *off* rhyme.

- **Half rhyme:** When the final consonants match exactly, but not the vowels, as in *rats* and *hits*.

- **Eye rhyme:** When words rhyme in sight, but not in sound, as in *cough* and *tough*. Eye rhymes aren't a good idea in children's books, because this particular rhyming technique may tend to confuse young readers who are still working out the right and wrong ways to spell and pronounce words.

- **Masculine rhyme:** A one-syllable rhyme, such as *pop* and *stop* or *soak* and *poke*.

- **Feminine rhyme:** A rhyme of two or more syllables, as in *jeepers* and *creepers* or *torrid* and *horrid*.

Rhyming patterns

When it comes to rhyming, sound is important, but so are the patterns of the rhymes you use. Two of the most common rhyming patterns are

- **End rhyme:** When words at the end of successive lines or sentences rhyme, such as "The more she ate the more she grew. Until she reached five foot two."

- **Internal rhyme:** When words rhyme within a line or sentence, such as "The old man on the moon sang his weary tune."

Keep your story moving with rhythm

Just as music depends on *rhythm* — a recurring pattern of notes or beats — to propel it forward, so too can the written word depend on rhythm. This rhythm in the written word is often called *meter*. When you read back your story, and something doesn't sound quite right, chances are that your meter is off, that is, it is not consistent or even. To check meter, you actually have to count the syllables and keep the same rising and falling tone and the same accented words in the same place for each matching line.

As a writer, you can select the rhythm for your story that sounds best to you, mixing different ones to provide variety and the occasional surprise or maintaining the same rhythm throughout. Different approaches to rhythm and meter impact how your story is received by your readers. The choice is yours.

The most basic unit of rhythm is the syllable. A *foot* (plural is *feet*) is a unit of stressed and unstressed syllables. The five most common feet include

- **Iamb:** One unstressed syllable, then one stressed syllable (da DUM), as in, "I *do* not *like* greens *eggs* and *ham.*"

- **Trochee:** One stressed syllable, then one unstressed syllable (DA dum), as in, "*Pe*ter, *Pe*ter *pump*kin *eat*er."

- **Anapest:** Two unstressed syllables, then one stressed syllable (da da DUM), as in, "'Twas the *night* before *Christ*mas and *all* through the *house.*"

- **Dactyl:** One stressed syllable, then two unstressed syllables (DA da dum), as in, "*Hick*ory, *dick*ory, *dock.*"

- **Spondee:** Two stressed syllables (DA DUM), as in, "One fish, two fish, red fish, blue fish."

As a writer, you can build a rhythm throughout your work by repeating these feet. When you build a line using one or more of these feet, the length of the line is measured by counting the number of feet you used. The following examples are iambic (can you tell us why?):

- **One foot:** "I *do*"

- **Two feet:** "I *do* not *like*"

- **Three feet:** "I *do* not *like* green *eggs*"

- **Four feet:** "I *do* not *like* green *eggs* and *ham*"

- **Five feet:** "I *do* not *like* green *eggs* and *ham,* I *do*"

- **Six feet:** "I *do* not *like* green *eggs* and *ham,* I *do* not *like*"

- **Seven feet:** "I *do* not *like* green *eggs* and *ham,* I *do* not *like* them *Sam*"

- **Eight feet:** "I *do* not *like* green *eggs* and *ham,* I *do* not *like* them *Sam* I *am*"

If you want to discover even more about rhythm, meter, and rhyme, pick up a copy of *Poetry For Dummies* by John Timpane (Wiley).

A final caution about writing in rhyme: The rhyme must be incidental to the story. The text still needs well-developed characters, a plot with a beginning, middle and end, no unnecessary words, good pacing, and so on. The rhyme should be the last consideration, simply adding another level to the book, not the first priority. In other words, don't manipulate the characters and events of the story or add unnecessary words, just because they make the rhyme flow.

Avoiding the kiss of death

Rhyming done poorly or even so-so is the kiss of death for a manuscript. Find someone who rhymes well (like a poetry teacher or a published writer of rhyming poetry) and have her look over your work. Ask a musician who writes and performs for children to do the same. If you don't have access to these talented individuals, and then try the method we call "pounding on the table." This method involves identifying your rhythm and pounding out the rhythm to your words to make sure your meter is even and consistent. You can use a drumstick and a drum, a finger on a piano, or your hand on a table. If you're uncoordinated, have someone else pound while you read. Another tip: Have someone who is not familiar with your rhyme read it out loud into a tape recorder. Listen to your story being read and notice where the reader stumbles over the meter. Also, don't force the meter by assuming the reader will stress a normally non-stressed syllable to make it fit into the meter of the surrounding lines. If you can't keep up the same rhythm throughout the manuscript, then the meter is off, and you need to fix it.

Using Humor to Your Advantage

Perhaps the quickest way to a child's heart is through humor. Children love to laugh, and after you get them laughing, you've truly captured their hearts (and their minds, for that matter).

In this section, we take a close look at what kinds of things kids find humorous and we discuss how to incorporate outrageous (and even gross) ideas into your writing.

What kids consider funny

Before you can start writing funny children's books, you need to understand the kinds of things that kids tend to consider funny. And, although there may seem to be no rhyme or reason for exactly what children find humorous, research shows that children go through different stages of humor development.

According to humor researcher (no, we didn't make that up) Paul E. McGhee, Ph.D., you can expect the following developmental changes in preschool children's humor:

> ✔ **Stage 0 (Age 0 to 6 months):** Laughs, no humor. During the first six months of life, children laugh not because they find something funny, but because something physically arouses them — like bouncing the little tykes on your knee or tickling them. To tickle this age group's fancy, write your story in a way that requires the actual reader (parent, sibling,

or care provider) to do something funny, like read in a funny voice or make unexpected physical movements or gestures. The content doesn't matter — how it's presented does.

✔ **Stage 1 (Age 6 to 12 months or so):** Laughs, with or at parent. During this period, children begin to find humor in the behavior of a parent or other significant people in their lives. Making silly faces or odd sounds all get a laugh from kids in this age bracket, as will a funny game of peek-a-boo. Write these kinds of actions into your story so that the parent or caregiver can act them out.

✔ **Stage 2 (Age 12 months or so up to 5 years):** Pretending that a particular object is something it's not. If you've ever seen a child sit in a big, cardboard box, making noises like a gasoline engine (pretending the box is a race car) or inviting her favorite dolls to an elaborate tea party (pretending they are real, live people), or turning a folded up piece of paper into a jet airplane (pretending it is coming in for a landing), then you've witnessed the power of pretend. Use the power of pretend in your stories to tap into this source of humor.

✔ **Stage 3a (2 to 3 or 4 years):** Playing with the names of common objects or actions. At this age, as language skills improve, kids begin to find humor in misnaming common objects. You can plumb this source of humor by calling a shoe a boat, or turning a dog into a cat, or a father into a mother, and so forth.

✔ **Stage 3b (2 to 3 or 4 years):** Opposites. This form of misnaming — particularly attractive to many children — involves stating the exact opposite of a particular word. Cold is hot, up is down, over is under, fast is slow, wet is dry. Every adjective has an opposite — consider the possibilities!

✔ **Stage 4a (3 to 5 years):** Playing with the sounds of words. At about age three, children begin to play not just with word meanings, but with their sounds. A common word such as *turkey* springs forth any number of variations including *lurky, wurky, perky* and so on. Children alter words for the humor of doing so and begin to create their own nonsense words to be funny. Use word sounds to create humor in your story.

✔ **Stage 4b (3 to 5 years):** Nonsense word combinations. Most 3 year-olds also begin to put real words together in combinations that make no sense. Examples of these kinds of humorous combinations include "I want some monkey juice" or "Give me that mushroom spoon." What nonsense word combinations can you insert into your story?

✔ **Stage 4c (3 to 5 years):** Distorting features. As children increase their command over the real names of objects, people, or animals, they find humor in distorting some aspect of them. They do this by adding features that don't belong (putting a fish's head on a dog's body), by removing features that do belong (a house with no doors), by changing the shape, size, location, color, and length of familiar things (a person with a grape-fruit head), and by ascribing impossible behavior to people or animals (a cat that talks).

> ✔ **Pre-riddle stage (5 to 7 years or so):** Sometime during this period, most kids discover the joy of jokes and riddles, and the verbal humor shared by older children around them. The ubiquitous knock-knock joke is an example of this kind of humor. ("Knock knock." "Who's there?" "Orange." "Orange who?" "Orange you glad I didn't say 'knock knock' again?")

Of course, you need to consider older kids, too, when it comes to using humor in your stories. Children in early elementary grades love broad physical humor, such as pie in the face, pants falling down to expose underwear, slipping on a banana, and so on. William Kotzwinkle and Glenn Murray's *Walter the Farting Dog* (North Atlantic Books) is the perfect example of poopoo humor. It's especially funny if a "serious" character (such as a parent or teacher) unwittingly does these things. Witness the popularity of the *Captain Underpants* chapter books for ages 7 to 10 by Dav Pilkey (Blue Sky Press/ Scholastic). From about third grade on, kids begin to appreciate verbal humor (witty banter, sarcasm, irony, and so on in dialogue) and have the patience to allow a joke to be set up over several scenes. Always funny is a character who just doesn't belong in his/her surroundings.

If you really want your humor to resonate with the children who read your book, then be sure to directly target the age group you're writing to with the right kind of humor. The wrong kind won't buy you many fans in the bookstore.

The outrageous and the gross

Would it surprise you to learn that kids love ideas and concepts that are either outrageous, gross, or both at the same time? Well, it's true. Of late, a number of books — including *Oh, Yuck: The Encyclopedia of Everything Nasty* by Joy Masoff (Workman) and *Grossology* by Sylvia Branzei and Jack Keely (Price Stern Sloan) — have tackled a wide variety of formerly taboo topics, much to the delight of young readers everywhere. Some of these topics include

✔ Vomit, barf, and burps

✔ Farts

✔ Animal eyeballs, hearts, and brains

✔ Boogers and snot

✔ Acne or other itchy red spots

✔ Leeches and worms

✔ Butts, poop, and related topics

Interview with Leslie McGuire, children's book author

Leslie McGuire, author of hundreds of children's books ranging from board books to picture books, and from easy-to-reads to middle-grade novels, is a talented writer with a very quirky outlook on life that often finds its way into her prose.

WCBFD: What role does humor play in your books?

LM: I don't always use humor, but when I do, it's usually a way to make children think. After all, laughter is really a shock reaction. Something unexpected gets said or done, and it's enough to get your diaphragm in your chest fibrillating — and that's what a laugh is — physically at least. That's what makes a good joke. The punch line is quite unexpected.

WCBFD: How do you use words to engage children in your books?

LM: Again, I use the unexpected, especially in descriptions of things. In one book — which wasn't funny — I described a baby owl's view of a luna moth as "A delicious, pale green moth." That makes children think about the eating habits of owls, and what may seem yucky to you might actually be gourmet-style wonderful to an owl. You could always describe a fancy sweater that has a feather boa trim around the neck and sleeves as "A bicycle accident with an ostrich." Language is so very powerful, it's a true shame that most writers for children (and everyone else, I might add) tend to rely on clichés or just boring exchanges. That's dreadful, especially when you consider that in a children's book most of the descriptions are in the picture, so unless you have something interesting to say, you really should avoid saying anything at all.

WCBFD: How do you make sure your rhyming works, both meter-wise, rhyming-wise, and in terms of making sense? What is the trick?

LM: Although this isn't as pompous as it sounds, I like to fall back on Gustave Flaubert at times like those. It took him seven years to write *Madame Bovary* because he yelled every sentence out loud until the music of it was correct. I don't yell it, but I say each sentence or sing it rhythmically until it has the correct meter. Not all that easy, I must say. Even worse, considering what I write, Flaubert would probably be horrified.

WCBFD: What are your tried-and-true ways for making your books fun to read?

LM: The trick is just to avoid overblown words — and when you must use one, define it in the very next sentence. Not only does that upgrade their vocabulary, it's a comprehension thing. Part of using humor is injecting an engaging way to make children think about what they just heard or read, and that's an opening for reading comprehension that's actually fun.

WCBFD: How do you vary your writing style for different age levels of readers?

LM: When writing for each age group, you have to see the world through their eyes, not through your own. Become a 5-year-old. Become an 11-year-old. If that's too hard, then pick a child of the age you're supposed to be writing for, one that you know, and tell that child the story as if that child were sitting right there with you.

WCBFD: What pitfalls should would-be authors watch out for?

LM: Low self esteem. That's the worst. Don't let it get to you. If you love what you wrote, then someone else will, too.

These topics tap deeply into the spirit of young people for the following reasons:

- ✔ Kids haven't yet been fully conditioned to pretend that these everyday things and events don't exist.
- ✔ These topics get a rise out of adults whenever they're mentioned.
- ✔ They're just plain fun to read about.

If your story merits their inclusion, then by all means don't hesitate.

Adults continue to debate about whether using these kinds of gross and outrageous topics and words is bad form or whether they should be acknowledged and celebrated. The message from kids, however, remains loud and clear: Bring it on!

The Mojo of Good Writing: Voice, Style, and Tone

After you figure out how to set your scenes, write scintillating dialogue, and inject so much humor that even *you* can't stop laughing, we still want you to be aware of a few more aspects to good writing. And these are the ones that, fortunately for the reader — unfortunately for you — nearly defy instruction. Let us explain.

When you read a particular author and are drawn in by everything you're reading, so much so that you savor every last page and hate for the book to end, then you have fallen for the writer's *mojo* (magic). Instantly addicted, you search frantically for other books by the same author, regardless of topic. You even order her books in advance so that you can get them the second they're released. That is falling prey to mojo. And as you know in your every cell, every nerve ending, mojo is pretty heady stuff.

So where can you get some? Well, we don't know any dealers, and wouldn't pass them on if we did, so you're just going to have to develop your own as a writer, just as your favorite writers have, and they do it with *voice, style,* and *tone*.

The only caveat is that you must remain consistent throughout the book, not changing voice, style, or tone suddenly on the reader midstream.

Capturing your mojo and suffusing your words with your particular tone, style, and voice takes a lot of practice. Beginning writers have so many aspects of writing to ingest and master that developing these other qualities

preschool participants and straightforwardly helping them deal with their problem. The tone of Robert Munsch's *Love You Forever* (Firefly Books) is tooth-achingly sentimental from start to finish — which is the secret to its bestselling success.

There are many tones you can take with your words and toward your characters, but the right ones will seal the meaning of your story and make your writing memorable.

Writing Exercises to Find Your Voice

Ever wonder what it's like for a child experiencing something for the first time? When the boundary between fantasy and reality is transparent — as it is for most young children — the possibility of magic occurring as one walks down a street is high. This is what is so amazing about being a child — and what most adults seem to forget. You don't need to spend any time explaining in a picture book why something magical has happened, because it's not so far-fetched for a child to imagine. As a matter of fact, much of what may have an explanation in the "real" world may appear to be magical to a child. Getting into this mindset is very important for you as a writer of children's fiction.

In this section, try a few different writing exercises. They are designed to fire up your imagination and get you into the place where children spend most of their free time: their minds.

Pretend to be someone else

Pretend that you're someone you know intimately. Write for 15 minutes in that person's voice. Don't judge, just write.

This exercise helps you get a handle on how writing in your book character's point of view feels.

Pretend you woke up this morning as your favorite animal

Describe your day from the moment you arise to the time you go to bed — all from the animal's perspective. Don't forget to write about the senses other than sight, too.

Using animals as your main characters is a device that adds both charm and distance to an issue a child may be facing. For instance, a kindergartener feels less anxious listening to a story about an anteater having trouble in anteater kindergarten than he does listening about another child going through the same difficulties in *real* kindergarten. Putting yourself in the shoes (or paws) of a smaller being is a great way to force your mind to start thinking differently. Writing for kids is all about thinking differently than adults do.

Pretend you swallowed a magic potion that makes you only three feet tall

Remember when Alice in *Alice's Adventures in Wonderland* by Lewis Carroll (PD) finds the bottle with the words DRINK ME on it and she does, suddenly finding herself only ten inches tall? Well, this exercise requires you to get down to about four times that height, but we don't have any more potion left to give you, so you have to exercise your imagination for this task.

This is one of Lisa's favorite pretending exercises: Spend an hour on your knees, shuffling around your house while you try to accomplish your normal tasks. Really pay attention to what you see at that level, what you smell, what you can reach, and what you struggle with. Then write about your experiences.

After ten minutes of this exercise, you may have sore knees, but you also have a better perspective on the child characters you're writing about. This exercise can also help you think about things a child experiences from down there so you can come up with new story ideas.

Pretend you have 30 days to live

What if you just found out that in 30 days you will disappear forever from the face of the earth? What would you do with that time? (Lisa's plans include traveling around the world with her husband and children — plus hiring three babysitters, one to help with *each* child; Peter's include lots of quality time sipping espresso on a particular piazza in Brescia, Italy.) If you can't be motivated to write by the urgency of your own impending death, we're afraid nothing can help you and you ought to take up some other creative endeavor besides writing. Just kidding — sorta. Anyway, this exercise is great for getting you to write and use your imagination even if you feel completely sorry for yourself and don't feel like writing.

Chapter 12

Writing Creative Nonfiction and How-To Books

As any writer who writes both fiction and nonfiction can tell you, writing nonfiction books is quite different from writing fiction. Although fiction allows you to pick any topic and create a unique universe around it, that's not the case when writing nonfiction, which must be factually correct. If you're writing nonfiction about Thomas Jefferson, for example, you can't ascribe superpowers to him. Although he may have been fit and strong, it's unlikely that he possessed X-ray vision or the ability to fly.

With that thought in mind, we dedicate this chapter to discussing everything you need to know about writing nonfiction children's books. We talk about some major similarities and differences between writing nonfiction and fiction. We consider how to choose fun and fascinating topics, and we take a look at why outlining your nonfiction story is a good idea.

Understanding Nonfiction

A *nonfiction* children's book is one that is not fictional and is drawn entirely from fact. Though the age groups and formats are similar for fiction and nonfiction, the nonfiction picture book format can go higher than age 8. Often nonfiction picture books can be for kids up to age 12, and the texts in these older books up to about 2,500 words — sometimes even more. Nonfiction easy readers and chapter books carry the same lengths as fiction and are used widely in schools.

Although fictional children's books most often find themselves in the spotlight — usually it's the *fictional* children's books that get turned into those matinee blockbusters that earn authors and film studios very big bucks — nonfiction works also play an important role in the lives of children.

The basics of nonfiction

A nonfiction book is one based on facts. It can be historical, focusing on an event (the Civil War) or a person (Susan B. Anthony), or it can home in on a topic, such as dinosaurs, insects, or mammals. Biographies are nonfiction, as are autobiographies (more on nonfiction genres in Chapter 2). The available subjects and topics for nonfiction are nearly endless.

The different elements that go into nonfiction books are often the same as in fiction, only the contents are different. For instance, nonfiction books often use *photorealistic* illustrations (illustrations done in a style that approximates photographs), photographs, line drawings, and simple diagrams, maps, and charts for the visuals. The ratio of text and visuals must be very well balanced, so that the text does not overshadow the images, cluttering up the page with too many words. (A pet peeve of many book buyers — see Chapter 3). The design of a nonfiction book may have to juggle many more elements per spread than a book of fiction; for instance, if there are main text, main visuals, charts, factoid boxes, text bubbles, and other visually stimulating graphics, all must be laid out in a way that encourages the reader to peruse everything without overwhelming her.

Nonfiction plays a very important part in the spectrum of children books. Teachers use nonfiction books in their curricula from preschool to high school. You will find nonfiction in every single format from board books to YA books, and everything in between. And nonfiction lends itself perfectly well to the parameters of all of the formats you can read about in Chapter 2. The only major difference is that although fictional picture books target ages 3 through 8 and max out at a word count of 1,500, nonfiction picture books can be aimed at audiences up to age 12, and the text can run up to 2,500 words or more — the page count increasing from 32 as well.

A great example of a nonfiction series that is appropriate for ages 9 through 12 and that so beautifully balances many different visual elements with the right amount of text (most of the time, in some volumes it's a bit excessive) is Dorling Kindersley Publishing's Eyewitness Books series. Each title, written by a different author or team of authors, offers an in-depth look at one subject, say pirates, or horses, or insects, and spends about 56 to 72 pages really digging into the aspects of the chosen topic that kids really care about. (For more about idea development and what your audience wants, see Chapters 5 and 6.) Instead of reading like dry reference books, these are like mini encyclopedias — fascinating and packed with information.

Nonfiction for the fiction lover

A nonfiction style that's written in a way that makes it read like fiction is called *narrative nonfiction.* It uses fiction techniques such as narrative, dialogue, and a story structure with a beginning, middle, and end — but everything that happens in the book is true. Biographies can be narrative nonfiction, as can books about events in history, or memoirs. Books with narratives focusing on the main character's diary entries fall into this genre, as do books in which the narrative consists of protagonists who wrote letters back and forth to one another. All the letters and correspondences in these books must be real documents — though verifying whether the writers of these documents were telling the truth about their lives would be a whole other book. Examples would be *Heads or Tails: Stories from the Sixth Grade* by Jack Gantos (middle-grade memoir; Farrar Straus & Giroux Books for Young Readers) or *The Boys' War: Confederate and Union Soldiers Talk About the Civil War* by Jim Murphy (young adult history; Clarion Books).

Children love to read nonfiction, too, and their teachers often build nonfiction reading into the curriculum. That means your easy reader about horses or your middle-grade book about pirates can be used in schools. So if you are into a topic and have always wanted to learn more and share it with others, writing nonfiction may be just the ticket.

Writing a nonfiction masterpiece

Writing fiction is different from nonfiction in a few ways. Though you may not have a main character (unless you are writing a biography or autobiography) or a plot tied to that main character, you will still have to make some decisions early on. For details about each of these, please refer to the chapters referenced, but here they are in brief as they apply to nonfiction:

- ✔ **Theme or subject:** This refers to the book's main idea or concept. What's your subject? See the "Choosing a Great Topic" section later in this chapter.

- ✔ **Characters:** Will you have a main character? What about supporting characters? (If your book is not about a particular person or group of people, the answer to this is usually no.) See Chapter 7.

- ✔ **Plot:** A plot is what happens in your book. You may not have a plot in nonfiction, but you still need to set up your work with a series of intertwined actions that progress from a beginning, to a middle, to an end in order to keep it moving and interesting to your young reader. Your outline will help you track and accomplish this. Check out Chapter 8.

- ✔ **Setting:** Where does the subject take place or is the place your subject? Many nonfiction books explore many settings. Flip to Chapter 10.

 ✔ **Point of view:** Except for many biographies and, of course, autobiographies, nonfiction is in the third person. See Chapter 11.

 ✔ **Format and target audience:** Although not necessary for you to begin writing, it can be helpful to know what format and what audience you think you might like to write for. (We cover formats and audience in Chapters 2 and 3 and researching your audience in Chapter 6.)

After you make these decisions and begin your writing, you have to make other choices that you do not have to when writing fiction. For example, in nonfiction, all dialogue must be factual and verifiable — many publishers require complete and documented accuracy. Will your book be long enough to need a table of contents? What about an index? How are you going to keep track of and credit those from whom you borrow information? (The two classics for researchers are Kate L. Turabian's *A Manual for Writers* [The University of Chicago Press] and *The MLA Handbook for Writers of Research Papers, Theses, and Dissertations* by Joseph Gibaldi and Walter S. Achtert [Modern Language Association].) What illustrations or other graphics will you seek to keep your text engaging? You have to get legal permission to use existing images from the originators — publishers will require copies of these signed legal documents. (Go to www.nolo.com for permissions information, books, and forms.) Or you may choose to create some of the visuals yourself or pay someone else to design them for you.

Aside from the visuals, how are you going to keep your text engaging? If you are writing about an event in history, and do not have a single historical figure you'd like to use as a main character, how are you going to keep readers engaged? Suspense, humor, and romance all still have places in nonfiction, and you still are the one to provide them. Chapter 8 gives ample tips about pacing and drama that you can apply to nonfiction writing as well.

The process for writing nonfiction, after you decide on the basics just described, is no different from that for fiction — until you hit the researching part. For instance, after you come up with a great topic and nail down the basics, you need to go out and make sure your topic is relevant and up-to-date and that kids will be interested in it — same as fiction. But then you jump into researching what your topic is all about — not necessary for all fiction, absolutely necessary for nonfiction. And the vast majority of nonfiction writers, unlike most fiction writers, do use outlines to organize their thoughts and help them flesh out their ideas. Then once you have down your first draft, your rewrites and your edits will involve the same sort of painstaking and careful attention to detail — if not more.

Librarians and booksellers tell us that the design and layout of a nonfiction book are paramount to their buying decisions. Chances are good they won't buy books with too much text and not enough pictures, or books in which the design is cluttered, illogical, or hard to follow. Although the publisher will design the interior of a nonfiction book, you can do much to encourage a good design. First, research nonfiction books that are well laid out and then note the elements they use that you can write into. For example, if little, interesting factoids are interspersed throughout the book using talk bubbles and cartoons that are different from the photorealistic illustrations you want to use, you can write text for these and include them in the manuscript. If you have lots of terms to define on each page, write them out separately so that the designer can figure out a cool way to incorporate them into the overall design. And if text blocks seem to work better in your mind's eye (and in the competition), then create actual text blocks of your manuscript paragraphs. And when you sell your masterpiece, you can even try to negotiate input in the design phase of the book.

Choosing a Great Topic

Writing a great nonfiction children's book begins with finding a great topic. You have an almost infinite variety of topics to work with. Of course, some topics will interest your audience — and you as a writer — more than others, so you must be selective when choosing the one on which you will focus your creative efforts.

In the sections that follow, we consider how to choose a topic that will both delight the children who read it and excite you to write it. We also take a look at sources for nonfiction book ideas and great places to test your ideas before you spend all your time and energy developing them.

Topics that float kids' boats

When it comes to fictional topics, you probably already have a pretty good idea of what gets children interested in reading: stories about wizards, flatulent canines, heroes with superpowers, princes and princesses, talking fish, cats with hats, Martians, girls from Kansas with ruby slippers, and many more. But what about ideas for nonfiction children's books? What topics float kids' boats? Here are just a few:

- Pets
- How bodies work
- Sports
- History and culture
- Dinosaurs
- Biographies
- Backyard nature
- Science
- Strange, terrible, gross, interesting facts

Choose a slant to the topic that will be unique and interesting to the intended audience. Younger kids (preschool through first grade) like topics presented as they apply to the kids' lives. For example, how to find and study bugs in your backyard. Kids in second grade and up use the books to write reports at school or do research, so tie the topics into the curriculum. And it's always good to add humor whenever possible, through the text, illustrations, or both. Consider the example of a nonfiction book in the picture book format for kids up to age 10 called *It's Disgusting and We Ate It! True Food Facts from Around the World and Throughout History* by James Solheim (Simon & Schuster Children's Publishing). It combines history and social studies, and it even includes recipes.

Topics that float your boat

When we say you should choose a subject that floats your boat, we mean choosing a subject that you have a strong personal interest in. Although it is ultimately of critical importance that your reader be interested in the topic you choose (otherwise, why buy it?), you have to be interested in it first. If you're not, it will show in your writing. To decide which topics float your boat, use the following indicators as a guide:

- **Choose a topic that you know a lot about.** If you know a *lot* about a particular topic, not only is that an indication that you probably like it, but it also means you probably have plenty of background knowledge to easily get started.

- **Choose a topic that you're curious about.** Perhaps there's a topic that you've been wondering about for a long time — maybe years — but that has never made it to the top of your list of things to learn more about. You may, for example, have a fascination with tornadoes — a topic about which you know little beyond what you learned from watching the film *Twister* years ago. This fascination may drive you to research the topic thoroughly — to the point that you become expert at it.

- **Choose a topic that you're passionate about.** Passion for something — an idea, a thing, a person — can really motivate you to achieve great things, including writing a great story. Tap into the emotion, energy, and inspiration that your passion releases by choosing a topic that you're passionate about.

- **Choose a topic that has personal meaning to you.** If you, your parents, or your grandparents immigrated to this country from, say, China or Mexico, why not choose a topic that allows you to further explore your own roots and your cultural heritage? Maybe a book based on Chinese New Year or Mexican Day of the Dead festivities.

Life is too short to waste your time writing books for which you have no passion or feeling of connection. Leave those books to someone else while you focus on finding the topics that work best for you.

Branch out into the real world

Beyond finding topics that interest your potential readers — and that interest you personally — it's a good idea to branch out and look at the real world and real topics that are going on today or that have happened in history. Perhaps it should come as no surprise that a glance through the pages of most any newspaper or magazine can reveal a wide variety of topics for you to consider.

The hot topics of the day

Kids are connoisseurs of all things current and hot. If there's something new out there, chances are that kids will already be in the know about it. Whether it's the latest teen idol, the hottest fashions and trends, or the coolest consumer electronics gizmo — or any number of other hot topics of the day — kids are likely already there. Be sure to check out Chapter 6, where we devote an entire section to dipping into the popular culture for ideas on what's hot and what's not.

Interesting historical topics that need more coverage

Another terrific source of topics for your nonfiction children's book is to look for broad subjects that are in deep need of more coverage. It's unlikely that topics such as dinosaurs or fire trucks are lacking in coverage in the children's book market, but other topics — such as the plight of American citizens of Japanese descent who had to abandon their homes and land when the government herded them into forced relocation camps during World War II, or great women scientists, or the impact of population growth on fragile ecosystems — may be.

Consider asking the following questions as you search for a subject that needs more coverage:

- ✔ Is the person, event, or thing historically significant?
- ✔ Is the person, event, or thing relatively obscure?
- ✔ Would a book based on the topic have a measurable and positive impact on its young readers?
- ✔ Are there other books on the topic? Do they leave certain issues unaddressed (that you can address in your book)?
- ✔ Is this a story that simply *must* be told because in your view it is particularly unique, timely, or compelling?

If you answer a number of these questions in the affirmative, you've created a compelling case for writing about the topic you have chosen. So, don't just think about doing it, do it!

Test your topic

After you have a topic picked out, how can you be sure it's a good one? By testing it. And who should test your ideas? We suggest getting feedback from kids and from teachers and librarians. Here are some suggestions for doing just that.

Feedback from kids

What better place to get feedback about your idea than straight from the horse's mouth, right? Kids can help you quickly determine whether your idea is a winner or something that should be put on the back burner. Here are some questions to ask to get the feedback flowing and to see whether or not you're on the right track:

- Do you like this idea?
- What about this idea do you like?
- What about this idea do you dislike?
- What would you do to make this idea more interesting?
- What idea would you like better than this one?

Be sure to check out Chapter 5, where we discuss going to kids to generate ideas for your stories. Many of the same ideas that we discuss there apply here as well.

Feedback from teachers and librarians

After you select your topic, get a second opinion. And why not get that second opinion from than someone who spends more time with eager young readers than most anyone else on the planet — librarians and teachers?

Librarians and teachers are on the front lines of every youthquake and mega-trend that passes through their libraries and classrooms. If the kids like something, librarians and teachers probably know about it weeks — perhaps even months — before you do.

Another way of finding out if a topic is good is to look at the public school curriculum for different grades, or for grades of the age for which you want to write. Most school districts have their curriculums on the Web. Then ask the teachers for those grades if they see a need for more books on specific topics that can be used in the classrooms.

Don't rely on last year's model — cast your lot with the people who are in the know — your local librarians and school teachers. (See Chapter 3 for more about choosing viable topics that appeal to wide audiences.)

Outlining Your Creative Nonfiction

After you figure out what kind of nonfiction book you want to write, choose your topic, and test it out on kids, and you further research your topic (see Chapter 6 for the lowdown on research), it's time to take the topic and the research and turn it into an outline.

Many nonfiction writers rely on outlines to help them develop and organize their stories. A good outline displays, at a glance, all the topics that need to be covered, in the order that they should be covered, and it helps avoid chronological or topical holes. Because an outline must cover the selected topic from beginning to end in a logical and sequential way, it essentially serves as a map for writers, telling them where they're at right now, where they've been, and where they're going.

Although outlines aren't used as much by writers of fictional children's books, especially shorter-length books like picture books, they're considered essential by writers of nonfiction children's books because they serve as guides to the writing process. Let an outline be your guide as well. But remember: outlines are guides, not the final word. Be ready to be flexible and to make changes to the outline as you research your topic and work through the writing process.

Create a simple outline

An outline's primary purpose is to guide an author's writing, which, ultimately, helps with the planning process. A simple outline has three main parts:

- ✔ **Title:** This is the title of your book. In the case of the sample outline that follows, the title is *Megalodons: The Real Story*.

- ✔ **Headings:** Headings are the major points that you will address in your book. In the finished book, they may become separate chapter titles, or they may remain headings. In the case of the sample outline that follows, the headings are

  - • What is a megalodon?

  - • How big were megalodons?

  - • What did megalodons eat?

  - • What about those big teeth?

- ✔ **Content:** This is the text that elaborates on the topic named by each heading (or chapter title). Under the heading "What is a megalodon?" the text includes the material in the bullet points directly under that heading.

When writing any kind of book, it's important to be organized and for your book to have a logical progression from topic to topic. An outline helps you plan ahead and to ensure that your book makes sense after you've written it. For example, it doesn't make much sense to go into details about what megalodons ate before you tell your readers what a megalodon was. Working through the outlining process will help you avoid potential problems like this.

Say you decide to write a children's book on megalodons, those gigantic, ancient sharks that roamed the seas from about 1.6 to 25 million years ago. Your outline may look something like this:

***Megalodons: The Real Story* (Outline)**

✔ What is a megalodon?

- Ancient shark (name means *big teeth*)
- Existed from 1.6 to 25 million years ago (Miocene and Pliocene epochs)
- Looked like present-day great white shark

✔ How big were megalodons?

- Estimated at 40 to 100 feet long
- At least three times larger than present-day great white shark
- Jaws could open 6 feet wide and 7 feet high

✔ What did megalodons eat?

- Mostly ate whales
- Squid

✔ What about those big teeth?

- Largest fossilized teeth discovered to date are 6 inches long
- Had three to five rows of teeth in mouth
- Megalodon didn't chew its food, gulped it down whole or in large chunks

---

An outline can be used to walk the author right through his story, from beginning to end. Because it's written down and planned out in advance, the author can see whether the story moves smoothly and can make minor (or major) adjustments as necessary. Not only that, but an outline provides the author with a detailed template of what he will be writing. After preparing a fully-developed outline, the actual writing will fall right into place.

A number of different approaches are available to you when it comes time to create your outline. You can simply type it out with your computer (much as we have done in the above example) or write it out by hand on a page of paper. Or you can write each of your headings on a 3-x-5 index card and write out detailed text on each card under the headings. The great thing about using index cards is that you can lay them out on a table and easily rearrange them, allowing you to try out a variety of different organizational options.

Whatever approach you take, the time you put into creating an outline for your nonfiction book will be paid back many times over when it comes time to write your manuscript.

Flesh out your ideas

After you've drafted an outline, you have a choice: Either start writing your book from the outline as it stands or continue to refine the outline, adding more material to flesh it out. Why bother with that? Because the more fleshing out you do, the closer you actually bring yourself to the finished product. And every step closer to the finished product brings you closer to accomplishing your goal: a children's book you can be proud of.

You can approach this process in a couple of different ways: either starting at the beginning and strictly working your way to the end or jumping back and forth between different sections of the outline, first working on what interests you most and then dealing with more challenging sections later. The exact approach you take to filling out your outline isn't so important; what is important is that you adopt the approach that works best for you.

In the case of a nonfiction children's book, fleshing out your outline likely requires you to do more research on the topic. (For more details on research, see Chapter 6.) Using the first part of the preceding example, a small part of a fleshed out, researched megalodon outline may look something like this:

Megalodons: The Real Story (Outline)

✔ What is a megalodon?

- A megalodon was an ancient shark that may have been an ancestor of the present-day great white shark. Megalodons roamed widely over the oceans, off the coasts of large parts of the earth — North America, Europe, South America, India, Oceania, and more. The name megalodon means *big teeth* — the largest megalodon teeth found to date are about 6 inches long.

- Megalodons roamed the world from 1.6 to 25 million years ago, and they are now extinct. Megalodons lived during the Miocene and Pliocene epochs.

- Megalodons looked like a present-day great white shark. They had many of the same features as modern-day sharks, including gill slits, front and rear dorsal fins, pectoral fin, pelvic fin, mouth, nostrils, and so forth. Their skin was rough and gray in color with sharp scales.

As soon as you're done fleshing out your outline, you can jump right into writing your children's book!

Enhance your outline with visual aids

As the old saying says, a picture is worth a thousand words. Some people are simply better and more creative thinkers when they see ideas presented visually rather than via the written word. If this is the case for you, it can be a good idea to draw out your outline so that it can be visualized.

Interview with Susan Goldman Rubin

Susan Goldman Rubin, children's book author extraordinaire, has regularly wowed her readers with well-researched and captivating non-fiction books.

WCBFD: How did you get started writing children's books and how was it that nonfiction became your strongest suit?

SGR: I started writing because I was an illustrator and had nothing to illustrate. So I wrote a little story about my kids sleeping over at their grandmother's house. I eventually illustrated that picture book and published it (after five years of trying). But I found that my writing won more interest from editors than my artwork. I turned to nonfiction because I loved art and wanted to share my enthusiasm with young people. My first nonfiction book was a biography of architect Frank Lloyd Wright. It came about when my husband and I were going to take our kids on an outing to Hollyhock House, one of Wright's buildings in Los Angeles. When we told the kids where we were going, my 10-year-old stepson (who had visited many museums) said, "Frank Lloyd Who?" That's when I knew I had to do the book. I published it with Abrams, a house known for their splendid art books. One project led to another. Sometimes my editor invited me to do a book for young readers in conjunction with an upcoming exhibition. Along the way, I began to write about Holocaust themes. This, too, came from the heart.

WCBFD: Many would-be children's book authors ignore the nonfiction genre — why is this a mistake?

SGR: When I teach or speak at a writers' conference, I strongly encourage would-be children's book authors to try nonfiction. I urge them to choose a subject that greatly interests them and find an approach suitable for a particular age group. About half of all published children's books are nonfiction, and there is a real need for fresh, new material. Chances for breaking into the market are greater with nonfiction.

WCBFD: What is it about writing nonfiction children's books that excites you?

SGR: I love research. Finding out secrets and gathering information about real people and actual events thrills me. The process is like a treasure hunt. One clue leads to another whether I'm looking for text information or for photos and art to use as illustrations. When I wrote *Toilets, Toasters and Telephones: The How and why of Everyday Objects* (Harcourt), for instance, I spent hours on the phone looking for a photo of an early Egyptian toilet seat dating from 1370 B.C.E. I called Cairo and wound up on a first-name basis with an Arabic-speaking phone operator as I searched for The Egypt Exploration Society. Finally I found that it was located in England

and the society provided me with the picture I needed — gratis!

WCBFD: How do you select a topic to write about?

SGR: I select a topic from the heart. Something that I feel passionately about, that I must do even if I think it may have limited sales. Perhaps the subject has never before been presented to children and I feel compelled to write about it. This happened when I stumbled upon the story of artist Friedl Dicker-Brandeis, an unsung heroine of the Holocaust. The true story gripped me. I put aside another book project under contract and with the permission of my understanding editor, focused on *Fireflies in the Dark: The Story of Friedl Dicker-Brandeis and the Children of Terezin* (Holiday House).

WCBFD: In what ways is writing a nonfiction children's book more challenging than writing a fictional children's book?

SGR: The challenge of writing nonfiction is to show, not tell, and use narrative techniques of dramatization with action and dialogue. However, scenes have to be based on reliable sources. A nonfiction writer has the responsibility of being accurate and truthful. Quotes can't be made up. Finding words that were actually spoken that will be clear and meaningful to young readers presents a difficult challenge.

WCBFD: Please describe the process of research you undertake when working on a typical project.

SGR: When I begin a project, I read everything I can get hold of on the subject. I read books and articles geared for adults as well as those written for children. I especially want to know what the competition is so that I can come up with something fresh. I watch videos on the subject. I interview people who can give me new information and quotes. When I was working on *L'Chaim! To Jewish Life in America!* (Abrams). I found out that Professor Jonathan Sarna, the eminent scholar in the field, was soon to publish a book for adults called *American Judaism* (Yale University Press). I did some research to find out his e-mail address, wrote to him, and asked him if I could possibly read some of his book before it was published to be sure I was on the right track. Professor Sarna generously sent me his entire manuscript via e-mail and even agreed to check mine for accuracy before it went into print. Research also often involves music. When I was writing *Degas and the Dance: The Painter and the Petits Rats Perfecting Their Art* (Abrams), I listened to Degas's favorite ballet music to immerse myself in his world. I went behind the scenes as Degas did and observed classes at the School of American Ballet in New York. Travel gives authenticity to nonfiction writing. When I wrote the book about Friedl Dicker-Brandeis, I managed to go to Terezin, the ghetto/concentration camp near Prague where she had been imprisoned. If I've taped interviews as I did for that book, I play them back at home, transcribe the words, then incorporate the best quotes for my purposes into the narrative. I write the book chapter by chapter, getting feedback from my supportive but critical writers' group. I keep going over the manuscript, "tightening and brightening," until it's ready to show to my agent and editor as a first draft. Even then, there's more research to be done when my editor and the copyeditor give me their comments and queries.

WCBFD: What advice do you have for prospective nonfiction children's book authors?

SGR: My advice for prospective nonfiction children's book authors is to follow your hearts. Write about subjects that truly excite you. See what else has been published and how recently. Maybe it's time for a fresh look at an old topic. Or perhaps in today's world it's appropriate to introduce very young readers to a subject formerly offered only to older children. Come up with a catchy working title. Find a unique angle. One of my editors says, "If you've got the hook, you've got the book."

A *storyboard,* for example, is simply a series of drawings that represent events occurring in sequence. You can use a storyboard to outline a single chapter or an entire book. If you're an extremely visual person, a storyboard may be helpful. Some writers buy cue cards, put their salient plot points on them, and arrange them on a corkboard. Others who are writing picture books or board books, paste the outline points on actual pages to help them visualize the progress the book must take and the word count they must keep in mind. Still others draw pictures, making dummies with illustrations or sketches in place of the action to show on the page what the words must express.

Other visual aids can be quite useful, too, including presentation software or even a simple paper-based flipchart that flips through the action as it's expected to happen.

Part IV
Making Your Story Shine

The 5th Wave   By Rich Tennant

AS A CONSCIENTIOUS FREELANCER, MONA ALWAYS HAD HER CONTRACTS CHECKED BY AN ATTORNEY, COPIED IN DUPLICATE, AND ROLLED FOR CAT HAIRS BEFORE SENDING THEM OUT

©RICHTENNANT

In this part . . .

To turn your rough stone into a polished diamond, you have to first have a vision for what your children's book will look like when it is finished and then shine it and buff it until it sparkles. In this part, we explore how to rewrite and edit your own book. We also take a look at how to format it, whether to illustrate it, and how to get feedback from others.

Chapter 13

Editing and Formatting Your Way to a Happy Ending

In This Chapter

▶ Rewriting your work

▶ Editing tips of the pros

▶ Hiring an editor

*F*ew writers — even the very best, most professional, writing-for-a-living types — are able to create books or stories that are absolutely perfect the first time around. In the real world (that place where we hope most of you live), writing is a repetitive process wherein you first put some words on paper or in your computer, and then you make some changes, and some more changes, add and delete a word or two here or there, and correct some misspellings or grammar issues. In short, you rewrite and edit again and again and again. Rewriting and editing are very much a part of the writing process, and a good rewrite and edit can turn a lackluster manuscript into a compelling, award-winning book.

Sometimes editing and rewriting are considered the same process. But for our purposes, we are going to separate them the following way: rewriting is the fixing process you do when you go back to check if the major parts of your book are working (all the parts we discussed in Part III); editing is the fixing you do after you are pretty sure the major parts are fine and you are working on more of the fine-tuning.

You may figure that your rewrites are all done and that your book is ready for the editing process. And you may be right — or not. Sometimes, even though we have rewritten our book a dozen times, during the editing process it becomes clear that we need to go back and rewrite some of the major components. That is not at all an unusual occurrence. So many little elements in a book are all tied together that when you move one little paragraph, you may create an avalanche. So just know that in practice, rewriting and editing go very much hand in hand.

We therefore dedicate this chapter to one of the most important topics when it comes to writing a children's book: rewriting and editing.

What to Check for at the Rewrite Stage

Before you get to the editing stage, it would behoove you to make sure all the major elements of your story are in order. Although we discuss these elements in great detail in Part III, which you can refer to if you have further questions, we repeat the major ones here.

When rewriting with major issues in mind, we have a way to make is easier to keep track. Each time you go through the manuscript from start to finish, attempt to tackle only one issue at a time. So if you are ready to rewrite your characters to make sure they are fleshed out properly, take one character at a time from start to finish of the manuscript. Then go back and do the other characters one by one. When you are finished, go on to the next issue. This way you won't go crazy wondering where you are as you work your way through.

Theme

Is there a clearly defined theme? If another reader (a friend, someone in your writing group) is unable to tell you in a word or two what your theme is, perhaps you have not homed in on one. If that's the case, you'll need to rewrite your story with theme in mind.

Be sure you *know* your story's theme. If you do, you need to make it apparent at the start of the story in the type of problem the character is going to have to solve. For example, if your story's theme is reassurance, you need to put your protagonist in a situation in which the solution leads to his being reassured. Then you need to insert reminders to the theme throughout the story. Furthering our example, you would need to show your character feeling insecure. You might even want to show other characters playing upon his insecurity. And in the end, you have to give that character the reassurance he needs. If you do not know your story's theme, you need to figure it out. And only you can tell what the essence of your story is. What is its heart? Keep it in mind while you rewrite your draft.

Characters

Your primary goal as a writer is to create unforgettable characters. Why? Because if your characters are dishrags, your manuscript may as well be, too.

In chapter books, middle-grade books, and YA novels, character is what makes or breaks a single title versus a book with series potential. If the character is poorly developed in the text, no amount of magnificent writing or perfectly crafted plotting will save you. In board books, so few words are used, you may conclude that the characters are made memorable by the illustrations alone, and in a lot of cases you would be correct. But most often, it is a marriage of the two that makes for success: complementary illustrations (where appropriate to the format) and great manuscript.

What makes a good character great is the way he sees the world and interacts with it. The character's quirks and preferences, the way he talks, the way he moves, the actions he takes, the reactions he shows — all the characteristics that bring the written character alive must make him seem like a real human being.

You need to have memorable characters to have a successful children's book because these are the people your readers are either relating to or rejecting. Are your main character and his supporting cast fleshed out? Are they interesting? Do they sound their age? Does your main character actively change from who he was at the start of the story as a result of his own actions or does someone else conveniently do the hard work for him?

Ways to check this include asking: In a picture book, does the main character appear in every important scene? In longer books, is the main character further developed in some way, no matter how small, in each chapter, through either plot events or dialogue or interaction with another character?

You are the only one who can answer these questions (until you seek feedback, that is). So go back in and check each character from start to finish. Make sure each one is active and has a definable core that is not stereotypical. Find at least five places for each character where a plot point (a place where the action moves forward in time) or dialogue contributes to developing that character beyond a name or a description. Remember: Seeing characters in action is what shows the reader who they are.

Plot

Plot is the order in which events occur. Every story has a beginning, middle, and end, and when these plot elements are handled clumsily, the resulting work exhibits major problems. Although huge surprises and plot reversals work well in children's books, you may be left with a disjointed mess unless you tie up the loose ends very carefully.

Is what happens in your story pretty clear? Can you point out the beginning, middle/climax, and end/resolution? Is there enough conflict between your main character and the primary issue he has to resolve?

If you haven't created a step sheet or outline or plot structure (see Chapter 8) to help determine these questions and you give you something concrete to check off, now might be the time to do this to help you rewrite. If you need to rearrange your plot for more impact, the step sheet is a great way to keep track of what goes where.

Pacing and drama

Pacing and drama are also intrinsic to a well-written plot. Are there enough dramatic moments to keep the story compelling and can you identify them? Is the pacing such that the reader will want to turn the pages?

You can check the pacing a picture book needs by breaking your manuscript into about 30 separate book pages. You then put each page of text onto a separate sheet of paper, stapling them together along the "spine," like a book, and reading them. The first page of text should be a right-hand page, the last a left-hand page. See if there is a different action on each page that the illustrator can draw, and if something happens on the right-hand page of each spread to make the reader want to turn the page to see what happens next. This division of the text is for your benefit only — don't send it in to an editor like this. (For proper submission formatting, see "Formatting: First Impressions Matter" later in this chapter.) In older children's books, make sure each chapter ends with a cliffhanger or an unresolved conflict. (See Chapter 8 for more on pacing.)

You're writing for children, an audience not known for patience. To maintain the interest of your reader, your story should move along briskly. When your pace lags, you'll quickly lose your reader to other pursuits (like grabbing a video game or watching the latest reality television show).

Setting and context

So you've created a character so memorable he haunts your dreams. Your plot is tight, and your pacing is clipped. But in various places in your story, we have no idea where the action is taking place.

When an author writes about a particular place, the reader should be able to picture it: to feel the wind blowing, smell the pine trees and cedar on a high mountain peak, or feel the grainy sand under her feet. If the reader can't picture a particular setting after reading about it, then the author hasn't done a good job. Try using brief descriptive words that evoke sensory experiences or metaphors that instantly bring up an image of a similar place or time. (More on metaphor in Chapter 11.)

Concise, consistent, and compelling writing

As any English major can tell you, there are enough rules for writing well to fill more than a book or two (although it was originally published in 1959, Strunk and White's pithy, 71-page *The Elements of Style* [MacMillan Publishing Company] remains our personal favorite). When it comes to writing well, keep three things — the Three C's — in mind:

✔ **Concise:** Never use 50 words when just 5 will accomplish the same goal. Your publisher isn't measuring the value of your book by how many words you write; your book is much more powerful when your message is clear and unfettered by flowery, verbose, or otherwise superfluous language. Pare your story to its barest essence and it will be better.

✔ **Consistent:** If you want your reader to be able to follow along (not a bad idea), plots, characters, chronologies, and storylines must be consistent from page to page, and from chapter to chapter. Take time to look at the big picture to ensure consistency throughout your work; you may even want to chart plots (we refer to this as a *step sheet* in the tools section of this chapter), chronologies, and the like to be sure that your story hangs together.

✔ **Compelling:** The best stories are ones that seem driven from within, that pick you up and move you along in an exciting journey to some new place you've never been before. Use action words to draw your reader into your story and to keep his interest after you've got it.

More often than not, you must be sure to identify the place or the particular context in which the story takes place, and you must do it simply so that your audience easily identifies with it. This doesn't mean cheating the reader by simply stating that it takes place in a city called Los Angeles. What if someone has never been there? You have to describe a bit of its flavor: What it smells like, what the main character sees, how the trees grow haphazardly around the house. Don't just include the run-of-the-mill details — write about the interesting things that color the story and character, making them more special than they would be if the story happened in Anyplace, U.S.A.

Adding a simple context that's interesting and different does *not* mean that you run on and on about a place, describing every little leaf and crack in the sidewalk. It means that you ground your story in a place, very briefly and simply, so readers know where the character is coming from or going to and can quickly understand what sets this place apart from all of the rest.

Does the reader know immediately where he is at the start of the story? Have you made apparent any contextual information that sets the story apart from real life (meaning, if the story takes place in 1750, do we know that right off the bat)? Are the setting and contextual clues elegantly intertwined within the action or are is the reader having to slough through long descriptive passages to get to the important information you are trying to convey? Go through and check each time the place and/or time changes and make sure the setting is clearly drawn without wordiness. Chapter 10 has more on setting and context.

Point of view

Have you chosen a POV and stuck to it consistently? The way to check is to see if in one part we are seeing the events through one character's eyes or mind and in the next part we are seeing through a different character's. If you get confused, chances are your reader is right there with you. Make sure if you have chosen to alternate viewpoints that you remain consistent.

We would argue that a lot of the points you need to check for in a rewrite of fiction also apply to nonfiction. Perhaps the correlation is not exact, but the major issues are often similar. The one main difference is that in nonfiction, you have to check and recheck facts, while making sure to provide for a balance in the text and other ways of conveying information such as sidebars, marginal factoids, illustrations or graphics, accuracy in headings, and the like.

These are the major issues you need to address in your rewrite. After you get these nailed down as best you can, you are ready for editing.

The Power of a Good Edit

Sure, you usually become a better writer as you write more, but even professional writers know that obtaining perfection in writing is a process; not very often is every word, phrase, paragraph, and page perfect the first time around.

Ernest Hemingway was one of America's greatest writers and even received the Nobel Prize in literature (1954) in recognition of his superlative writing skills. If anyone could write a great story in his first shot up to bat, you'd imagine it would be Hemingway. Guess how many times he rewrote the final page of his classic book *A Farewell to Arms*. Five times? Ten times? What do you think? Would you believe 39 times? How many times do you think Hemingway revised the opening paragraph to another one of his classics, *The Sun Also Rises*? Almost 100 times.

Pros know that good writing takes a lot of work. Every time you make a *pass* through your story (editing your work from beginning to end), your story will improve — sometimes in small ways and sometimes in very big ways.

Editing can fix some of the common writing problems discussed in the next section. For example, take a look at this:

> The rabbit went back at a not so fast pace and acted kind of anxious as he did. He looked at the ground and all around him like he had lost something. He wondered how his whiskers and paws would fare if the Duchess made him pay for the lost objects with his life. The little girl who was watching him figured out that he must be looking for the fan and the white pair of gloves, and she started looking for them to help him out, but she could not find them. No matter where she looked, everything she had seen the first time she had been there was now gone.

What's happening here? It's clear that we have a frightened rabbit who has lost his possessions and a little girl who is trying to help him. But the writing is boring, passive, and vague: What's the rabbit's name? What has he lost? Who is the girl? What exactly had changed from the first time she had been in the place?

Here is the passage as Lewis Carroll wrote it in *Alice's Adventures in Wonderland* (PD):

> It was the White Rabbit, trotting slowly back again, and looking anxiously about as he went, as if he had lost something; and she heard him muttering to himself "The Duchess! The Duchess! Oh my dear paws! Oh my fur and whiskers! She'll get me executed, as sure as ferrets are ferrets! Where can I have dropped them, I wonder?" Alice guessed in a minute that he was looking for the fan and the white pair of kid-gloves, and she very good-naturedly began hunting about for them, but they were nowhere to be seen — everything seemed to have changed since her swim in the pool; and the great hall, with the glass table and the little door, had vanished completely.

Notice the difference between our butchered passage above and Carroll's. Carroll names both characters, instantly giving them some personality. In the single word *anxious* he conveys the tone of the passage, whereas ours is toneless, boring, and has no rhythm. By giving us dialogue instead of reported speech, he brings the White Rabbit alive, further fleshing out his character as forgetful, nervous, and slightly harebrained. The sentences about Alice further flesh her out as a good-natured girl who wants to help. And the setting detail setting lets us know we are in a place that was formerly quite grand.

Seasoned writers know that the editing process is just as important to the final result as is getting that first draft down. In fact, a good rewrite and edit is often *more* important than the first draft. So don't fear the edit, embrace it. Look forward to it. Send it an invitation for lunch and take it out for a date. Believe us: A good edit is every writer's best friend.

Hot Editing Tips

In cooking, when you boil a substance down to its essence, it's known as a *reduction*. The resulting mixture is thickened or made richer. When you edit successfully, you have reduced your story not to its bare bones, but to its true essence, making it richer and better-tasting (so to speak). In this section, we recommend ways to easily reduce your stories to their entertaining cores.

Sometimes there is something wrong with your manuscript, and you can't tell what it is. When you're editing your work, you need to not only know how to recognize the problem, you've got to know what to do to fix it. Most likely, if you've addressed the major issues in your rewrite, it will be one of the smaller (yet still mighty important) issues we describe next. In this section, we outline some of the most common problems writers face and hand over tips from professional editors to help you more quickly tackle these issues.

If you've got a hook, you've got a book

You need a strong opening sentence. This may sound like a no-brainer, but it's really quite important. It's just like when you are watching a movie on TV: If the plot or characters don't grab you right away — click! — you're on to the next channel, looking for something that can hold your attention.

In order to hook in your reader right away, your opening lines should contain some suggestion of conflict, apprehension, suspense, or promise of such. Tricks for creating good ones include starting off with a bit of dialogue or a conversation, piquing the reader's curiosity with a little anecdote or quote that sets the mood of the story, or describing the main character and his problem in one short sentence:

> Kathryn Camille had a big, fat problem and if she didn't solve it by 8 o'clock, she was a goner.

And don't worry if it takes a while for a good one to come to you. Most writers leave that task till the very last. Lisa creates her first sentences in her sleep, by posing the task to herself for coming up with a good opening before she goes to sleep, and waiting till the right one comes along.

Keep your dialogue on target

Take a close look: Are your characters' personalities reflected in their speech patterns, tone, or the content of their dialogue — or do you have a five-year-old character who speaks like a teenager or a mad scientist who has trouble articulating even basic scientific concepts? Dialogue that doesn't fit well with the characters makes your writing seem unbelievable or confusing.

For example, here's a kindergartener whose dialogue sounds like a teenager's:

> Five-year-old: Yo, man, do I gotta secret for you! And aren't all the girls gonna be chasing after me when they find out what it is!

Go through all your dialogue and make sure each character sounds appropriate for his age and occupation. Also check that the characters sound different from one another.

Another issue is excessive use of dialogue. Ever hear someone talking and instead of finishing what they are saying, they end their sentence with, ". . . and blah, blah, blah."? In general, blah times three is used as shorthand to indicate that whatever followed in the dialogue isn't worthy of the time it takes to say it. When too much dialogue is used in children's books, the readers' minds automatically switch into blah-times-three mode. They start skipping what's on the page to get past all the blah-blah.

Dialogue is a great way of get information across to your reader through an interesting avenue: the character. But a character who just blabs on and on can be boring, so watch out while you write.

Characters who talk to themselves or spend too much time wondering aloud are not effective characters. Dialogue must be interaction that moves the plot forward.

Check out the discussion about writing realistic dialogue in Chapter 9 and then pass through your manuscript, reading your dialogue aloud to see if it rings true for each character, if it moves the plot forward or further develops a character, or if it's just plain blather.

Transition effectively

When you're having a conversation with your best friend, you can jump from subject to subject without confusing him. Your hand gestures, body language, and tone of voice can all add to your story, allowing your friend to follow you from one topic to another. But in a book, you must help the reader move from scene to scene, from place to place, from character to character.

Transitions are passages that connect one thing to another. Transitions move you forward in time without getting you lost and are necessary when your character changes locations, activities, conversations, or time frames, or when your story alters its focus. Transitions can be as simple and as brief as one word or as long as a sentence. Here's a trick: Use one word from the last sentence of a paragraph in an obvious way in the first sentence of the next paragraph to indicate change but to promote continuity.

One example of a good transition is:

> Mary was trying on a pair of glitter-pink shoes when the ceiling fell in. *Miraculously,* she escaped unscathed. Her favorite purse was not that lucky. Brushing herself off, Mary left a twenty to pay for the shoes and scooted out of the rubble.
>
> "Speaking of *miracles,*" Mary said into her cell phone as she left the store and headed for home, "can you believe . . ."

Notice the one word that allows Mary to change venues without leaving the reader confused about the fact that one minute she's trying on shoes when disaster occurs and the next minute she motoring around town with bits of plaster in her hair? That's a sneaky but effective transition.

When you have managed to put together all the little pieces that make for a great story, make sure your transitions are also effective.

Wordiness is not next to Godliness

Many would-be writers think that because children's books are short, they must be really easy to write. We wish! It's actually *more* difficult to write shorter works. When you have a lot of words to work with, you can be lazier. You can beat around the bush, decorating your words with popcorn strings and colorful lights. What's an extra word here or there when you've got *thousands* to work with, right? When you have a limited word count to work with, though, every single word counts.

And even if you are writing a novel for children, that doesn't mean your words should work any less hard. For example, instead of writing your sentence like this:

> The orphanage was a gray place, with gray walls, a gray ceiling, water-stained gray floors, gray furniture, and even a sort of grayishness floating in the air. The children themselves, possessing a gray pallor, seemed to emanate an unhappy gray mood.

You may consider instead:

> The orphanage and its inhabitants were gray as rain. The floors, the furniture, even the children seemed muted.

Although the first sentence explains the dismal context, setting a mood and letting us know that the even the orphans themselves (the characters) are unhappy, it is too wordy, using 41 words to say and accomplish what 18 do just as well. Why does the writer get to keep that rewritten, tightened sentence in the book? Because it sets up the context where much of the plot takes place; therefore, it contributes to plot development. The writer can defend it because there's a reason for it — so it stays.

Children's books have typical word counts for each format, which we discuss in the sidebar in Chapter 2. Because of these word-count requirements, the shorter the work, the more carefully you have to build your plot and your characters. Whatever excess verbiage you have should be gotten rid of. Here's a trick we use: If you find yourself overwriting because you are having trouble expressing exactly what you mean, sit back, say what you mean aloud to yourself, then try writing it again. Another trick is to read your work aloud; often this will help you tell if the writing really works or not.

Check overuse of adjectives, adverbs, and eliminate long, descriptive passages. Go through every sentence of your book with a fine-toothed comb, always seeking to tighten, to replace a weak word with a more evocative one, to eliminate redundancies. It's hard work, but it's so worth it!

Keep your chronologies in order

Time is a constant. But when timelines are violated with no clear and apparent milestones, or when time becomes unclear or loses its grounding in reality, then readers get lost. And a lost reader is not a happy reader.

For example, if you had your main character bunny speaking to his teacher before he goes to school that day, you have your chronology of events out of order. We don't mean to sound like a broken record, but a step sheet like the one we describe in Chapter 8 is a great way to make sure your beginning, middle, and end (and all the important plot events in between) are in order.

Don't assume

How do you feel when you're with a bunch of physicists and they start going on and on about muons, string theory, and particle accelerators, and you, the English major, have nothing to say or contribute because you don't understand a word they're saying? Not great, right? Well, you wouldn't want your reader to feel similarly left out in the cold, now would you?

Often, writers assume that their readers understand what they're writing about, without really thinking about whether that's likely to be the case. Perhaps they use jargon or refer to an historical event that the reader is not familiar with. Make sure you clarify any subjects that you feel may be confusing or little-known just as soon as you mention them in your text.

Axe out awkward writing

Some words were just never meant to go together. When writers *do* put these taboo words together, the result can either be a brilliantly executed subversion of common writing conventions, or an unmitigated, awkward disaster. If your writing falls in the latter camp, then you've got a problem.

There are so many different ways to write that we cannot really give you any better advice than to read the short (but absolutely right on) classic, *The Elements of Style* by William Strunk Jr. and E. B. White (MacMillan Publishing Company). Hey! Did you notice that the second author of this seminal work is the very same one who wrote the children's classics *Charlotte's Web*, *Stuart Little*, and *The Trumpet of the Swan?*

It's time to stop editing when . . .

Always take a break after a complete pass through your work. Each time you check an issue from start to finish, take a breather of at least a few minutes, even a day if you can. If you go back to it the next day, and it seems that you have ceased to improve your work or, worse, that you are only creating more problems for yourself, then it's time to stop editing. At this point you can choose to look at how to format your work for the submission process (see later in this chapter) or you can get some professional feedback.

Hiring an Editor or Editorial Service

So you've followed all the rules, and your writing group thinks you're the next Francesca Lia Block. Now you're ready for a professional editor or editorial service to check each word, line, and paragraph to ensure that you're ready to submit your manuscript to an agent or publisher.

An editor is someone who corrects a work to prepare it for publication. An editorial service can simply be one editor's business, especially if she offers many different services (proofreading, line editing, and ghostwriting for example, are three different services), or it can be a business composed of several editors with expertise in different areas.

Some editorial services list one editor's credentials to bring in business and then send out the work to some other editor. Check to make sure that you are getting the services from the person whose credentials are listed and that your work is not being farmed out to a subcontracting editor. Or if it must be subcontracted out, that you can review and approve the new editor.

How do you find an editor or service you can trust? You need someone who has the experience and the education to serve your interests — and who doesn't charge you an arm and a leg. But before you can choose someone to work with, you need to know exactly what kind of service you are seeking.

- ✔ **Book doctoring:** Editing and fixing a manuscript that has already been written.

- ✔ **Line editing:** Going through a manuscript from start to finish and editing every line for everything from grammar, spelling, and style to drama, pacing, and characterization, and anything in between. Usually done on a hard copy (printed out) of the manuscript or using a change tracking tool for an electronic document.

- ✔ **Copyediting:** Type of editing that involves mostly fact and grammar checking; usually used for nonfiction books.

- ✔ **Read-through and evaluation:** A general, overall reading of the work for its literary merits (or lack thereof) that points out the major flaws that need to be addressed without necessarily telling the writer how to go about executing them in detail.

- ✔ **Ghostwriting:** When an editor or writer writes or rewrites the original manuscript from start to finish and isn't credited on the book, but does get paid and often shares in the royalties — or gets a flat fee.

- ✔ **Proofreading:** Checking one proof of a book against another printed proof of the book to make sure it doesn't have misspellings, nothing is missing, images correspond to text, and all the edits were performed as indicated. Side by side, the two proofs should be mirror images of one another after a proofread.

- ✔ **Literary consultations:** Consultations between a seasoned writer and an editor that determine the literary merits of a work in progress and that range from a read-through of the work and a citing of general impressions to more involved editing for character development to complete line editing.

  Before the manuscript is ready for submission, the editor and writer exchange it back and forth a few times so that the editor can check that the author has executed the feedback. Sometimes the author even involves the editor during the publication process to help the writer through the edits mandated by the publisher.

- ✔ **Writing coach:** Service offered by an editor who acts as editor, teacher, and mentor to the writer throughout the entire publishing process. A writing coach may work one-on-one with the author or may lead a writer's workshop. But unlike a critique group, in which every member participates equally, the workshop leader may do most of the critiquing.

Editors don't agent, and agents don't edit

One piece of misinformation shared by many new writers is that their professional editors should *agent* them (represent or sell their book to publishers) after the editing process or refer them to a particular agent or publisher.

In our opinion, charging a client for an edit with the promise of a referral to an agent or publisher is unethical. If an agent charges a client for an edit prior to or as part of representation, this practice is also unethical. Although many editors may have a list of agents they refer clients to, and agents may choose to refer new clients to a list of editors, no money should change hands between the agent and editor — ever. (See Chapter 16 for more about agents.)

An independent editor and an agent are two separate but equally important parts of a writer's life that should remain separate. Use The Society of Children's Book Writers and Illustrators (www.scbwi.org) to research agents. Membership in this organization allows writers access to a list of agents who are willing to take on new clients. Again, be sure to do your homework, because some agents don't accept all formats. The Association of Authors' Representatives (www.aar-online.org) provides a canon of ethics for all their members.

Choose line editing if you aren't sure what kind of editing you need. Line editing covers every type of editing your manuscript probably needs to make it the best it can be — and it usually comes with a detailed critique letter to help you accomplish what the editor suggests.

Find a good editor

When you are in the market for a professional editor, you need to do some homework before you hire someone. These are the issues we think you ought to consider to get the most out of your experience:

✔ **Find a professional children's book editor.** Children's books have different requirements than adult books. You want someone who has at least ten years under his belt as a children's book editor at a reputable children's book publishing house that has published books that contain Library of Congress numbers, that have been sold in major bookstores, and that can be located in a walk-in library.

✔ **Ask whether your editor has had her own children's book or two published.** If so, you can assume that she's had experience on both sides of the line: editing and being edited. An editor who is also a published writer knows what it's like having words critiqued and may carry this sensitivity into her work with you.

✔ **Find out what the editor's clients and colleagues say about him.** Look for quoted accolades in his advertising. You want someone who is spoken highly of by at least a few industry professionals who can be reached by e-mail for verification. Ask the editor's clients and colleagues whether he has won any awards as an editor or writer that indicate respect on the part of his peers. (For more on referrals, see the next section.)

✔ **Do you like any of the books she has edited?** When the editor provides a list of the books she has edited, go to a bookstore and read a few to see if you like what you read. However, know that there is a chance that the writer chose to ignore her comments, to the benefit — or detriment — of the final work; or that there might be many other wordsmiths who have altered the manuscript after she has. There's really no way for you to know the extent of her involvement in a particular book without asking.

✔ **Inquire about your editor's education.** Although university education shouldn't make or break your decision (a few editors are self-taught or may have been mentored by the best in the business), knowing that your editor has a passing familiarity with quality written material through the ages is a comforting feeling.

✔ **Find out how much the editor charges.** Some charge a per-page rate of $2.50 to $5.00, and some charge by the hour. Others charge a flat-rate minimum to start and then more money depending on how many pages the manuscript is. Still others offer professional discounts for repeat customers. Only you can determine the kind of editing you need, how much you can afford, and what price is fair.

Here's a publishing insider's trick: If you want to know who really appreciates your editor, check out the dedication and acknowledgements pages of her client's books (mostly applicable to longer children's books). If your editor's name appears in either place, chances are the experience was mutually satisfying. If it doesn't appear on either, its omission could be the result of the author's oversight or of a mutually *un*satisfying experience. Or the publisher doesn't give space for dedications or acknowledgments. Another possibility, though remote and usually related to celebrity ghostwriters, is that the writer doesn't want to divulge the name of the editor or her existence in the writing process in order to take the credit for himself.

To avoid any price surprises later, give your manuscript to the editor before he quotes you a rate. Not all manuscripts are alike, even if their word count is similar. The writer's writing style, previous experience, and formatting all affect how much time is needed to edit a manuscript. So it's important for the editor to peruse your manuscript before giving you an accurate price quote.

The moral of this story: don't preach!

Cindy Chang, a publishing professional who has authored several children's books, now runs one of the most successful children's licensing divisions at a major entertainment company. Throughout her experiences, Cindy has discovered that one of the worst things a writer can do is point out the moral to the story, which more often than not just comes off preachy.

WCBFD: What do you look for when you edit a children's book?

CC: Real characters in a great story with an emotional hook. I love it when I'm editing a manuscript and I start getting hooked into the story. There is nothing better than when I begin reading [a book] to see what happens instead of reading it because I have to finish editing it.

WCBFD: What are the most common mistakes you see in manuscripts?

CC:

- No story. By that I mean [a book] that doesn't have a beginning, a middle, and an end. Some writers are strong in one or two of the three but forget that all three make a strong manuscript.

- Missing or weak conflict. Unrealistic or weak resolution.

- Flat characters.

- Preachy stories. I've actually seen manuscripts that end with "And the moral of this story is . . ." That is just horrible. Who wants to read that?

WCBFD: What advice do you find yourself giving over and over again?

CC: I seem to repeat the following over and over:

- Ask yourself "What is the story I want to tell?" If your story is based on an actual event or real people or relationships in your life, forgot about the "real" people or the way that things really happened. You're writing a story and have the power to move things around to make a better story.

- Make the characters realistic, with both strengths and weaknesses. Nothing is black and white — especially people. Giving your characters both good and bad qualities is a way to make them real. It gives readers a way to relate to the characters.

- Don't get stuck giving too many details that aren't relevant to your story. If your story is about how a third-grader saves his town from invading aliens, you don't need to start the story when he is born and give every single detail of his life up until that fateful day when the aliens invade. Get to your story or else you will just bore — and lose — the reader.

- It is all about having a relationship with your readers until the last page of your book. Respect the readers (no matter what age you're writing for). Never write down or preach to them.

Most editors don't require contracts, but they do require up-front payment in full with the understanding that they return any *underages* (money not used) with the manuscript. You can expect to be called or e-mailed to approve any *overages* (more money required to complete the job).

Ask the right questions

Here are some essential questions to ask the editor or editorial service you're about to hire. Whether the answers please you depends on what services you've decided you need:

- Do I get a written evaluation or report along with manuscript comments? (These are very helpful because they offer guidance as to how to go about making the changes suggested by the editor.)

- If I have questions, do I get to talk with you for free after you send back my edited manuscript? (Usually the answer is no.)

- Do we correspond by e-mail or phone?

- Do you charge extra for a pre-editing consultation? How much?

- Are you willing to work electronically with a track-changes edit and commentary? (Whether an editor is old-school, working on the hard copy, or knows how to use tracking-changes software doesn't affect the quality of the edit you will get. It depends on your preference for how to work: on hard copy or on an electronic document with running changes from draft to draft kept all in one place.)

- How much do you charge for editing my revisions?

- Can you provide a client list or a few referrals that I may contact by e-mail or phone?

- Do you give any discounts for members of professional writing organizations, published writers, need-based clients, or repeat customers?

The editor should also specify what *formats* (types) of children's books he has been paid to edit. (Refer to Chapter 2 for more on formats.) If an editor indicates a preference or a predilection for editing a particular format — let's say, middle-grade books or picture books — consider that information in your decision-making process.

Ultimately, your experience with an editor or an editorial service should be fun and informative. You should walk away from the process with specific ideas and methods for making your manuscript the best it can be and the secure knowledge that the money was well spent regardless of whether the manuscript ultimately sells. A good edit will avail you of the type of information about writing and editing that you can use again and again. Asking the right questions before you hire someone will help insure that your experience goes more smoothly and that there are no misunderstandings.

Formatting: First Impressions Matter

If you don't make a good first impression, you'll likely get your manuscript sent right back to you accompanied by one of those dreaded rejection letters (see Chapter 17 for more on dealing with those nasty things).

So how do you make a good first impression? And almost as important, how do you make sure you don't make a *bad* one? It may surprise you, but figuring out how to correctly use formatting, fonts, and headers is a good start. And another thing: Keep it simple. Your manuscript needs to reach editorial desks in a clean, easy-to-read format. Don't let misspelled words get the best of you. Don't send something in that shows the signs of an argument you had and lost with the typewriter's correction tape (or with the computer printer's ink cartridge, which most of us still can't figure out). And for goodness sake, don't forget your contact information.

The reason that all these little nitpicking issues are important is that editors see a gazillion manuscripts every day, and the sight of certain common errors makes them sigh with impatience. With so many resources available to writers of children's books, it seems crazy to submit anything other than a clean and well-edited manuscript.

Keep your presentation simple

When you're about to send off your manuscript, you need to make sure to restrain your creative impulses in everything but writing your story. You're selling your words, not your graphic talents (unless you're also an illustrator). Let your manuscript wow them, and not your attempt to blind them with fluorescent paper. It may look plain — perhaps even homely to you — but your unadorned manuscript will look simply beautiful to the publishing pro who receives it. Here's how you can make sure of it:

✔ Submit your manuscript on regular white typing paper or laser paper, 20-pound weight. Sure, 24-pound paper might feel better to you, but it costs a lot more than regular old 20-pound paper and it's not going to score you any brownie points with your editor.

Kinko's now offers a rainbow of regular and fluorescent paper to choose from, along with a dozen different bindings, embossing, debossing, and sparkly glitter pens. Don't use any of these. All they do is distract from your work.

✔ The manuscript, if picture book length or shorter (1,500 words or fewer), can be either stapled with one staple in the top-left corner or paper clipped together. If it is longer than that and will fit in a binder clip, use one of those. If your manuscript is still too long, then place a big rubber band around it and put it in a manuscript box or a large envelope. And if it's longer than 300 or 350 typed, double-spaced pages, chances are that unless it's a young adult novel that it's altogether too long anyway and you haven't properly edited. Kinko's also offers binding services, but you don't need them because the manuscript rarely lies flat when opened, and some editors feel that attaching the pages in any permanent way makes reading the manuscript more difficult.

Become a formatting pro

You may think formatting isn't important. Think again. You want an editor to focus on your story and your words (and maybe your illustrations). Sticking to the following submission conventions will assure that she is not distracted by common errors.

It used to be that every manuscript, *de rigeur,* was sent out with a cover sheet. These days, cover sheets generally get torn off and tossed, and if your contact info was on that page only, tough patootie! So save a tree and forego the cover sheet (but make sure your contact info is on the first page of your manuscript).

Here are some do's and don'ts to assist you in submitting a manuscript:

✔ Do type your manuscript double-spaced with at least 1.25-inch margins on either side and at the top and bottom of each page. Although the left margin type should be justified, the right margin should be *ragged right*, meaning that you let the lines end however the length of the words and the 1.25-inch margin dictates.

✔ Don't allow your word processor to break words at the ends of lines in children's books.

✔ Do put all your contact information in the upper left-hand corner: name, address, city, state, zip code, phone, fax (if any) and e-mail address. Nothing more. Like this:

Lisa Rojany Buccieri
1234 Some Street West
Some City, California 90000
310.555.1212
esola@editorialservicesofla.com

✔ Do center the title about a third of the way down on the first page (it can be in all capital letters, or in capitals and lowercase). Then skip a line and start your text.

✔ Don't supply your social security number, your residency card information, your height and weight, or anything cutesy with your contact info.

✔ Don't repeat your name under the title with a "by" line, *nor* do you need to indicate what kind of manuscript it is, for example, "A graphic novel by . . ."

✔ Do make sure your text starts at least two line spaces down (one double space) to separate it from your header.

✔ Do indent all paragraphs 10–12 single spaces (usually one hit on the tab button in default word processor settings) or about ½ inch.

✔ Do indent all new dialogue (each time a new speaker takes a turn) 10–12 single spaces in, one tab hit, or ½ inch.

✔ You may leave a blank line in the story where a page break might occur — but only if you really feel you need to, because most editors will decide that on their own.

✔ Do make sure your pages are numbered consecutively.

✔ Do list the word count. Your word count should be exact, excluding title, headers, page numbers, and author's name and contact info. Longer manuscripts can have a word count rounded to the nearest 50 words. Put it at the far right-hand top line across from your contact name, like this:

Lisa Rojany Buccieri   WORD COUNT: 1,238
1234 Some Street West
Some City, California 90000
310.555.1212
esola@editorialservicesofla.com

✔ Don't add art directions to your text unless you're illustrating your own book. (*Art directions* are notes to the illustrator indicating what image should be illustrated and where it should be placed in relation to the text.) Your words need to stand on their own, evoking strong images in the reader's mind, without any prompting. If you need to explain what the editor or agent — your first reader — should be seeing in his mind, then your words aren't working.

✔ If you are writing a chapter book, middle-grade book, or a young adult novel, the first page of each new chapter should have the word *Chapter* with whichever number it is, centered, about a third of the way down the page, with the story starting two double spaces below that.

Why editors love Courier

It used to be that all typewriters had the same or a similar font, so you had no choice until a book was being designed and typeset. Then word processing software came along, and Courier became the font that was believed to most approximate the typewriter font in which every character was the same width. Many editors of the old school still prefer to get manuscripts in Courier font, 12-point size, especially if the manuscripts are for longer children's books or novels.

The reason is that using Courier 12 point, double-spaced, yields an average of 250 words per page, a number that editors and agents were used to seeing when estimating word and page counts. Now that word-processing software allows you to calculate word count immediately, and it's something you should list on your manuscript, estimating is no longer necessary if the author follows professional submission guidelines. And that professional would be you, right?

Fonts

Today, a million fonts are available, and, unfortunately, many children's book authors-to-be think that they should try out at least half of them in their manuscripts. Not only does this make your manuscript hard to read, it screams out "Unprofessional!" to the editor on whose desk it lands. We therefore strongly recommend using good old-fashioned Courier. If you can't stand Courier (or the fact that most word processors limit alternate key configurations in this font), it's okay to go for Times or Times New Roman, but that's it.

Don't ever use fancy fonts or typesetting. Avoid colors, bigger letters (known as initial caps) on the first words of a new chapter — all that fun stuff you see in finished books. These are decisions made by page designers and art directors at a later stage. Right now, all they do is distract from the story you're trying to tell.

Don't use *sans serif* fonts (a typeface in which the characters don't have *serifs* or strokes at the ends or tips of the lines that form the characters) because they are hard to read and generally not used on final printed children's books. **Arial** and **Helvetica** are sans serif fonts. The most common *serif* font is **Times** or **Times New Roman.**

Overusing **bolded words**, *italicized words*, WORDS IN ALL CAPS, or punctuation, such as exclamation points (!!!) or question marks (???), can indicate that your words aren't doing what they're supposed to do. If you find yourself relying on these formatting tricks, it's a strong sign that your story is due for a rewrite.

Headers

Every page — except the first page of your manuscript with the contact info on it — should have a header to indicate title and author flush left and page number flush right, like this:

WRITING CHILDREN'S BOOKS FOR DUMMIES/Rojany Buccieri & Economy   2

Headers are important because they allow you and others to keep track of your pages. If the editor loses a page on her desk and finds it later, she'll know where it belongs because the header identifies your book's title and you as the creator. Also, if you are having a conversation with her about it, you can use the header to make sure you are both referring to the same page. It's a good idea to print yourself a copy of the version you send to the editor (in case you've made changes in the meantime).

All these specific formatting requirements are used to tell editors that you take your work seriously and want them to give you serious consideration as an author. Do images along with your text help you do that? We discuss that in Chapter 14.

Chapter 14

To Illustrate or Not to Illustrate

Do you need to first get your manuscript illustrated to give it a better chance at getting accepted? And how do you go about finding an illustrator if you are not one yourself? How do you figure out who does what and for what?

This chapter gives you answers to those questions, but here's the bottom line: If you aren't an illustrator, you shouldn't illustrate your book. Simply said, bad or amateurish illustrations turn off editors and agents in a big way. And turned off editors and agents aren't in the mood to represent or buy your story. Even if a story is well written and may very well be the Greatest Children's Book Ever, there is a chance that it will get rejected solely because of the recipient's reaction to the art.

In this chapter, we talk about why not to illustrate your own book, explain what happens when you leave the art to the publisher, and help you decide whether and how to hire someone to illustrate your book.

Editors Match Manuscript to Illustrator

Illustrations need to both complement the text and add personality to children's books. Editors and art directors work together with page designers to create a vision. The words and the illustrations together must be better than each alone. At least that's the goal.

Editors like to pair up authors with their own choice of illustrators. They choose someone they think can add yet another dimension to your words with images, truly complementing and completing your work with the illustrator's own. Your editor may choose to pair you, an unknown writer, with a known and recognized name illustrator to help sell the book. Or perhaps she wants to pair you with a newbie illustrator who has just created a style that she thinks will take the world by storm. Maybe she has been waiting for just the perfect writer to pair up with her most favored and beloved illustrator. Whatever her decision, it's hers to make.

Leave the art to someone else

Glenn Murray is co-author, with William Kotzwinkle, of the bestselling *Walter the Farting Dog* (North Atlantic Books), a book that took a lot of detours before it finally found a publishing house. Glenn recommends that you leave the illustrations to the publisher if you aren't an artist yourself. Read on and see why.

WCBFD: Your collaboration with an illustrator, prior to finding a publisher, on your bestselling book, *Walter the Farting Dog*, was an exception. What have you learned since then about how most publishers work?

GM: One thing I notice is that many writers of children's stories are unaware that most publishers don't want you worrying about the artwork. Publishers have editors and art directors and designers in-house to handle the images and do not necessarily want or need your input as the writer. Publishers also often choose experienced illustrators who understand the process as well as page design, formatting, and all that. I have found that most authors and illustrators have never met or talked — all arrangements were made through the publisher's art department and the editor in charge of the project. Editors seem to like it this way, but most novice writers don't understand this. Novice writers feel they

need to submit a whole package [text and art] and don't realize that they are a) making unnecessary work for themselves, and b) possibly limiting the potential acceptance of the manuscript.

WCBFD: What else have you learned since you wrote that first *Walter* book?

GM: I've also learned an awful lot about the legal relationship between authors and illustrators [who pair themselves up prior to submission] that most people don't realize — why, for instance, if you insist on submitting art with your story that you might want to simply contract an illustrator with a flat fee rather than offer them a percentage. And I've met a few other children's authors who've had hassles later on from contractual arrangements they made early on with wide-open but ill-informed eyes. On the other hand, there are some author/illustrator partnerships that bring themselves together before submission that last happily for decades. So go figure.

WCBFD: So what would you tell a writer if she is considering finding an illustrator prior to submission?

GM: You just need to write a good story and get that story to an editor to read. If the editor likes it, she'll know what to do with it.

Chances are that you, the writer, will never even meet the illustrator during the publishing process unless you two decide to reach out and make the effort to communicate on your own. When your manuscript goes into the process of being turned into a book at a publishing house, after you and your editor have worked together to make your words the best they can be, you will most likely not see your words again until they appear in print. We discuss more about the process in Chapter 18. But suffice it to say that editors tend to keep their authors separate from their illustrators.

We know that you have images in your mind of how to bring your characters to life. Unless you're a professional illustrator, though, keep them to yourself for now. Board books and picture books (formats that always come with pictures) are really half the job of the author, and half that of the illustrator. It's the illustrator's job to add another level of story with the pictures, and the illustrator can't be restricted by the author's ideas of what the pictures should be. You may be surprised what professional artists will come up with.

Word people (as opposed to picture people) often assume that no one will ever be able to create images that are as unique and creative as their written characters or their stories. But artists often see the world in a slightly different way (how could they not? — they even favor a different side of the brain from word people). And these differences often interpret words in the most astonishing and gorgeous manner — and totally differently from how a word person may have envisioned them.

Illustrating Your Own Book

Nothing surprises new writers more than this: Unless you're an artist with lots of artistic talent, you shouldn't be illustrating your own manuscript. Nor should you bother paying or contracting with someone else to do it. Period. Seriously. We're not joking. Amateurish illustrations make your manuscript look unprofessional. They also distract from the words. And if the editor likes the words but absolutely hates the illustrations (or vice versa), he is likely to reject both because the assumption is that the writer and illustrator are already connected and to rip them apart would invite a host of complications best avoided.

If you're a talented illustrator as well as a writer, congratulations, you are a rare breed indeed. If you decide to go ahead and illustrate your own picture or board book, you need to submit to the publisher a *dummy,* which is a to-size paper mock-up of what you envision the book looking like. And that's just what we discuss in the following section.

Hiring an illustrator without going broke

If you absolutely insist on submitting illustrations with your book (and you aren't an illustrator), consider the following tips:

- **Find an illustration style to match your book.** There are as many ways to illustrate a book as there are to write it. Look at books that have already been published and see how various illustrators realize their styles. Decide on a few that you like. Then you can track down that illustrator, or you can take the example of a style you love and use it to find other illustrators who create art in a similar style.

- **Find an illustrator.** Go to places both online and in the real world where children's book artists hang out and promote their wares. If you can't find anyone through the Society of Children's Book Writers and Illustrators (www.scbwi.org), you can check out art colleges, Web sites, book conferences, and the annual comic book convention in San Diego. In addition, artist's reps (agents who specialize in representing illustrators) are listed in sources such as *Children's Writer's and Illustrator's Markets* by Alice Pope (Writer's Digest Books) and *Literary Market Place: The Directory of the American Book Publishing Industry* (Information Today).

- **Put together a written agreement.** Before contacting the illustrator, decide whether you want to pay the illustrator a flat fee or partner with him, sharing in the proceeds. Then get a contract that you both sign and date, which usually involves getting an entertainment or publishing attorney involved and should cover, at minimum, the scope and quantity of illustrations to be produced; formatting instructions, including size, black-and-white versus color, and so on; amount to be paid (for example, a flat fee or a portion of the book's royalties) and schedule for payment; whether the illustrator will transfer or retain rights to the illustrations; and a schedule for delivery of the pencil illustrations and the final color art.

- **Establish open communication.** Open communication between the two of you about what you both expect in terms of your involvement in the illustration process and its details ensures that you start off on the right foot and stay there. One way to make sure you're on the same page is to create a sample page together.

- **Pay attention to the details.** The images should not only complement the text but must provide spark and personality as well. Some illustrations may even replace text or insert further meaning into the text. Each page or spread has to come alive with an exceptional interpretation of the story. In addition, the images need to employ different perspectives from page to page, focus on different aspects of the main characters, and take place in different parts of the scene or context of the story. Color and texture, shading and line, consistency and perspective all are aspects of illustrations that an editor considers when reviewing a submission with art. And although different illustration styles require different focal characteristics, all must have that little something that appeals to children — be it charm, personality, simplicity, sweetness, humor, quirkiness, or expressiveness. Good illustrators pay attention to all of these issues as well as the little details, such as consistency regarding characters and backgrounds.

Submitting art and text together

As an author illustrator, you want to show off both your talents. After you have your manuscript in proper format, break up your book into pages (most picture books are 32 pages long, with at least two pages taken up for title and copyright pages, 2 to 4 more if there are endpapers, leaving you with 26 to 30 actual manuscript pages. For consistency's sake, throughout this section we assume 30 pages). If you work with software that allows you to place text and create space to import your scanned-in art, by all means do so if that doesn't rob your art of its appeal.

Otherwise, you can cut up the type and paste it on each page and then create black-and-white pencil illustrations for the corresponding images. If you're not an expert in cutting and pasting (the end result should be pristine), then simply separate the text and art on different pages.

The illustrations ought to be detailed enough to give the editor and art director a solid idea of what you see on each page. Try to vary full-spread and single-page art (more on spreads in Chapter 2). Paperclip or binder clip the pages together, adding a cover idea if you have one. You should always include two or three samples of your color work (but never send original art work). Make sure to include your contact information on the dummy itself in case the cover letter gets lost or misplaced. And *paginate* (put page numbers somewhere on each page) no matter what.

The cleaner and more professional your work looks, the more likely you are to get taken seriously. If you're illustrating your work, make sure that the dummy is complete and doesn't look rushed — even pencil illustrations can look finished and well thought-out. Make sure your pages are clean and that no paste-up glue remains on your dummy, that no smudges or white-out appear, and that the copies of your art are clean, cut evenly, and on sturdy paper that doesn't wrinkle or rip easily.

Many art directors use a few shortcuts to determine whether an illustrator can handle the usual objects he may be assigned to create in a children's book. Some of these include having the illustrator draw a child's face, a child's body, an infant (in its entirety), or a domestic animal (think puppies or kitties). Send along sketches of these up front, and you'll save an editor from spending time questioning your skills. Send these images from different perspectives (from the front, at a three-quarter angle, and the like), and you're even more ahead of the game.

Tooting your horn (as an artist)

We talk about cover and query letters in Chapter 17, but because you're taking the leap and choosing to illustrate your work, you may need some extra selling help. Make sure your query letter to the agent or editor includes the following types of information about yourself as an artist:

✔ Has your art ever been published? Where?

✔ Do you have a formal art background? From which school(s) or super-famous mentor(s)? If you mention someone that non-artist types may not know, supply enough information so that they can check them out online or otherwise. Name dropping should be used judiciously.

✔ Are you flexible and open to art and text suggestions, both minor and major?

✔ Do you take art direction well?

✔ Are you open to having someone else illustrate your text or to illustrating someone else's words? This can double your chances of getting a contract from a publisher who likes your stuff and will keep the text from being rejected if the editor likes the words but not the pictures.

You need to keep your query letter to one page. If, however, you must exceed that limit by an extra paragraph in order to list your illustrating credentials, we won't hold that against you.

Chapter 15

Finding Feedback and Encouragement

*A*lthough the words *practice makes perfect* certainly ring true in the writing profession, *every* writer can benefit from candid feedback and constructive criticism from others. Most writers do plenty of rewriting and editing before their stories ever make it to an editor at a publishing company. (Chapter 13 discusses the rewriting and editing processes in detail.). But even producing multiple manuscripts doesn't change the fact that having someone else take a look at your work brings a fresh perspective that can lead to invaluable improvements in the manuscript.

You may be wondering, where's the best place to get feedback? When should I get it? And from whom? In this chapter, we answer all those questions and more, first considering the most common source of outside feedback — friends and relatives — and then moving on to writing conferences, workshops, and writing groups.

Feedback is the breakfast of champions, and good, timely feedback can make the difference between a story that is merely so-so and one that knocks the socks off everyone who reads it. And, guess what? Good feedback can make the difference in whether your children's book ever finds its way to a bookstore shelf.

Why You Need Feedback

Here's the first rule for getting feedback from others: You have to ask for it to get it. You can't sit back and wait for it to magically find its way to your front door. Seek feedback wherever and whenever you need it to move your story forward.

The reason feedback is necessary is because we writers get very close to our work. How can we not? We become enamored with the words we write. We pour our feelings, research, desires, and dreams (not to mention our neuroses and ignorance) into our work. And after the manuscript is printed out, it *feels* so final, so hard copied, so finished. But it's not. Both authors of this book still seek feedback, because after years of writing and editing, we're both familiar with the "enamored" phenomenon and how it can mislead a writer into thinking that a less-than-perfect manuscript is ready when it's not.

You can't hide from feedback. Feedback is a very powerful tool, but because it introduces the possibility of being criticized for personal failings or shortcomings in the writing skills department, many people do everything they can to avoid it.

Criticism, when given constructively, is a *very good thing*. The right feedback can help you hone your story, making it more compelling and powerful (and saleable) in the process.

Keep your manuscript from running off the road and into the dreaded "writing ditch" by getting feedback at several stages throughout the writing process:

- ✔ **In the beginning:** You may not have any words down on paper, but in the beginning you have an idea — an idea of what your story is about, where it will take place, who (or what) will be in it, how it will progress, and how it will end. Before you've written a word, you can get feedback on your idea from others to find out if your idea is derivative or novel, intriguing or limp. This early feedback lets you know if you need to develop your idea further or toss it aside and move on.

- ✔ **After you've written a few pages:** Here's a common story: A writer is so turned on by a particular idea, so convinced of its inherent greatness, that he huffs, and he puffs, and he knocks out a complete book manuscript in several days or weeks of nonstop, caffeine-fueled computer love. Unfortunately, when he shows the manuscript to his agent, the response lies somewhere on the low end of the Richter Scale — a total snoozer. Getting feedback after you've written only a few pages can help prevent this kind of outcome by identifying major story flaws before you go too far down the wrong path.

> ✔ **When the manuscript is complete:** Before you send your manuscript off to an agent or publisher, get it critiqued. As the other old saying goes, you only have one chance to make a first impression; getting feedback on your manuscript before it gets to an agent or publisher is the best way to ensure that the first impression you make is the best one.

What questions should you ask to get the feedback you need? If you have a complete manuscript, check out Chapter 13, where we talk about the most important issues to check on while rewriting and editing. However, if you are unsure about whether something is really working, it's best to bring that to a feedback session. And even if you are just at the idea stage, you might still ask questions, such as

> ✔ Is this an interesting idea?
>
> ✔ Can children relate to it?
>
> ✔ Is it a current or timeless topic?

Ask for feedback throughout the writing process and use different sources along the way to get a variety of observations. Anytime is a good time to get feedback, and the more the better.

Do be sure to tell the person you seek feedback from exactly what kind of feedback you're looking for — *before* she provides you with the feedback, not after. For instance, if you want a critique of your dialogue only, don't wait until she's line edited your entire manuscript to tell her so. Your guidance helps her focus her efforts in the direction that provides you with the feedback you seek. You have no reason to play hit-and-miss when you can clearly describe the target to the other party.

Getting Help from Friends and Relatives (or Not)

Many writers feel most comfortable testing their work on the people closest to them. They sit down with their children, their significant other, or their best friend's dog, and they read their manuscript aloud. And — almost invariably — they're showered with kudos and accolades (or dog licks).

After a response filled with praise, how could a writer *not* believe that he's destined for great things? But getting help from friends and relatives has its pluses and its minuses. Do the most honest critiques really come from the people who know you and care most about your success or failure as a writer? Well, maybe yes, and maybe no.

Delving into the pros and cons of friendly advice

The good thing about having friends and relatives read or listen to your manuscript is that you will get some initial feedback that is most likely going to be very enthusiastic. It's important to be appreciated and to feel that you are doing a good job, and friends and family are great at providing that kind of support. Also, if someone within that close circle is an avid enthusiast of children's literature (or has children they read to a lot) then you may get some helpful criticism as well.

The bad thing about soliciting help from friends and family is that although they are usually a willing audience, they aren't always the most discriminating. Or objective. Or professional. According to editors we've interviewed, the one item that leads to an almost immediate rejection of a submission is hearing the writer gush about how much their spouse, grandkids, or very own children loved it. Of course they did! Would any kid say he or she didn't?

Truth be told, pretty much every editor in the universe feels this way. So do yourself a favor: Get your material in front of a real writing group where you receive some honest and pointed criticism or find a professional editor who can do the job. A familiar audience is fun, and you can get great initial feedback from children regarding certain parts of your story and its pacing and drama, but it doesn't constitute a professional critique that you can feel confident will pass muster at a publishing house. When in doubt, farm it out.

Having a friend in the business

If you have a friend in the children's book business, do you approach him with your manuscript? Do you take advantage of this connection for yourself or your other friends?

The simple answer is: Of course you do! But if you want that person to respect you, show him respect by doing a few things before you go to him for feedback:

✔ Have your manuscript carefully (perhaps professionally) edited beforehand (see Chapter 13 for more on hiring an editorial service). Yes, we know this person is your friend; but that does not mean you should not put your very best effort forward. We know, you may have to shell out some dough to get this done. But, believe us, making a positive first impression by being professional in your work is particularly important in this stage of the game. (You have all the time in the world to be unprofessional after you have your first hit book — just kidding.)

✔ Do your homework. Research what *imprint* (publishing division) in the company your manuscript fits best with, plus the name of the editor in charge of that unit.

✔ Ask whether you can submit a manuscript and a *query letter* (cover letter) to the particular editor at their publishing house because you have done some research and think your work may prove a good fit with that editor's imprint. (When his eyes widen with newfound respect for your brilliant sleuthing, you'll know you're halfway there.) Then whip out the manuscript and the query letter from behind your back and present them to your friend (complete with self-addressed, stamped envelope, of course), and then turn tail and run like heck, yelling out thank-yous over your shoulder before he changes his mind.

This approach assumes that your friend in the children's book business has a few years under his belt and isn't the newly hired editorial assistant (see Chapter 18 on the hierarchy of publishing houses). And even if your friend is new to the company, you owe him as much respect as you owe the veteran.

Attending Conferences

Writing conferences and workshops are great places to go to get support from fellow writers and immerse yourself in the world of children's publishing. You can also learn so much just by listening to the speakers, attending the gatherings, even lunching next to someone new. Writers, editors, illustrators, librarians, agents — it's great to be surrounded by a lot of people who all share a love and respect for children's books. However, you need to figure out first what kind of feedback you are seeking and then choose a conference or workshop that can deliver just what you want.

Getting critiqued at conferences

Conferences can be a great source of feedback for your writing efforts, assuming that they're structured in a way that allows for the feedback you're seeking. If a conference doesn't offer specific workshop sessions, manuscript reviews, or individual face-to-face critiques, then the conference may be a lot of fun where you can learn a lot about the children's book business, and you could even get to network with some heavy hitters — all valuable experiences — but you will not get specific feedback.

Although different conferences have different kinds of sponsors, most children's book conferences are similar in structure in that they usually run for several days, offer presentations and workshops conducted by published authors or industry professionals (such as editors, public relations experts, or literary agents), have cocktail parties and group luncheons or dinners to allow attendees to meet other writers and industry professionals, and offer critique groups or manuscript reading services.

If you're turned on by the idea of writing children's books now, you can't imagine how pumped up you'll be after attending a well-run conference. Particularly for an aspiring author, being immersed in a total children's book writing experience for several days and nights can be a very heady brew indeed. We highly recommend it!

Please note that we don't endorse any particular conferences or workshops or vouch for their effectiveness. Before you spend hard-earned money on a particular conference or workshop, thoroughly check it out. Find out the answers to these questions: What are the credentials of the people running it? Why are they qualified to put it on? Are the headlining presenters noteworthy? Does it have lots of positive reviews? Can past attendees be contacted for their candid feedback? In addition, keep in mind that the costs we list here may change.

The following two conferences are but a tiny sampling of the multitude of conferences available to you. Ask around for recommendations or do an online search for **children's book conferences** using the Google search engine (www.google.com).

SCBWI Annual Conference

The Society of Children's Book Writers and Illustrators (SCBWI) offers two extremely comprehensive annual conferences each year — one in Los Angeles, and one in New York City. Chock-full of presentations and workshops (including sessions such as *Bunny Eat Bunny: Surviving the Kid-Lit Jungle, Writing a Humorous Picture Book*, and *The 411 on Working with Independent Literary Agents*), the most recent conference in New York City pulled in more than 700 people. Critique groups and opportunities for individual manuscript reading and consultation services are a very popular part of SCBWI conferences. Nonmember registration costs $330, with discounts offered to SCBWI members. To find out about SCBWI membership and conferences, check out its Web site at www.scbwi.org.

Check out your regional SCBWI organizations (see the SCBWI Web site), which often have their own conferences.

BYU Writing for Young Readers Workshop

Sponsored by Brigham Young University in Provo, Utah, this conference (ignore the word *workshop* in its title) brings together a stellar roster of published authors, working editors, and literary agents for a one-stop shop for aspiring children's book writers. In addition to spending lots of time meeting and greeting, attendees see presentations like *The Nuts and Bolts of Writing Well, Writing Your Own Fairy Tale, 1000 Story Ideas,* and more. The events also provide opportunities for critiques and feedback. The price for this six-day conference is $399. Go to `http://ce.byu.edu/cw/writing` for more info.

Participating in a Workshop

A *workshop* is just a fancy name for a class or course about some aspect of the children's book writing process, usually lead by a teacher or publishing pro. Depending on the particular workshop you enroll in and the way it's structured, a workshop may or may not be a good source of feedback for you.

To ensure that you get the feedback you seek, consider the following when signing up for a workshop:

✔ **Quality of presenters:** Who is presenting the workshop? If your instructor is a current bestselling children's book author or an acquisitions editor at the children's book imprint of a large publisher, you're likely to get much better feedback than if your instructor has only shopped around a couple of book proposals and has yet to be published.

✔ **Length:** You're much more likely to get the quality feedback you seek in a workshop that lasts at least a day or more.

✔ **Number of attendees:** If you're jockeying for your instructor's attention along with 100 other eager children's book writers-to-be, your chances of getting any sort of usable feedback are greatly reduced. Small workshops of, say, 5 to 15 people, are much more conducive to getting you the feedback you seek than the let's-see-how-many-people-we-can-pack-into-this-room variety.

✔ **Structure:** Some workshops specifically set aside time for critique and feedback of attendees' work; some don't. Be sure to take a look at the workshop schedule to find out whether feedback is a part of the plan. If it's not, you should pass.

With such a plethora of workshops available around the country, we don't list any specifics in this chapter. Ask other children's book writers for their recommendations, or do an online search for **children's book workshops** on `www.google.com`.

In general, workshops are smaller and more intimate than the large national or regional writing conferences and offer you a much better chance of getting direct feedback on your writing from the person(s) running the workshop.

Joining a Writing Group

Have you ever read a book by an established writer, and the story seems like a good idea, but the execution is poor or the length is excessive? Although an editor is ultimately to blame (for not brandishing the editorial whip no matter how famous and influential the writer), so is the writer who probably failed to get adequate feedback during or after the writing process.

If you join or create your own writing group, chances are your fellow members will not let you get away with such sins. A *writing group* is a gathering of committed writers — typically composed of at least two members, but often many more — who get together on a regular basis to critique one another's work and make it the best it can be.

What better way to get feedback during the writing process than by joining a weekly, semiweekly, or monthly writing group? A good writing group can shave years off the time required to refine your writing skills. A bad writing group can really set you back or derail your writing career altogether.

Find the right writing group

Before you can hop into the ideal writing group, you need to *find* it, which leads to the $64,000 question: How in the heck do you go about doing that?

An acceptable avenue for finding a writing group is to visit local community colleges or universities that offer writing programs. These programs often have bulletin boards that list writers who are looking for other writers interested in forming a group. Bookstores and coffee shops now have these boards, and you can even visit a message board online at The Children's Writing Resource Center at www.write4kids.com. But in our experience, message boards are a bit too random and impersonal for many writers and may or may not help you find the group you're looking for.

Check out your local Society of Children's Book Writers and Illustrators (SCBWI) chapter. You can find the chapter nearest your home and contact the regional advisor about joining a writing group through SCBWI's Web site, www.scbwi.org.

Other resources that can help you find a writing group that's right for you include the following:

- ✔ **Writing classes:** Take a class in writing, and join up with some of the people you meet in the class.

- ✔ **Word of mouth:** If you personally know writers in your area and are friendly with them, ask whether they know of any writing groups or are interested in starting one.

- ✔ **Online writing discussion groups:** Functioning like a group chat, online discussion groups consist of writers who get together online to share ideas and offer feedback. Manuscripts are sent as e-mail attachments or posted on a Web site. The manuscripts are read by a certain deadline, and members get together online to discuss the chosen manuscript. We have certain issues with the public nature of this option, given that anyone could *potentially* steal your manuscript, but if the only time you have to yourself is during the middle of the night, participating in an online writing discussion group is better than nothing.

Tons of online resources can help in your search for a writing group or online writing class. But again, we urge caution: Make sure the Web site is a reputable one before committing yourself and your precious creative energies.

Sift through your feedback

The major benefit of writing groups is that you get free feedback from the many different writers who participate. The biggest potential drawback inherent in writing groups is that the feedback you receive comes primarily from other new writers who may not know any more than you do and may not steer you in the right direction. So how do you get the right feedback from the right people?

If you're in a writing class where everyone takes turns reading aloud, and everyone else is allowed to comment, your best bet is to listen carefully to the teacher's critiques and to take into consideration the participants in the class who consistently make solid observations. Who you decide to listen to is a strictly subjective choice on your part, so consider everything, but choose only what seems to make sense to you. This may sound like common sense, but sometimes new writers are so eager to learn or so unsure of their abilities that they listen to everyone and try to incorporate all helpful comments — and end up with a manuscript mess. Focus on the positive aspects of the creative atmosphere and the exchange of ideas back and forth.

Although we can't promise that everyone always comes prepared to a writing group discussion or that each member listens and offers constructive critiques, we can assure you that a writing group that bonds well often produces both successful books that sell well and lifetime friendships.

The difference between critiquing and criticizing is very important — and you don't find this difference in any dictionary. When you give a *critique,* you offer well-reasoned, pointed, clear criticism with an eye to possible solutions. When you *criticize,* on the other hand, you offer a judgment about why something is bad. Writers tend to be a sensitive lot, and a critical evaluation that is mean-spirited isn't helpful to the writer's creative process. So watch your tongue. You could be the one at the other end some day.

A great way to insure that you get clear feedback is to ask pointed questions when you finish reading your piece aloud to the members of your writing group. Here are some good questions to consider for making sure you get the feedback you need:

- ✔ Is my main character believable? Why or why not?

- ✔ How can I improve the secondary character(s)?

- ✔ Is my story exciting or interesting to you? Do you want to learn more or find out what happens next? If not, why?

- ✔ Is the action consistently paced, or did you feel the story lag anywhere?

- ✔ Is my point of view consistent?

- ✔ What do you think about what the characters said to one another? Does the dialogue ring true?

- ✔ Does anything in particular bother you about my story/chapter/scene? Something you'd like to see improved? (Only the brave of heart need apply here.)

- ✔ Do you think the humor worked?

Usually the audience's response while you're reading lets you know whether your humor is effective, but asking is a nice way to find out how you can make something funnier if the response fell flat. As you read, pay attention if you get grimaces from the audience in unintended places.

Questions like these and others tailored specifically to your work elicit answers that you can use as opposed to criticisms that you can't. And although you aren't usually allotted the time to ask all your questions at one reading, asking the right one or two can make all the difference to your rewriting process.

Ask people to be specific in response to your questions. This way, when your time is limited in a group meeting, you can quickly get to the heart of what someone thinks about your work.

Start your own group

Having a hard time finding the right writing group? Why not start your own? All you need to form a group is one friend who wants to write and is serious enough to commit to writing and meeting on a regular basis. If you're in a writing class, choose a few people who impress you and seem tolerable — ignore whether they love or hate your work — and ask them if they're interested.

Choosing the perfect group

Although we suggest that you recruit more than two members (if you only have one member, and he decides to drop out for personal reasons, then where will you be?), we also believe that more than eight is too many. In our experience, at a critique group's inception, everyone has something to read and wants time to share her work. So if your group has ten members, and they each get a half-hour, your meeting lasts five hours — way too much time for most of you juggling busy careers, families, and extracurricular pursuits. As a group matures, every member doesn't usually want to read his material at each meeting, and some members typically miss meetings here and there. A group of eight ensures that enough people have new or revised material for consideration at most every meeting.

Take discriminating notes

In Lisa's very first writing class, being a diligent, apple-polishing, A-student, she wrote down every darn thing everyone, including the teacher, said about her writing. And she didn't separate one comment from the other. She took notes this way throughout the ten-week class, even though she began to figure out about halfway through the class that perhaps not everyone's comments were as educated or on the mark as the teacher's. Alas, when the class was over, and Lisa tried to apply what she had learned, she was extremely confused as to whose advice and commentary to pay attention to and whose not to. She had no way of distinguishing the teacher's comments from the yahoos', so she had to put aside the rewrite of her story for a good year until she forgot most of the remarks and could start from scratch. The subject matter was timely the first time around, but unfortunately, by the time she got back to her story, it was no longer so.

When you want an open-book career, bring an open mind

Stephen Mooser is an author and president of The Society of Children's Book Writers and Illustrators (SCBWI). A founder of SCBWI, he knows all about writers' conferences and workshops and how to get the feedback you need.

WCBFD: We all agree that writers' conferences can be a very valuable experience for a new writer. How can a new writer be sure to get the most out of his experience?

SM: Be prepared to listen. Lots of what you hear will be helpful, and every once in a while something will be said that will be startling in its insight into a problem you could be wrestling with.

WCBFD: Are there scam conferences out there? How can a writer find out if a conference is reputable and worth the money?

SM: I've never heard of scam conferences — though some are obviously better than others. Make sure the conference has been held at least once before and then research the faculty. Good people are not likely to waste their time speaking at a conference they don't respect.

WCBFD: When hunting for writers' conferences, should a new writer focus on those sponsored by literary agencies or not?

SM: The SCBWI conferences are probably the best for new writers because of the feedback opportunities available as well as the range of speakers and workshops for different levels of writing expertise. Others like Chautauqua Institution (www.ciweb.org) and Haystack (www.cannonbeach.org) that have been around for a long time also are quite good.

WCBFD: To get the most out of a conference what should writers bring with them?

SM: An open mind. It's also probably worth it to do some research on the publishing houses represented by editors who will be speaking.

WCBFD: Do you believe that a writing group is of value to a new writer? Can it make the difference between getting published and not getting published?

SM: Writing groups are very valuable, but you'll need to find one that best suits your level. If you are just starting out as a writer, choose a supportive group, but one in which you can also offer something valuable to the other members.

WCBFD: Is it realistic to expect that an agent will discover you at a writer's conference?

SM: Probably not, though it can happen. Don't expect to hand a manuscript to an agent or an editor just in passing, but if you have a critique with an editor or agent, then it could work out that they might later take you on.

WCBFD: If one gets feedback on a manuscript at a conference, how does one know that the feedback is on target, especially considering that the writer usually does not get to choose his editor or reviewer?

SM: It's hard to tell. If it makes sense to you then go with it. If in doubt, try to get an opinion about the feedback from another writer you respect or your critique group.

WCBFD: Let's say a writer cannot or does not want to pay for an edit. What are his alternatives?

SM: Working with a critique group is a great alternative. As well, many colleges offer extension classes in writing. These can be good places to hone your skills and get valuable feedback.

WCBFD: Anything you'd like to rant or rave about?

SM: Conferences are valuable for a number of reasons, and I urge people to attend them whenever physically and financially possible.

Conferences offer excellent networking possibilities, give you an opportunity to improve your craft, and demonstrate a commitment to pursuing children's literature in a professional manner.

Make sure, if you can, that your group has a balance of skill levels. You want some writers who are your peers, some who are more experienced, and some who have been published or who have some professional writing experience. A balanced group is a happy and productive group.

Establishing your group's ground rules

If you start your own group, establishing some ground rules helps avert problems later on. Here are some good rules to consider:

- **Number of participants:** Allow eight participants maximum, and after you choose a number, stick to it. Only consider new members if membership falls below this number and a majority of the group votes them in.

- **Size of submission:** Limit the size to one picture book manuscript (or its equivalent of 1,500 words max) or one middle-grade chapter.

- **Type of critiquing:** Does each member read aloud and get verbal feedback? Or does each member submit a written manuscript and get written feedback the following week? Or a combination of both? If your members do not like the idea of "homework," they may prefer simply to listen to the writer read aloud during the workshop while they take notes, offering a verbal critique at the end of the reading. If they like to read in peace and quiet, take notes, and then offer their critique aloud during the next workshop, that's also a possible approach. All the members need to decide together how they want to conduct the critiques.

- **Required critiquing:** Does each member have to critique each submission? How long does she get to critique her peers? In most workshops, everyone can participate in critiquing if they have something productive to add to the discussion. And the time taken to offer a critique is totally up to what the members consider appropriate. If the critique required is written, everyone who gets a hard copy should offer at least some comments.

- **Participant behavior:** Certain behaviors shouldn't be tolerated and should lead to dismissal from the group. For example, if a member misses a certain number of meetings in a row, the group should require that he drop out, opening up a place for a replacement.

Mean-spirited criticism, sarcasm, and *ad hominem* comments are not acceptable and do not help create a forum for open and creative discussion. Make this a basic ground rule for your group.

✔ **Meeting location:** If the meetings take place at the same private home, you need to decide how to deal with refreshments. Does everyone contribute a sum of money to be applied every month toward coffee and donuts? Is it BYOM (bring your own munchies)? If the group alternates between different members' homes each week, should the weekly host provide the refreshments?

✔ **Structure of readings:** You also need to decide whether the participants' readings or critique times will be timed in order to keep a big group from running overtime each week. How much time is allowed? Who marks the time for the group?

If you are putting together the group, print out the preceding rules and considerations and hand them out at the first meeting. Suggest that each member read one rule aloud and open up the floor to discussion so you can all decide together how your group will work. You quickly get rule-making out of the way so your group can get to writing.

At the first meeting, pass around a piece of paper that asks for each member's name, address, home phone number, cell phone number, and e-mail address. You can promise a roster of names and contact information for each member at the second meeting.

Part V

Getting Published and Promoting Your Book

The 5th Wave — By Rich Tennant

"I'm not sure we're ready to publish a children's book described as '...ripped from today's headlines'."

In this part . . .

Despite its fun leanings, publishing children's books is ultimately a business, and the key players — agents, publishers, and even (many, if not all) authors — are in the business to make money. This part gives you an overview of the publishing process and helps you find the right publisher. It also sets you on the right foot in your search for an agent or attorney to help you deal with the paperwork and other legal mumbo jumbo, such as publishing agreements, financial concerns, and contractual conditions. Or you may decide to walk your own path to publishing success. We explore what to do if your book is rejected and then take a close look at self-publishing. Finally, we consider the most effective ways to promote your book and get it noticed.

Chapter 16

Getting an Agent to Represent You

· ·

· ·

*B*elieve it or not, children's books don't sell themselves to prospective publishers — you have to get your manuscript in front of the right person at the right time if you hope to see your children's book move from dream to reality. Two key options can help get your manuscript in front of the right person at the right time. You can engage a literary agent to sell the manuscript for you or you can try sending off your manuscript to every appropriate publisher you can find with hopes of someone actually opening your package and liking what they find.

In this chapter, we discuss what you need to do if you go with the first option: finding an agent. We cover where to find an agent, what to look for in one, how to get his or her interest in your book, and then what to expect after you've hired him. We also tell you what to do if you decide to part ways with your agent. (Want to have a go at selling the manuscript yourself? Sure, no problem. You'll find a bit of information on that approach in Chapter 17.)

Defining the Perfect (and the Not-So-Perfect) Agent

An *agent* is someone who works to sell your book to a publisher. Agents may own their own businesses or may work for a larger agency among many other agents. In exchange for selling your book, agents work on commission — a percentage (usually a flat 15 percent, sometimes increased to no more than 20 to 25 percent for selling foreign or other specialized rights where your agent has to engage the services of a subagent) of the advance and royalties stipulated in your publishing contract.

Agents can work magic because they're in much better contact with publishing companies than unpublished authors are. Publishers rely on good agents to filter out the riffraff — the vast number of manuscripts that just don't make the grade and have little or no chance of being published — and present them with the cream of the crop. The best agents know exactly what children's book editors at different publishing houses are looking for and do their best to provide it.

Your agent will probably bill you for costs that are out of the ordinary, such as extensive copying, manuscript retyping, long-distance or overseas phone calls, and overnight delivery, but you should be clear on these charges and agree on them in advance. On the other hand, most legitimate literary agencies include in their regular cost of doing business (the 15 percent agency fee) items such as reading your manuscript; providing you with general advice on the publishing process and tips on improving your manuscript; local phone calls, fax, and computer time; and routine photocopy and mailing costs.

Your agent can be your best friend and advisor, your teacher, and your literary confidant. The relationship you form with him or her can play an extremely important role in your success as a children's book author and can last the rest of your life. If you decide to work with an agent to sell your work, be sure to get a good one.

Many of the big children's book publishers (as well as many of the smaller ones) deal *only* with agents. They won't even *look* at unagented manuscripts submitted directly by prospective authors.

What good agents can do

Agents provide a vital service to authors, and a good one is well worth whatever fee she charges. From advice, to hand-holding, to negotiating, good agents do a lot of work for their authors:

- Help you shape up your manuscript by offering free editorial advice or by referring you to a professional editor or *book doctor* (someone who fixes manuscripts for a living).

- Help you find a publisher for your work by sending your manuscript to one or more selected editors, *pitching* your idea by assertively touting the general wonderfulness of your manuscript (perhaps explaining to the editors that you are the next Judy Blume, or that your manuscript is perfectly timed for an emerging trend in the marketplace), following up to gauge interest, and then negotiating and closing the deal. An agent may also sell or license your work in other markets such as foreign or television and film.

✔ Hold your hand through the publishing process, from manuscript to finished book and beyond. There are a variety of things to consider after a book is published, such as getting the author's rights back if a book goes out of print, or selling foreign, film, electronic, and other rights that may have been excluded from the primary publishing contract.

✔ Negotiate the terms and conditions of your publishing contract, including such things as advances, royalty rates, submission and payment schedules, rights, and much more. (See Chapter 17 for a discussion of contract terms and conditions.)

✔ May be contractually empowered (in your agency agreement and in the publishing contract) to receive your advance and royalty payments, take their cut, and then send you a check for your portion of the earnings. In this case, they also monitor publisher royalty statements and keep accounting records of your earnings and payments.

✔ If your work is licensed to other parties, the agent may monitor how they use your work to ensure that such use complies with the terms and conditions of your licensing agreements.

✔ Advise you on standard industry practice and on new trends in the publishing industry.

Watch out for bad agents

Although we wish the world of literary agents was all fluffy bunnies, sweetness, and light, we're here to tell you that it can sometimes be ugly — *very* ugly. Although many children's book agents and agencies are completely reputable, ethical, and honest, there are some whose primary goal is to devise efficient and effective ways to separate you from your hard-earned cash.

Real agents are paid out of the proceeds (the advance and royalties or flat fees) of your publishing agreement and the sale of any other rights. Bogus agents will want you to pay them for their services out of your own pocket (in most cases because they have no intention of actually selling your book to a publisher).

Here are some warning signs. Definitely watch out for

✔ Agents who ask for money up front, before they do anything.

✔ Agents who ask for a fee just to read your manuscript.

✔ Agents who have little or no publishing industry experience.

✔ Agencies that have been in business for only a very short time.

> ✔ Agents who are unwilling to give you names of clients they have handled or recent sales.
>
> ✔ Agents who offer to make your work saleable by editing it for a fee before the agent will consider handling it.
>
> ✔ Agents who refer you to an editor from whom they get a kickback sum, depending on how much the editor charges you, before the agent will consider handling it.

For a general discussion of potential pitfalls, be sure to check out the agent warnings and cautions at the Science Fiction and Fantasy Writers of America Web site, right here: www.sfwa.org/beware/agents.html and Harold Underdown's excellent rundown on children's book agents at his Purple Crayon Web site: www.underdown.org/agents.htm. The money (and the writing career) you save may be your own.

Finding an Agent

Okay, so you've decided that you would like to work with an agent. Now what? The next step is to find a great one who will not just sell your book to a publisher, but who is ethical, who will take the time necessary to properly develop your work and present it in the best light, and with whom you can develop a long-term working relationship. In this section, we show you where to find agent referrals, how to use an agent directory, and why you may need to head to some more writing conferences. And after all our helpful information has helped you find this person, we offer up a few tips so you can make sure you've really found the agent of your dreams.

Keep in mind that agents are in business to make money. This means that they're very selective about the authors they choose to work with. Many agencies receive thousands of queries, proposals, and manuscripts from prospective authors each year — some good, but many others not so good — and they of necessity reject far more authors than they accept. If an agent turns you down, don't let it slow you down — submit to another agent or consider submitting your manuscript directly to a publisher (covered in Chapter 17).

Get referrals

Do you have a friend, relative, or acquaintance who already works with a good literary agency? Or do you frequent Internet forums where people share stories about their children's book publishing experiences? Or do you ever enroll in writing workshops led by successful children's book authors? If so, approach the people you meet who already have an agent they're using.

Your new best friend: Your agent

Many agents come from publishing companies where they held various positions that have given them true insider info. Deborah Warren, the principal owner of East-West Agency, is one of these agents, and she always has a lot of great information to share with her clients.

WCBFD: Why should a children's book author have an agent — can't an author just approach publishers him/herself?

DW: A good agent will submit your work to targeted editors (having established and grown those relationships); negotiate the publishing contract; possibly retain some subsidiary rights (selling the work to book clubs, foreign publishers, and so on) to sell on your behalf (allowing you to keep more of the money from these sales than if the publisher sold them for you); keep track of deadlines and royalty statements; and generally act as go-between for you and the editor on business issues. Retaining an agent allows you to concentrate on what you do best: writing. Having representation allows the writer and editor to keep their relationship focused on the writing of the book and not the negotiations surrounding it.

WCBFD: What things turn you on (and off) when you're approached by a potential client?

DW: I'm impressed when clients have an appreciation for, and knowledge about, the industry — in particular, about the acquisition process.

WCBFD: What do you do to earn your fee?

DW: I'm a long-term advocate for my client. I work for — and with — her to best represent her interests, passion, and vision. As her new "best friend," I'll also nurture, guide, inspire, promote, market, and help shape my client's work. For this, I'm paid a 15 percent commission on domestic rights sales, and a 20 percent to 25 percent commission on foreign rights sales of the work,

in perpetuity, for as long as it's in print. As far as expenses: I deduct actual, out-of-pocket expenses from the first royalty check.

Believe me, a good agent is with you for the long-term. *Your* best interests are *her* best interests. It'll be easy to spot one that's not on your side.

WCBFD: What are some danger signs for an author to look out for when approaching an agency?

DW: Run away, don't walk, if an agent doesn't promptly return your phone call, e-mail, or postal query. A red flag should go up if the agency demands money from an author upfront for representation.

WCBFD: What can an author do to help you do your job?

DW: A large percentage of submissions are rejected. Despite the pile of manuscripts beckoning the agent (or editor), she or he must be immediately convinced that this one is special and deserves recognition. Furthermore, publishers are extremely cautious in today's marketplace. If you're a new talent in children's books, you're challenged to earn "credentials." To that end, if you haven't already done so, join your local chapter of SCBWI (www.scbwi.org), a national writers' and illustrators' organization with annual bi-coastal conferences. As a result, you'll network with other writers and industry professionals, benefit from a manuscript critique and/or portfolio review which allows members to obtain feedback on their works-in-progress, and receive marketing news through their newsletter. (SCBWI also sponsors awards and grants, including the Sue Alexander Most Promising New Work Award for unpublished manuscripts, and the Kimberly Colen Memorial Grant for unpublished authors and illustrators.)

Literary agencies are businesses, but they don't advertise in a traditional way. Although they can perhaps run a small advertisement in the back of a writer's magazine — soliciting manuscripts for the next children's megahit — it's unlikely that you'll see an agent's face on a highway billboard or a 30-second spot after the Super Bowl halftime show. Instead, agencies mostly rely on word-of-mouth advertising as well as their own recruiting efforts to bring them new authors.

Authors who are happy with their agents will usually be very willing to refer you to them. So the next time you're chatting with a children's book author, be sure to ask him who his agent is, whether he's happy with her, and whether he can make an introduction for you. Or if you've found an agent you like, ask for a list of clients you can contact for feedback. Looking back someday, you may realize that taking this simple step was the smartest thing you ever did to get your children's book published because of the information you will learn about this person with whom you are about to enter into a very important relationship.

Use an agent directory

There are a number of terrific directories — both online and in print — for finding literary agents and agencies. Directories — both hard copy and online — provide you with agency names, contacts, mailing addresses, phone numbers, and detailed information about what kinds of books the agency specializes in representing. Simply find an agency that looks like it meets your criteria, get the contact information, and get in touch. As you look through these directories, be sure to focus only on agencies that specialize in children's books. You'll be wasting your time (and the agency's time) if you try to pitch your children's book to an agency that specializes in cookbooks or Westerns or chick lit.

Here are some online sources for agent directories:

- The Association of Authors' Representatives (www.aar-online.org)
- Association of Authors' Agents (Great Britain — www.agentsassoc.co.uk)
- Publishers Marketplace (www.publishersmarketplace.com)
- Agent Research and Evaluation (www.agentresearch.com)
- WritersNet (www.writers.net)
- Society of Children's Book Writers and Illustrators provides a list of agents to their members (www.scbwi.org)

And here are a few books to help you out if you don't have access to the Internet:

- *Children's Writer's and Illustrator's Market* by Alice Pope and Rebecca Chrysler (Writer's Digest Books)
- *Guide to Literary Agents* by Kathryn Brogan (Writer's Digest Books)
- *Writers Market* by Kathryn Brogan and Robert Brewer (Writer's Digest Books)

Attend conferences

Agents sometimes participate in conferences and workshops to find promising new talent — some agencies even sponsor them. Because that promising new talent may very well be you, and because it's in your interest to do everything you can to get your book in the hands of a great publisher, you should consider attending writers' conferences for the express purpose of hooking up with an agent. Here are a few ways to increase your chances of finding the agent you're looking for at a conference:

- Check out writers' conference or workshop agendas and participant lists to see whether agents will be making presentations or otherwise be in attendance.
- Contact the agent in advance of the conference or workshop (e-mail is the best bet here) to let her know that you would like a minute of her time to introduce yourself.
- Be sure to bring copies of your pitch or manuscript to hand out to agents at the conference or workshop. Although they're unlikely to have time to look samples over at the meeting, chances are good that they will after they return to their offices.

Agents attending conferences and workshops are often very popular people, so it may be hard to corner one to make your pitch. They may be leading roundtable discussions or making presentations, plus getting pitched by other prospective authors. You can get a jump on the competition by making contact with the agent before the conference, letting him or her know that you'll be there and looking forward to a personal meeting. Be patient, be polite, but be persistent — eventually, you'll have an opportunity to make your pitch. Be ready for that opportunity when it presents itself, and jump as soon as it arrives.

Self-addressed stamped envelopes say a lot

When you submit an idea to an agency in written form, be sure to send along a self-addressed, stamped envelope (SASE) as a courtesy so that the material can be returned to you if it is rejected. To save on mailing costs, you *may* consider sending a small SASE for an acceptance or rejection and tell the recipient to simply toss the manuscript if it's rejected (but see below for our feelings about that).

Just so you know: We're aware that postage costs account for a large portion of your expenses. And you may be saying to yourself as you lick the 40th envelope of the day that you don't want to waste another stamp (or more) on the return of your work if it's rejected. Why bother, if you have a printer and can print out your own new copy every time you need to? Well, stuff it! Who wants to represent an author who doesn't care what happens to her manuscript, rejected or not? That stamped envelope shows you care, and it's a courtesy the agent may use when she sends you an acceptance letter instead! So use the small SASE option only if the manuscript is truly long and therefore costs a lot to mail. You don't want to send the wrong message about your pride and joy.

How to know when you've found "the one"

After you've found an agent you want to work with (and who wants to work with you), the Association of Authors' Representatives (www.aar-online.org) suggests that you ask a number of questions to help ensure that the agent you've selected is the right one for you:

- ✔ Are you a member of the Association of Authors' Representatives? (AAR requires its members to adhere to a strict code of ethics and business practices.)

- ✔ How long have you been in business as an agent?

- ✔ Do you have specialists at your agency who handle movie and television rights? Foreign rights?

- ✔ Do you have subagents or corresponding agents in Hollywood and overseas?

- ✔ Who in your agency will actually be handling my work? Will the other staff members be familiar with my work and the status of my business at your agency? Will you oversee or at least keep me apprised of the work that your agency is doing on my behalf?

✔ Do you issue an agent-author agreement? May I review the language of the agency clause that appears in contracts you negotiate for your clients?

✔ How do you keep your clients informed of your activities on their behalf?

✔ Do you consult with your clients on any and all offers?

✔ What are your commission rates? What are your procedures and time frames for processing and disbursing client funds? Do you keep different bank accounts separating author funds from agency revenue? What are your policies about charging clients for expenses incurred by your agency?

✔ When you issue 1099 tax forms at the end of each year, do you also furnish clients upon request with a detailed account of their financial activity, such as gross income, commissions and other deductions, and net income, for the past year? In the event of your death or disability, what provisions exist for my continued representation?

✔ If we should part company, what is your policy about handling any unsold subsidiary rights in my work?

Different agents will answer these questions in different ways, and answering one question in the negative shouldn't necessarily disqualify the agent from consideration. But use their answers to help you make the very important decision of who will represent you and your work. And don't forget to ask other authors what they know about the agent, do a search for information — good or bad — about the agent or his agency on the Internet, or check with the Better Business Bureau.

How do you cut through the competition and get your idea in front of an agent in a way that will maximize your possibility of success? Read on to find out.

Follow submission guidelines

The number one mistake that many prospective children's book authors (well, authors in general) make when submitting an idea to an agency is that they don't first find out what the agency's submission guidelines are. Instead, they create an epic work — a sight to behold, a wonder to handle — that violates every rule that the agency lays down for prospective authors. The result? A lot of beautiful manuscripts lining a lot of ugly, gray wastepaper baskets. Don't let this happen to you. Check the agency's Web site or give it a call and ask for a copy of its guidelines.

Depending on the agency's preferences, you may be asked to submit your idea in a variety of different forms:

- A query letter (which contains a short synopsis of your idea as well as your contact information and brief biography — see the sample in the "Send a query letter" section later this chapter)

- A complete manuscript (you have one of those, right?)

- Sample chapters and an outline (especially if you're pitching a young adult novel or other longer work)

- A proposal (which contains a synopsis of your idea, a proposed table of contents, marketing and biographical information, analysis of competitive works, and perhaps a sample chapter or two). We cover proposals in Chapter 17.

After you have the agency's guidelines, make sure to follow them to the letter!

Stand out from the pack

How can you stand out from the pack of hungry authors beating down agents' doors? Here are a few tried-and-true tips:

- **Choose the right agent for the job.** You're not going to make a positive impression (or engage the agent's services) if you send your epic children's fantasy to an agent who specializes in selling crime novels, mysteries, and horror. Make sure you have the agent who specializes in the type of children's book you wrote.

- **Follow the agency's guidelines.** You wouldn't believe how many authors don't follow submission guidelines — suffice it to say that it's *a lot*. Just following the agency's guidelines automatically makes you stand out from the rest of the competition. Visit their Web site or call and ask for the guidelines before you do anything else.

- **Be sure your manuscript is complete and polished before you submit it.** Either get feedback from a writer's group or a writing class or engage the services of a professional children's book editor or book doctor (see Chapter 13 for a detailed discussion on this topic) to make your manuscript all it can be.

Send a query letter

Keep your query letter short and sweet; one page should do the trick. You'll have plenty of time to write a book after you get your contract.

Ever wonder what a query letter looks like? The following is a generic sample, but be careful to tailor it to a prospective agency's guidelines (which you'll find on the agency's Web site or in writing if you request them from the agency) before you submit it.

Your Name
Address
Home Phone
E-mail Address

Date

Agent's Name
Agency Name
Agent's Address

Dear Ms. _____:

A Dog's Life is a completed 20,000-word young adult fantasy set on a distant planet some time in the future. I have selected your agency because of your success in placing young adult books in the science fiction genre.

Sirius is a dog with a difference: He has discovered the secret to time travel. Using his machine, he travels forward and backward in time with ease, zipping to and fro across the universe at will. That is, until he lands on the planet earth in the year 2005 and his time machine breaks. This causes all sorts of problems for Sirius, beginning with the human family that mistakes him for a regular dog and ties him up to their RV in Florida. Only by convincing his new owner's 10-year-old daughter that there's more to this dog than Alpo and Milk Bones can Sirius hope to escape his fate and get his machine fixed in time to save the earth from the asteroid that has coincidentally just moved into a trajectory that will intersect with its orbit in exactly three days, fifteen hours, thirty-seven minutes, and four seconds!

I have been writing science fiction stories for fifteen years, and I have had a number of stories published in the popular magazine *Asimov's Science Fiction*, as well as at a number of online science fiction sites. I'm a card-carrying member of Science Fiction and Fantasy Writers of America and the Society for Children's Book Writers and Illustrators, and I was a finalist this year in a local writing contest.

Please let me know if you are interested in seeing this manuscript. I would be happy to send you the first couple of chapters of this story or the complete manuscript — whichever you prefer. I have enclosed a SASE for your reply. Thanks for taking the time to consider this query.

Sincerely,

Your Name

When communicating with agents or publishers in a query letter (see more on going directly to a publisher without working with an agent in Chapter 17), always make sure to identify the format of your book (we talk extensively about formats in Chapter 2). In the preceding query letter, the format is identified twice as young adult. This shorthand allows the agent or publisher to immediately understand your intended audience as well as the approximate page count and size of the book. It also assures that the right in-house editor will receive your submission. And, perhaps most importantly, it shows you have done your research and separates your submission from those of the wannabees who refer to their work only as a "children's book" (and who most likely will receive only a rejection letter in return for their limited efforts).

Understanding Typical Agency Agreements

Depending on the literary agency you select, you may or may not be required to sign a written agency agreement before an agent will represent your work to publishers. Although a handshake agreement may work out fine for you and your agent, our preference is for agency agreements to be in writing. Life is complicated enough; it's always better to get it in writing. Here we discuss the standard terms and conditions that go into most agency agreements, as well as give you tips on how to negotiate your end of the deal.

Standard terms and conditions

A variety of terms can make their way into a typical agency agreement, including some of the following:

- **Scope of the agreement:** This part of the agreement spells out exactly what the agency is going to do (represent your work), where the agency is going to do the work (within your country or throughout the world), and whether the relationship with you the writer is exclusive or for a specific project (see the next section for more details on this distinction).

- **Duration of the agreement:** Does the agreement last for six months? A year? Forever? Many agreements last for the duration of a specific project — from the initial pitch to publishers until the book eventually goes out of print. Other agreements are for minimum of one year and apply to all projects sent out during that year (see the "Exclusive and by-project services" section later in this chapter); after the one year it may be assumed that the relationship will continue until either party decides, at will, to pull out. Read this part of the agreement, and you'll soon find out.

Suppose you've been with an agent for over a year and really feel that she's not the right fit for you. Your contract may allow you to terminate the agreement from that point on, but any project the agent has submitted to publishers and that is accepted after you terminate the agreement will still be covered under the old agreement. In other words, for any work that she has done for you on any particular book that you gave to her during the time of your agreement, your contract applies in perpetuity.

✔ **Handling of funds:** This part of the agreement spells out how funds will be handled. Typically, the agency will receive payments from publishers, disburse your portion to you within a certain amount of time, and keep an accurate accounting of all financial transactions.

✔ **Commission rate:** The amount of each publisher check that the agency gets to keep for doing its job is typically 15 percent (or 20 to 25 percent for sales of foreign and other rights involving subagents).

✔ **Authorization to sign on your behalf:** The agreement may contain a provision that allows the agent to sign contracts or checks on your behalf. We are personally uncomfortable with turning over that much control to an agent — we want to review publishing agreements and sign them ourselves. But as far as payments, if your agent disburses funds to you after taking his cut (typical in the industry), then it's fine for him to sign checks.

✔ **Expenses:** The agreement may spell out exactly what expenses the agency will bear as a part of its standard commission (typically, routine overhead items like local phone calls, small copying jobs, computer, fax, employee time spent editing your manuscript and presenting it to publishers, and so forth) and what expenses will be billed against the author's royalties (typically extraordinary expenses such as overnight shipping, messenger, large copying jobs, long-distance phone calls, and the like). Avoid agents that charge reading fees. These border on being unethical, and are expressly prohibited by the Association of Authors' Representatives' Canon of Ethics.

✔ **Indemnification:** Some agencies may want the author to indemnify (protect) them against legal claims resulting from acts or omissions on the part of the author that exposes the agency to legal claims. Such provisions are not in your interest, and you should consider trying to negotiate them out.

✔ **Termination:** This part of the agreement spells out the conditions that each party must undertake to end the agreement. It usually involves waiting a specific amount of time from signing, typically a year, and then allows either party to bow out at will, in writing.

Make sure your agency agreements contain a specific mechanism for termination. It's better to have these understandings spelled out in advance — when you and your agent are cool, calm, and collected — than trying to sort out a big, bloody mess when emotions are running high.

Exclusive and by-project services

One question you may face when working with agency is the issue of whether your relationship is going to be exclusive or by project. The difference between the two is major, and it can have a significant impact on your writing career:

- **Exclusive agreement:** When you enter into an exclusive agreement with an agent or literary agency, you're turning over representation for all of your work for as long as the agreement is in effect. Although this may make your life easier because someone else is worrying about placing your projects with publishers, on the other hand, your flexibility in being able to try different avenues to getting published is greatly reduced — perhaps for many, many years.

- **By-project agreement:** This kind of agreement is for one project only, including any sequels or derivative works that may spin off of the original work. Although your agent takes full responsibility for selling a particular work to publishers, you can take your other projects to other agents, or submit them directly to publishers yourself — whichever approach makes the most sense to you at the time.

For your first book, you may choose to pursue a by-project agreement. With this kind of agreement, you have the opportunity to see if you and your agent work well together before you make an exclusive commitment to one another. It's kind of like going steady or getting engaged before you tie the knot.

Negotiate like a pro

As is often the case with business deals in other industries, you may find that the terms and conditions of your agency agreement are negotiable. Of course, you will also find that agents will be more flexible with the terms and conditions when they really, really want you to sign up as a client. So, for example, you may find that the agent who was adamantly insisting last week that you sign an exclusive agreement is willing to accept a by-project agreement when you drop a hint that you may soon start looking elsewhere for an agent.

In the mood to negotiate? Here are some tips guaranteed to turn you into a negotiating pro (okay, maybe an advanced intermediate) in no time:

- **Be prepared.** Being prepared gives you a definite advantage in *any* negotiating situation. So much so that the downside of not preparing for a negotiation far outweighs the small amount of time and effort that it takes to prepare.

✔ **Leave plenty of room to maneuver.** Nobody likes to be boxed into a position with no room for compromise or flexibility in meeting the *mutual* goals of both parties. When you develop your negotiation goals and positions, build in enough flexibility so that you can achieve your agent's goals, *while* you achieve yours.

✔ **Have lots of alternatives in mind.** For every possible reason that your agent gives for *not* agreeing to one of your positions, you should have one or more alternatives ready to go. So, for example, if your agent-to-be insists on an exclusive agreement in perpetuity, but you don't want to be locked in for more than a year, then be ready with an alternative that gives your agent exclusivity she seeks but only for a year.

✔ **Keep your word.** In business — as in life in general — your word should be your bond. Negotiation is built on a foundation of trust and mutual respect. If you aren't willing to keep your word, then you'll quickly lose both respect and trust. It's okay to make an honest mistake, though — that's something that most anyone can understand and deal with.

✔ **Listen more than you talk.** One of the most important negotiating skills is an ability to listen — *really* listen — to the other party. If you ask the right questions and then let your counterpart talk about the answers, you'll usually find out exactly what it will take to successfully negotiate and close a deal. Don't forget — if you're talking, you're not listening.

✔ **Don't give up too much too soon.** In our experience, it pays not to give up too much too quickly when you're dealing with a tough negotiator. Not only will you appear weak and perhaps a bit desperate, but you'll miss out on getting any significant concessions from the other party. Take your time when you're negotiating. It's much better for *them* to be in a big rush to close the deal than for *you* to.

✔ **Be able to say no.** Telling someone no is a very difficult skill to acquire. Everyone wants to tell business partners yes and encourage positive relationships. However, when you're negotiating a deal, sometimes you must say no to achieve your own goals. So, if you're not happy with the terms and conditions of a proposed deal, just say *no*.

For more on how to negotiate with ease, check out *Negotiating For Dummies* by Michael C. Donaldson, Mimi Donaldson, and David Frohnmayer (Wiley).

If you're uncertain what terms and conditions you should accept or reject, or if you're uncomfortable negotiating the agreement yourself, seriously consider engaging the services of an attorney who specializes in the practice of entertainment law. Although such representation isn't cheap, you may find that hiring a lawyer will put you way ahead money-wise in the long run.

Terminating Your Agency Relationship

In the previous section, we alluded to the fact that entering into a long-term relationship with an agent can be like getting married — there are a lot of expectations on both sides of the aisle, and when things go wrong, breaking up can be rather like getting a divorce. But sometimes you have no choice, and breaking up isn't just the right thing to do; it's the *only* thing.

When things go from bad to worse, don't hesitate to terminate your relationship, invoking the termination provisions in your agency agreement. Typically, this would involve simply mailing a letter to the agency stating that you are terminating the agreement. Your particular agreement may or may not require a certain number of days prior notice before the termination becomes effective. Be sure to send the letter via certified mail, return receipt required, so that you have a record of the mailing.

Before you break up with your agent, make sure both of you have been on the same page about the particular problem. If you have an issue to address with your agent, always try talking about it first, hammering out the details between the both of you. But if you have tried to work through whatever your issues are and truly have reached the end of your rope, then take the high road and behave like a perfect gentleperson. Get your divorce agreement in writing and then move on. Above all, be professional, be polite, and do whatever you can to avoid burning bridges along the way. The children's book industry really is a small world, and the relationship you save today may be one that will serve you well years down the road.

Chapter 17

Finding the Perfect Publisher and Signing a Contract

* *

In This Chapter

▶ Determining which publisher is right for you

▶ Creating compelling query letters and proposals

▶ Copyrighting your work

▶ Understanding traditional publishing agreements and contracts

▶ Dealing with rejection letters

▶ Deciding whether self-publishing makes sense

* *

*B*efore you can get your children's book published, guess what? You have to find someone to publish it. Now, in these days of self-publishing and print-on-demand, you have more options than ever before to get your children's book into print. But to truly *get published* — to have a real live publisher pay you an advance and royalties, promote and market your book on its own dime, distribute your book to all the bookstores, and hire salespeople to sell your book — is truly something special. It's so special that, each year, thousands of aspiring children's book authors send manuscripts to agents and publishers — all hoping to be one of the lucky ones chosen to get a publishing contract.

There's no reason that you can't be a lucky one. In this chapter, we focus on identifying and approaching the right publisher to sell your book.

Identifying the Right Publisher

There are many, many publishers out there in this wide and wonderful literary world. Some are small — publishing only a book or two a year — while others are relative giants — publishing houses with many different *imprints* (smaller publishing divisions within the publishing house), each with its own publisher, churning out catalogs full of books and other published products. Not only that, but each publisher and imprint has its own distinct personality. Some are buttoned-down and corporate, whereas others are impetuous and quirky. Some love to make a big splash in the marketplace, and others cater to a distinct niche of readers.

We suggest that you make a chart of the publishers you are considering, listing the imprint name, the acquiring editor's name, and the formats, genres, and subject matter they specialize in. You can expand this same chart when you are ready to submit to help you keep track of where your manuscript is, when you sent it, and what the response was.

Take yourself and your work seriously

Doug Whiteman, President of Penguin Books for Young Readers, has some pointers for writers submitting books for consideration at any publishing house.

WCBFD: You started out in the publishing business as a book salesperson and now you're running one of the top three children's publishing companies, so you know your stuff. Tell us what in a submission identifies a children's book writer as a pro who knows her stuff?

DW: That's actually pretty simple: It's all about the homework. The writer who has gone out to the stores to see what her potential competition is and who has presented her submission in a way that distinguishes it from the rest of the field gets my attention immediately. And you really have to go to the stores; simply looking things up on Amazon or going to the library doesn't do it because you need to see the space stores are giving to the various genres; you need to see the jackets against each other; and you need to see what is drawing the customers' attention.

WCBFD: In your experience, what is one of the most common mistakes new writers make?

DW: Not listening: To your editor, your publicist, your booksellers, and your readership. It's really imperative that you soak up everything you can about our business and the way things work if you're going to succeed over the long-term. And that includes advice, particularly in the editorial area.

WCBFD: Anything you'd like to rant/rave about?

DW: I wish you'd asked me this one first! I'm always willing to rant. I think the thing that annoys me most is the new writer (or veteran adult writer) who assumes that writing for children is easy, and gives me a half-hearted, half-baked submission that they'd never do for an adult book. One should come to children's writing with at least as much respect as you would for an adult project, and many would argue that it takes even more effort to connect with children. It's not easy for an adult to communicate with kids via the printed word, and all prospective writers need to remember that!

Gathering info at bookstores and libraries

Checking out bookstores, libraries, and online booksellers can help you gather more information about the publishers you should pursue.

Hit the stores and walk the aisles to find books organized by overall category — fiction and nonfiction. Not only that, but board books have their own area, as do chapter books, young adult novels, and everything in between. Then check out the back covers or copyright pages to see who is publishing what. Doing this can help in a number of ways:

- ✔ You can compare your book to already published books to see where yours fits. Then when you submit, you can mention how your book trumps the competition.

- ✔ You can find out which publishers are publishing books like yours so that you can target them during the submission process (write down editor names and contact information from the front matter).

- ✔ You can see whether any other books approach your topic in the same way you do, so you can make sure that yours is different.

The Society of Children's Book Writers and Illustrators (www.scbwi.org) offers to its members a list of which popular books were edited by which editors at which houses. This information is valuable, because it tells you exactly which editor acquired or worked on what — presupposing that this is the type of material they will continue to seek out.

Writer's guides and directories

Writer's guides and directories — both printed and online — can be terrific aids in identifying the right publisher for you *and* in giving you all the information you need in order to determine what kinds of communications the publisher prefers, along with editors' names and mailing addresses.

Here are a few of our favorite books:

- ✔ ***Children's Writer's & Illustrator's Market* by Alice Pope and Rebecca Chrysler (Writer's Digest Books):** This book is an absolutely essential tool for figuring out the best publishers for you to approach and how to reach them. If you're serious about succeeding in the world of children's books, buy a copy — *now*!

✔ *Writer's & Illustrator's Guide to Children's Book Publishers and Agents* by Ellen Shapiro (Three Rivers Press): Another solid reference book for finding the right publisher for your work.

Here are a couple of Web sites that can give you some help:

✔ **Children's Book Council Member's List** (www.cbcbooks.org/html/memberlist.html): A comprehensive list of all members of the Children's Book Council, a trade group representing children's book publishers. Contains publisher names, contact information, publishing interests, and brief submission guidelines.

✔ **Literary Market Place** (www.literarymarketplace.com): Lists publishers by subject and type of publication; sorts by specific city, state, or zip code; can help you find an editor's name and title; and can even help you produce mailing labels.

✔ **Canadian Children's Book Centre** (www.bookcentre.ca): A national not-for-profit organization and registered charity, the Canadian Children's Book Centre (CCBC) was founded in 1976 to promote, support and encourage the reading, writing, and illustrating of Canadian books for children and teens.

✔ **U.K. Children's Books** (www.ukchildrensbooks.co.uk/pubs.html): A detailed listing of children's book publisher Web sites with an emphasis on publishers in Great Britain.

Drafting Query Letters and Proposals

Publishers don't have time to review mountains of full manuscripts. Instead, they require prospective authors to either submit a *query letter* (a brief letter of introduction that invites the publisher to ask for more details about your project) or a *proposal* (a longer document providing additional editorial and marketing information about the book).

Checking submission guidelines

Most publishers have guidelines for how they want your material to arrive, regardless of whether you're sending a query letter or full proposal. Always find out the guidelines — and follow them.

Take one of these three easy routes to getting a publisher's guidelines:

✔ Write a letter to the publisher requesting its submission guidelines (and include a self-addressed stamped envelope).

✔ Consult a written or online guide to children's book publishers, such as *Children's Writer's & Illustrator's Market* by Alice Pope and Rebecca Chrysler (Writer's Digest Books).

✔ Visit the publisher's Web site. This is probably the best source because you get the information faster than if you write a letter, and it is probably be more up-to-date than any printed or online directory.

Whatever approach you take, be sure to take the time to find the publisher's submission guidelines and follow them exactly. Ignore them at your own risk.

Submitting query letters

The point of submitting a query letter (one page only, please) is to give the publisher a quick rundown on your idea, describe how it fits into their current offerings, how it fits into the marketplace, and show some indication of your ability to write the book and promote it when it is published.

Lisa has a tried-and-true approach to writing query letters and she shares this approach with everyone who asks. Here's what you need to put into your one-page query letter to publishers:

✔ What your manuscript is about (one sentence)

✔ Audience, age, format, and word count

✔ A bit more about the book

✔ Why you chose this particular publisher/imprint (scores major brownie points by showing you did your homework)

✔ Competition (similar books in the marketplace)

✔ Unique marketing ideas (the more interesting the better)

✔ Your publishing background (if any, or relevant professional experience)

✔ Your contact information

See Chapter 16 for a sample query letter.

Pumping out proposals

In some cases, you may be required to submit a proposal to a prospective publisher. A proposal is a document that resides somewhere between a one-page query letter and a full-on manuscript and is generally appropriate only for longer books — particularly nonfiction works. You would never do a proposal for a short board book, for example.

Not counting the introduction and sample chapters, a proposal typically runs 10 to 15 pages. It should be unbound, double-spaced throughout, and have 1-inch margins.

Here's an outline of the contents of a typical book proposal:

- **Overview:** This is a synopsis of the book and typically *pitches* (sells — in a catchy, pithy manner) the idea to the publisher; it is a brief statement (1 to 4 pages) of the project's overall concept.

- **Marketing plan:** Describes the target audience for the book.

- **Promotion:** Explains how you plan to market or promote the book, whether through speaking engagements, book readings, videos, television appearances, radio, advertisements, and so on.

- **Competing title analysis:** This is a list of other published books (no more than five) that cover similar subject matter in a similar way; be convincing about how your book is unique in its approach, style, and subject, and why it is important enough to be published.

- **Author bio:** A shortened résumé, this shows the publisher that you have the background and/or credentials to write this book.

- **Introduction to the book:** Should be written as you would like it to appear in a published book. If the book would not ordinarily have an introduction, such as a work of fiction, this section can be a prologue that gives the reader an idea of the essence of the book's concept, drawing the reader into your world.

- **Chapter summaries:** Gives the publisher a glance at how the entire book will read, especially if only a few sample chapters are provided in the proposal. One paragraph per chapter is adequate. This lets the publisher know you have the book planned from beginning to end.

- **Sample chapters:** The chapters should be in chronological order and begin with Chapter 1; at least two or three sample chapters should be provided to give the publisher a true sense of how you write.

✔ **Attachments:** Attach any relevant, supplementary information you have about the book project, including speaking and seminar schedules; sales figures for previously published material (including books, videos, and audio); and a *client list* if applicable.

Copyright: Protecting Your Work Before You Send Anything

You may think of your children's story as a wonderful beam of heart-warming light in an otherwise dark and cloudy world. That's all well and good, but your story is really something a bit less ethereal; it's property and, like any other property, it needs to be protected.

What? Protected? But why would anyone want to steal your story?

Although your children's book-to-be may never turn into a full-blown, raging bestseller, there's always a possibility that it may. And guess what? Full-blown, raging bestsellers can be worth a lot of money, especially if your characters are turned into licensed products (to be used on T-shirts, lunchboxes, board games, or as dolls or action figures) or your story becomes a Saturday morning television cartoon or major motion picture. And if your rights aren't fully secured from the very beginning, then you can kiss all that money (and the fame and glory, too) goodbye.

The most commonly used — and perhaps most commonly misunderstood — way of protecting a literary work is by a copyright. A copyright is simply a legal protection of an original work. This includes literary, dramatic, musical, artistic, and other intellectual works. Only the owner of the copyright (or someone the copyright owner expressly authorizes) may reproduce the work in copies, prepare derivative works based on the work, perform the work publicly, and display the copyrighted work publicly.

You're probably familiar with the famous mark that signifies an item is copyrighted, the letter *c* within a circle: ©. The copyright symbol is one-third of what is known as a copyright notice. A copyright notice consists of the copyright symbol (©), the year of first publication of the work, and the name of the owner of the copyright, like this:

© 2005 Lisa Rojany Buccieri

Works in the public domain

A story falls into *public domain* (PD) if it is a creative work that is not protected by copyright and can be used by anyone. This includes many fairy tales and works such as *Alice's Adventures in Wonderland* by Lewis Carroll. What do you do if you want to use a story that's in the public domain as a starting point for your own story? You first have to find out if you can.

To find out whether anyone owns a story, and whether you can retell it in your words without getting in trouble, use the fairly reliable test: If you can find three different sources of adaptations or retellings in the public domain then you can fairly assume the story is up for grabs.

But make sure to actually get your hands on the book the story comes from, checking the copyright and permissions pages, and ascertaining that they haven't obtained permission from someone to use the story — because if they did, they would have to credit it, and if the credit is in the book, they may have had to pay for the privilege of using it or adapting it — something you may not want to do. And a word of caution: If you choose fairy tales, make sure to go back to the originals and not to the Disney adaptations, because certain additions to the Disney tales are not public domain. For example, Disney's addition of the characters Flounder (a fish) and Sebastian (a Jamaican-accented crab) to Hans Christian Andersen's classic tale *The Little Mermaid* is not public domain.

Although legally you aren't required to place a copyright notice on your work for it to be protected under copyright laws (before March 1, 1989, your work *did* have to have the notice to be protected), our advice is to put the copyright notice on everything you write (or, if you hope to illustrate a written work, everything you draw or paint). It won't cost you a dime and the work you save may be your own.

Ideas, procedures, methods, systems, processes, concepts, principles, discoveries, or devices, as distinguished from a description, explanation, or illustration, can't be copyrighted (but, boy, you can sure patent and trademark the heck out of some of these things — visit the U.S. Patent and Trademark Office for more details: www.uspto.gov).

What does this mean to you in practical terms? It means that even though you have an idea, you cannot protect it until you develop and write that idea into an actual story. You might submit a query letter to a bunch of publishers about your idea for a story about a girl who finds a lost puppy. You get rejected everywhere. Then months (really often years) after you do, three different books with the same premise come out from three different publishers. Have they stolen your idea? They can't! Ideas are not protected therefore they cannot be stolen in the first place. Regardless of copyright law, the chances of three publishers, or really even one, taking an idea from a query letter they have rejected and going out and soliciting the story from another writer are slim to none.

Although copyrights don't protect your work forever, they do last a pretty long time. For works created on or after January 1, 1978, the copyright lasts for the author's entire life *plus* 70 years after her death. When the work is a "joint work prepared by two or more authors who did not work for hire," the copyright lasts for 70 years after the death of the last surviving author.

So, what, you might ask, happens to ownership of your work after the copyright expires? When your copyright expires, your book enters the *public domain* (see the "Works in the public domain" sidebar); that is, no person or organization has an exclusive right of ownership in the work, and anyone can then use the words you wrote in any way he or she sees fit. Eventually, all copyrighted children's books meet this fate.

A common misconception about copyrights is that you need to fill out a form or hire an attorney or pay a fee to copyright your work. Although any number of attorneys would love to have you spend big bucks to hire them to secure a copyright for your work, you don't necessarily have to do this. According to U.S. copyright law, your work is automatically copyrighted the moment it is created in fixed form (meaning that it is tangible — such as a published story or written song or a printed photograph — or if not directly perceptible, that it can be communicated with the aid of a machine or device), and the copyright immediately becomes your property as the person who created the work.

Advances, Royalties, and Work for Hire

One of the greatest moments of a writer's life comes when you get the news that a publishing company wants to publish your book. Quite quickly following that wonderful moment comes the (very) scary part: signing the publishing agreement.

Understanding publishing agreements

There are generally two types of publishing agreements: a *work-for-hire* or *flat-fee* agreement and the traditional *advance against royalties* agreement. For our purposes here, *contract* and *agreement* refer to the same thing. We're going to walk you through the standard contents of both.

✔ **Racking up royalties with the traditional agreement:** Before a publisher can publish your book, the company first needs a signed publishing agreement. A *publishing agreement* is a legal contract that spells out the terms and conditions under which the publisher will publish your book, including such important areas as payment, schedule, copyright, and much more.

The traditional form of a publishing agreement has long been the standard *royalty agreement. Royalties* are a percentage of the proceeds from the sale of each book, minus the advance. The advance is money the publisher pays you up-front.

✔ **Giving up royalties in a work-for-hire agreement:** When a publisher engages an author under a *work-for-hire agreement*, the publisher pays the author a fixed amount of money for a specific piece of work. When the work is delivered, the publisher pays the money and takes all rights to the work with no residual payments, such as royalties due the author.

In contrast to a traditional publishing agreement, which has a life long after a manuscript is delivered, a typical work-for-hire agreement ends upon delivery of the manuscript. If the book becomes a bestseller, the author won't see a single dime more than what was already paid (unless the author has negotiated some sort of bonus provisions based on number of units sold).

Publishing agreements usually contain all kinds of provisions, including grant of rights, payment, reversion of rights, and more. Check out *Getting Your Book Published For Dummies* by Sara Parsons Zackheim with Adrian Zackheim (Wiley) for the lowdown on contract pitfalls or consult with an attorney with experience in publishing agreements.

Getting what you want in the contract

Whatever you may find in your publishing contract, be sure that the contract is carefully reviewed before you sign it — either by you if you're sufficiently qualified or by an attorney if you're not. And don't sign it until you understand exactly what you're signing and are in full agreement.

Although new authors often give in on a lot of issues because they're so excited to have their first book published, take a look at some of the aspects of a contract that you should try to have a say in:

✔ **Front cover byline:** New authors especially should require that their name appear on the front cover and the spine of the book in a font size that is large enough to be read without difficulty, and that it's as big as the illustrator's name.

- ✔ **Free copies:** Make sure you get enough free copies to give away to your family and friends, as well as to hand out as promotional copies.

    Many publishers will send out promotional copies, including an introductory letter at no cost to the author, to important media contacts provided by the author. Find out their publicity department's standard practice and see if you can negotiate more copies if necessary.

- ✔ **Additional copies:** Make sure the price at which you can purchase additional copies is at a deep discount, typically the publisher's cost or 50 percent of the suggested retail price, which is what publishers sell the book at to most retailers (though in some cases the discount to retailers may be even steeper).

- ✔ **Option to purchase:** Just before it's about to go out of print, your book may be remaindered (sent off to discount retailers at a price significantly lower than the suggested retail price). Make sure your contract states that you'll be notified first so you have the option to purchase those copies at a certain (low) price per unit before they're sent away.

- ✔ **Royalty rates:** Royalties are specific to the format and territory, generally 10 percent total on hardcover sales and 5 to 8 percent total on trade paperback sales. Push for a *gross royalty rate* (royalty based on the suggested retail price without publisher's cost subtracted from the price) versus the *net royalty rate* (royalties based on the retail price minus the publisher's costs). Why? Because it's often hard to quantify ahead of time what the publisher considers fair, fixed costs to charge against the royalty monies owed to you, often resulting in a lower net royalty rate than you may have expected when you negotiated your contract. It's always best to go for the gross royalties. (Read the "Interview with Phalen "Chuck" Hurewitz, Esq." sidebar for more details.)

- ✔ **Escalating royalty rates:** This means that the more books you sell, the more royalties you get paid. While first-time authors often won't get the option to push for this, you can always try. Why? Because you only make more if the publisher makes more — a win-win situation as far as we are concerned. And be sure that sales for a revision to your book are counted in as additional sales for the initial edition (instead of being counted as a new book).

- ✔ **Royalties from other countries:** Make sure your negotiated royalty rates are specific about countries and languages, specifically English. Do you get the same amount of royalty for books printed in the U.S. in English and sold in Britain as you do for books sold in the U.S.? Or are Britain or Canada considered foreign sales with applicable royalty rates?

- ✔ **Copyrights:** Make sure that the agreement provides that the copyright will be in your name, not in the publisher's name. (You will not have this option in a work-for-hire agreement.) For more on copyright, see the Protecting Your Work Before You Send Anything" section earlier in this chapter.

✔ **Schedule for manuscript delivery and acceptance of manuscript (timeline and format):** If the work is not accepted, the publisher should explain, in writing, why this is so and allow for good faith changes within a designated period of time. Assuming the work has been rejected or there has been a failure of timely delivery, negotiate a kill fee that allows you to retain a portion of the advance. In the case of termination, negotiate a *first proceeds clause*, which allows for the repayment of any amounts advanced by the publisher. Make sure that it shall be from — and not greater than — the first proceeds (or the first money) paid to the writer from the work by another publisher. In the event of advance recoupment, make sure to delete the term "other payments" to ensure that the advance is repayable only from your royalties and not from your split on the licenses for the various sub rights. To be clear, add language like: "in no event shall an unearned advance be considered an overpayment."

✔ **Accounting statements (annual, semiannual, or quarterly):** Make sure that the publisher is not using *cross accounting* (sometimes called cross collateralization), meaning that this agreement is for this book only and won't be tied into the royalty accounting for subsequent titles that may or may not earn out.

✔ **Indemnity/insurance:** It's highly unlikely that you'll be able to obtain any concessions in the indemnity clause, but you should try nonetheless. If the publisher has the ability to settle claims without the prior approval of the author, make sure there is a dollar amount limitation. Furthermore, the withholding of legal expenses should be held in an interest-bearing account. Query as to whether the author might be included as an additional insured on the publisher's insurance policy.

✔ **Right to audit:** Every publishing contract should give the author the right to audit the publisher's accounting records for that book.

✔ **Publisher bankruptcy:** Some authors try to include a clause in their contract stating that if a publisher goes bankrupt, the rights to the book will revert to the author immediately.

Keep in mind that a publishing contract is drafted by the publisher and is written to minimize the publisher's risk and maximize the publisher's financial return, not the author's. You must decide for yourself the degree to which you'll give up provisions (such as getting a net royalty rate versus a gross royalty rate) in order to secure the publishing contract for your book.

Interview with Phalen "Chuck" Hurewitz, Esq.

Chuck Hurewitz is an experienced entertainment and publishing attorney with Isaacman, Kaufman & Painter, a firm in Beverly Hills. He says that it's often very difficult for new writers to get an agent, so attorneys are your next best advocates. However, the reality of what happens to new writers in negotiations is worth reading:

WCBFD: What are some of the publishing contract hot buttons today?

CH: The hot-button issues for children's book writers are about the same as the hot-button issues for all writers. The author should expect an advance appropriate to the author's talent and credentials, the amount of work involved in completing the book, and the anticipated book sales. Advances will depend on the "heat" surrounding the book — if other publishers are interested in bidding and/or if the writer has had some prior success as a writer or is a celebrity. A non-celebrity, first-time writer whose book hasn't generated a lot of heat is not likely to command a large advance. If the author of a book and the illustrator are two different individuals, the advance and royalty will be shared.

Publishers like to pay the advance in multiple installments over a longer period of time. An author would prefer fewer payments over a shorter period of time with the final payment upon delivery and acceptance of the completed book and not on publication. But many publishers will insist that the last installment be paid at the time of publication.

Most large commercial publishers still pay royalties based on the list price or retail selling price of the book, typically, 10 percent on the first 5,000 books; 12½ on the next 5,000 and 15 percent on the rest. Those royalties are referred to as *gross royalties.* But a number of smaller publishers are now paying royalties based on their net receipts. *Net receipts* represent the balance remaining after deducting the publisher's publication costs and other expenses. Gross royalties represent royalties that are calculated as a percentage of the list price of book sales proceeds without deducting any costs or expenses. The same royalty percentages based on net receipts represent about half the amount of royalties based on the list price of the book. An author should also make sure that increased royalties will be paid out at the same escalating plateaus, based on the sales of the book. So if the language of the agreement talks about net receipts rather than list price or retail selling price, you need to do the math. The royalty percentage on a net receipts basis should be twice the percentages of royalties calculated on a gross basis.

WCBFD: What terms and conditions will publishers rarely if ever give on?

CH: The basic royalties won't change. The royalty split or division on the so-called subsidiary rights is negotiable.

However, many publishers will make some adjustments in the contract form. The adjustments can include such matters as including the writer as a named insured on the publisher's errors and omissions liability insurance policy, more favorable splits with regard to licensing subsidiary rights of the publisher, the pass-through of subsidiary licensing revenue (although the publisher will rarely, if ever, allow the pass-through before the publisher's recoupment of the advance), changes in the time periods for notification in the event the publisher fails to timely publish, delivery of the manuscript, a definition of "out-of-print" and time periods to take action if the condition occurs, and limitations on the publisher's option rights regarding the author's "next work." In the case of children's books, the issue of merchandising could be significant, and the writer should attempt to reserve and retain merchandising rights.

WCBFD: What should new authors be aware of?

CH: On a first book, it is very hard to negotiate any substantial advance or significant contract changes. If the first book is successful, there will be some leeway on the agreements for future books; including the amount on the advance.

For a new writer, a publishing contract with a reputable publisher is a significant achievement. You should protect your own interests as best you can in the negotiation, but in the final analysis you should try to make the deal. A published book is an important marker on your career path as a writer.

Dealing with Rejection

A *rejection letter* is notification from someone you sent your manuscript to — usually a literary agent who you hope will represent your work to publishers or an editor who acquires new titles for a children's book publisher — that your manuscript isn't being accepted for publication. If you sent along an appropriately sized, self-addressed, stamped envelope (SASE), then your original manuscript may also accompany the rejection letter, or your manuscript may have simply ended up in someone's round file (otherwise known as the wastebasket).

Rejection is all about tenacity

Glenn Murray, co-author of *Walter the Farting Dog* (North Atlantic Books), knows all too well what it feels like to be rejected. No one wanted Murray and Kotzwinkle's story of a farting dog. Until one dark and windy night . . .

WCBFD: Tell that great story about how your book, the bestselling *Walter the Farting Dog,* finally came to be published after ten years of solid rejection.

GM: I've had a lot of requests to read manuscripts since Walter's rise to success — as if I have anything to offer! My co-author was the guy who wrote the novel *ET: The Extra-Terrestrial* (Putnam) and that still wasn't enough to get our book published. Walter's story of getting published shows that even when you try to cover all the bases, and you have an agent, it's not always enough. There's a certain amount of luck, of being in the right place, and of timing. It's amazing the difference a little time can make, especially in matters of taste or propriety. The problem was that we used the F—word [farting] in the title and throughout the book. We went out on the edge a little before the publishing world was ready for us. What's acceptable today was not acceptable ten years ago.

WCBFD: Where did the idea for *Walter the Farting Dog* come from?

GM: One night, when we were working on this kids' adventure screenplay, my co-author, Bill Kotzwinkle, was reminiscing about this dog he had met in an office supply store in town. This dog had a prodigious capacity to produce gaseous emissions. The dog was famous for this. When he let go, the entire store would clear out, it was that bad. I asked Bill if he remembered the dog's name and he said, "Yeah, it was Walter." Immediately, I could see it, the title — *Walter the Farting Dog* — blazing across the skies. "Gee, that would be a great title for a children's book!" And we sort of let it go, like a joke. Then circumstances changed, and we had to put our children's adventure screenplay away for a while. As a consolation to ourselves, I said, "Let's write that farting dog story. And we did. We laughed all day long and had a pretty good time. We wrote about a dog who was making the best of a bad situation, turning his liabilities into assets, which was what we, as writers, were trying to do as well. It was a simple, but satisfying, story, and I knew, having spent a great deal of time reading to kids in the school system, what kids like and what would grab their attention. Little did we know that we would have such a hard time selling it.

WCBFD: So what happened next?

GM: Bill has been published a bunch of times, so we sent it to his longtime agent as well as to the illustrator he had been paired with on previous books. And before we even got the agent's reaction, we got rejected by the illustrator who was not interested. But we still had high hopes. And it didn't take long before a lot of responses came in.

WCBFD: What were those responses?

GM: "We laughed and laughed, but we cannot publish this." No one wanted poor Walter. Then after five years had gone by, we sat down again and tried to soften up the manuscript a little by changing a bunch of F-words to "and he did it" and the title to *Get That Dog Outta Here!* — a change that made me pretty unhappy. But we wanted to get published and we thought it would help. It didn't; the rejections kept coming. Then, in 2001, Bill was at a dinner party, and the host asked him to get the dog story out and read it to everyone as sort of an after-dinner mint. So he did, and the entire room fell off their seats roaring with laughter. One of the guests was a publisher who said he had to publish it, even though he didn't publish children's books. That's how it all started.

WCBFD: What advice would you give fledgling writers regarding rejection?

GM: You can't be too sensitive at the beginning. The people at the other end have their guidelines about what their company wants to publish, and they have their own idea of what they are looking for. There is not much that we can do about it. But they are not out to get us. So as soon as the manuscript comes back, send it out again. If you have a manuscript in the mail, you have hope. If you don't, you are just sitting around kicking yourself in the head and no way anything will ever happen. Remember Ted Geisel. His first manuscript was rejected 26 times. That was *To Think That I Saw It on Mulberry Street* (Random House). And he, as Dr. Seuss, is the most loved children's book writer in America today. Do you think we would know about him if he were easily discouraged? Rejection is all about tenacity. As I tell the children I speak with: If you are gonna give up the second time you fall off a bicycle, you are never going to learn to ride a bicycle, either.

The bad news: You are going to get a lot of rejection letters as you travel along the path to getting published — from literary agents, editors, publishers, and maybe even from your local dogcatcher.

So what should you do when you receive a rejection letter? After having a quick cry (always keep a box of tissues handy when you open letters from publishers), you can do a number of things to turn this particular lemon into lemonade and to grow from the experience:

✔ **Take some time to cool down.** A rejection can bring your dream of getting published to a screeching halt, and it can be a very emotional event. If you find yourself upset by the rejection, take some time to cool down before you do anything related to your manuscript. Relax. Take a deep breath. Don't throw your manuscript in the fireplace.

✔ **Look for clues.** Is the rejection letter one of those form letters where someone wrote in your name after the typed-in "Dear . . . ," or is it an actual personal letter in which the editor offers advice or encouragement? If advice specific to your book is included in the letter, read it closely! These bits of info — like how to improve your manuscript or where you can find a more appropriate publisher for your book — can help you create a better book (while giving you a greater chance for eventual publishing success).

✔ **Revise your manuscript.** If the person who sent you the rejection letter took the time to give you specific advice on how to improve your manuscript, by all means take it and revise your manuscript accordingly. Editors and agents know what books will sell. Sure, they make mistakes from time to time — launching books that sink in the marketplace faster than you can spell Titanic and rejecting books that another publisher picks up and turns into a raging success — but their advice is as straight from the horse's mouth as you'll ever get, and most of the time it's dead-on accurate, as painful as it may be. Not only that, but the advice costs you nothing. In some cases, a rejection will suggest that the editor or agent will be interested in seeing the manuscript again after you make the suggested changes. This is a *big* hint to you that you're very close to selling your book, so long as you make the changes. Our advice? Make 'em!

✔ **Redo your research.** Did you send your manuscript to the right agent or publisher? Different agents and publishers specialize in different genres and types of children's books (see our extensive coverage on these topics in Chapter 2). Does your manuscript conform to the common publishing standards for that type of book? If not, then your manuscript may be rejected for that reason alone. Do your research and double-check that you sent the right manuscript to the right agent or publisher.

✔ **It's business, not personal.** Book publishing is a business. If your manuscript was rejected, the editor didn't believe the book would sell enough copies to be a profitable venture for the publisher. It's that simple. Move on and keep looking for the right publisher for your book.

Self-Publishing

Most every author has fantasized at least once or twice about the possibility of self-publishing. In the case of unpublished authors who can't seem to get an agent or publisher interested in their work, self-publishing offers the promise of still getting a book into print. For established authors who have one or more traditionally published books to their credit, self-publishing not only allows them to be free of the constraints put on them by their publishers, but also puts all the profits in their own pockets. And for the author who finally realizes that he's only making 50¢ from every book his publisher sells — and that he'll have to sell 250,000 copies to kickstart his royalty-based personal retirement plan — the siren song of self-publishing can be a very intoxicating melody indeed.

Regardless of your motivation, self-publishing is definitely worth considering. With today's digital word processing and printing technologies, prices are lower than ever to produce professional results very quickly. Of course, self-publishing involves more than just printing up a bunch of books — you also have to figure out how you'll get them distributed and sold.

Reasons to self-publish

Maybe you've huffed and puffed and still no one is interested in your book. Maybe you want complete creative control and the only way to get that, of course, is to do everything yourself. Or maybe you just want to rake in all the money. You may have one of several good reasons for taking the self-publishing road less traveled:

- **If a publisher won't take on your book, self-publishing offers you a viable (and perhaps only) alternative for getting your book into print.** Some children's book publishers reject 95 percent or more of the manuscripts they receive for consideration. Thousands of children's book manuscripts each year fail to find a home and are left languishing, lost, and unloved. Self-publishing offers rejected authors a path to being published that traditional publishers may not be willing to provide.

- **It's all yours, baby!** When you publish your own book, you keep all the rights, you decide exactly what words and illustrations lie between the covers, and you control when and where it's sold — no pesky editors or publisher marketing people to get in the way. If you're organized, willing to learn about the business, and have a knack for marketing, you can make just as much money or more as you would if your book were published by a traditional publisher.

- **You get to keep all the profits.** When you sign with a traditional publisher, the financial picture is heavily weighted in the publisher's favor and against you, the author. Of course, it's the publisher that is taking the majority of the financial risk by laying out its money to pay you an advance and direct internal resources to the development, editing, printing, distribution, and promotion of your new book. So, it's no surprise that publishing contracts reward the publisher accordingly. By controlling your costs of production, distribution, and promotion — while selling lots of books yourself — you can end up with a very healthy profit, every penny of which goes into *your* pocket!

- **You may be able to turn your successful self-published children's book into a successful, traditionally published children's book.** Very occasionally, a self-published book can sell a lot of copies or garner significant attention in the marketplace — enough to attract the interest of a traditional publisher who will then beat a path to your door to get you to agree to allow them to publish it for a second run. Traditional publishers still have an advantage over self-publishing because of their extensive distribution and sales relationships with booksellers.

Richard Paul Evans's path to self-publishing success

Are you familiar with the book *The Christmas Box* by Richard Paul Evans? According to Evans, he originally wrote and self-published the book because "I wanted to express my love to my girls [his daughters Jenna, then 6, and Allyson, then 4] in a way that would be timeless." Evans photocopied 20 copies of his manuscript and sent them to family and friends, who encouraged him to get the book published by a traditional publisher.

After he sent the manuscript to six different publishers — all of which flatly rejected his work — Evans decided to spend $5,000 of his own money to have 8,000 paperback copies of the book printed. He distributed these copies to local bookstores, where they were quickly sold at a price of $4.95 each. Flush with his initial success, Evans spent another $13,000 to have 19,000 more copies printed. One thing led to another and,

within weeks, *The Christmas Box* became a bestseller in his state — selling 240,000 copies nationally by the end of 1994 and attracting the attention of a novice editor at Simon & Schuster when it became the first self-published book to reach the number-one position on *The New York Times* bestseller list. The editor liked what she saw and signed Evans's book (along with its prequel, *Timepiece*) for $4.25 million.

Evans offers the following advice for authors considering self-publishing: "Before you decide to self-publish, start sharing your book with people around you — family, friends, and business associates. Be sure you are convinced that you have something special, because it takes a lot of work to take your book outside your own circle. And I would start with agents, not publishers."

You have a much better chance at making a success of a self-published book if it's nonfiction, or fiction geared to a very niche market. General fiction (Richard Paul Evans aside) is much harder to self-publish because it doesn't have a "hook" and is competing directly with all the other fiction in the stores. Also, you have to really understand marketing and have a way to reach consumers via a newsletter, Web site, targeted mailing lists, trade shows, and so forth to sell anything approaching a significant quantity of books. For example, a picture book about a child who has to have an operation and stay in the hospital can be displayed in doctors' offices and in hospital gift shops, and the author can attend medical conventions, send out flyers to medical centers, speak to support groups for parents of children with diseases, and the like.

When you shouldn't self-publish

Just as you may have plenty of good reasons to put your own book on the market, you're going to run across a number of reasons to pass off the work to someone else. Here are just a few:

✔ **Self-published books are taken less seriously than traditionally published books.** When your manuscript is powerful enough to attract the interest of a real, live publisher, that accomplishment says to the world that you've really achieved something (and you have). When you self-publish your manuscript, some observers automatically assume that the only thing going for it is the fact that you had enough money in your bank account to finance its publication. Truth be told, few reviewers bother reviewing self-published books, and few bricks-and-mortar bookstores carry them. Three strikes, and you're . . .

✔ **Self-publishing is hard work.** Sure, you get to put all the profits from your book directly into your pocket, but writing, designing, illustrating, laying out, and arranging for printing, distribution, and promotion of any book is no small task — that's why the first choice of most authors is to approach a publisher or agent when they have a manuscript they want to turn into a book. Believe us: The amount of success you'll achieve by self-publishing your book will be directly proportional to the amount of work you devote to the task. Even then, you get no guarantees.

✔ **Self-publishing isn't cheap.** If you think self-publishing your book means that you're going to print out an original of your manuscript on your computer and have Kinko's make and comb-bind 10 or 15 copies to send to friends as gifts, then self-publishing can be very inexpensive — you'll get by for well under $100. But if you want to do a first-class job (getting everything professionally edited, designed, illustrated, and laid out, and then having hundreds or even thousands of copies printed), then you're talking big bucks, potentially many thousands of dollars. Fortunately, the recent emergence of print-on-demand (POD) publishing, explained in the nearby "Only when you need it: Print-on-demand" sidebar, can make self-publishing much more affordable.

✔ **You may expose yourself to legal problems.** Say that you find some really beautiful photographs on the Internet that would be just perfect to illustrate your book — no problem, right? Wrong. Whenever you use someone else's work without permission, you're setting yourself up to get sued. Depending on how much money is involved, you may find that not just your book's financial standing is in jeopardy, but your own as well. Get permission for everything you use that is not your own and make sure an attorney handles all the written agreements.

✔ **You can get scammed.** A number of shady operators know that some people will do most anything to get their books into print, and these folks are very well aware of exactly what buttons to push to separate you from your hard-earned money. Be careful with self-publishing promises that seem too good to be true — they may be just that.

To self-publish often requires a renegade's personality — a willingness to go against the grain, push huge boulders uphill, scoff off rejections as misguided, and simply forge ahead. Ready to give it a try?

Only when you need it: Print-on-demand

There's a new kid on the block, and this kid's name is *print-on-demand* publishing, or POD for short. The print-on-demand process works like this: You first send your children's book (including illustrations) to a print-on-demand publisher. You pay a fee, and then the publisher's staff designs and lays out your book and submits it to you for review. After you give the green light, your book is immediately made available for anyone to order — in any quantity they want.

Although many print-on-demand publishers are in the marketplace, the big three are currently Xlibris (www.xlibris.com), a "strategic partner" of publishing giant Random House; iUniverse (www.iuniverse.com), partly owned by large book chain Barnes & Noble; and Author's House (www.authorshouse.com). So what does a typical print-on-demand publisher offer?

The primary purpose of a print-on-demand publisher is to sell publishing services to you, the aspiring children's book author. Some services include designing the interior and covers, getting your book listed with the big distributors and online stores, printing on-demand as orders come in, and paying royalties on each sale. Here's a list of what a typical publishing plan offers its customers (at the time this book is about to go to press):

✔ **Basic service:** If you want some control over the look and feel of your book, the basic service is for you. You can choose from various interior templates and cover templates to help you customize your book. Your book is available in trade paperback edition. This service costs you around $500.

✔ **Professional service:** This is where they hand you the steering wheel and let you drive. You have even more templates to choose from than basic service, and you get to customize them. You can also add tables and an index to your book, which is available in hardback and trade paperback editions (see our sidebar discussion on what this means in Chapter 2). It's also registered for a copyright. This service costs you around $900.

✔ **Custom service:** This service offers the highest possible control over your book's design. Custom includes all features of professional service but allows you to talk to a designer, combining your creative input and their expertise to achieve the personalized design you want. This service costs you around $1,600.

Of course, in addition to these up-front fees, you pay every time you order a copy of your book (beyond the author copies included in your plan, if any). Print-on-demand books can be rather expensive — from $15 to $50 or more per copy for a trade paperback. Ouch!

Chapter 18

Following the Publishing Process

*B*efore your manuscript makes its way to a child's eyes and ears, it has to go through an entire publishing process. And the better you understand this process, the more enjoyable it will be for you — and for the publishing professionals with whom you will soon be working.

In this chapter, we give you a general look at what the publishing world is like. Chapter 16 gives you additional information on how to find an agent, and Chapter 17 shares the ins and outs of finding the right publisher for you, signing a contract, and self-publishing.

Moving through the Publishing Process

You've hit the big time! Your manuscript has been accepted by an editor who seems to think you're the hottest writer since Lemony Snicket; you've signed your contract; and you're wondering when you get to start signing copies of your masterpiece at bookstores all over the country. Hold onto your horses. The process has only just begun. Your main contact in the publishing house will be your editor, who may be called an assistant editor, an associate editor, a senior editor, an editor-in-chief, an editorial director, or George. Regardless, this professional guides you through the editorial, layout, and design stages with the production and art departments. Last but not least, your book reaches the marketing stage. Read on for details.

The editorial process

Your manuscript might have been acquired by an editor with a heady title (editor-in-chief) or one not so (assistant editor), but you should realize that titles mean different things at different houses, and whereas the assistant editor at one house may be the newbie just out of college, the assistant editor at another house is next in line to the editorial director's job. (For additional info, check out the nearby sidebar, "Who does what? A cacophony of titles.") There are enough checks and balances along the way in the editorial process that you do not have to worry — you are in good hands. The editorial department will take care of you and your manuscript.

Who does what? A cacophony of titles

Although titles and duties and hierarchy differ vastly from house to house, here's a quick overview of who does what in the editorial department.

Editorial assistant: This is most likely the person who discovered your manuscript in the *slush pile* — that stack of unsolicited manuscripts that aspiring children's book writers send to publishers with a hope and a prayer that their book will make it past the big bad wolf's world of rejection. The editorial assistant is usually relegated to reading slush, photocopying, posting letters, straightening up the production samples, organizing the reference library, and doing other people's research. Despite their busy schedules, we have found that these people are often the most diligent communicators, so if you're looking for someone who may take a minute to answer your many questions, the editorial assistant is a good person to start with.

Assistant editor: The next person up is the assistant editor, sometimes known as an associate editor. This person has some time under his belt. He may be the right hand to a higher up or a full-fledged editor making slightly better than entry-level pay. This person usually has a degree in English, an appreciation for children's literature, and enough ambition to run his own department one day. He edits, maintains in-house style

guides, shepherds projects through the editorial process — but is never the last word, handing over final sign-off to a more senior editor.

Copyeditor: A copyeditor (often spelled *copy editor*) looks at grammar, spelling, punctuation, bolding or italicizing, continuity of details, and accuracy of facts. If you've written a nonfiction book, with lots of facts to be verified, though you are the one ultimately responsible for accuracy, chances are a copy editor will be looking closely at your manuscript.

Proofreader: The proofreader makes sure all the editor's changes, your changes, and the copy editor's changes have been incorporated into the final text, as well as looking for errors in layout such as extra spaces between words, a paragraph that's not indented, dropped quotation marks, repeated text, and the like. Sometimes the copyeditor and proofreader are the same person.

Editor: The editor acquires and edits manuscripts, helps choose illustrators for projects, reviews or writes catalog copy (used to sell your book to bookstores), and manages a list of titles. The editor usually has at least three years of actual editing experience in children's publishing and is an up-and-comer. This is the most common title in the editorial department.

Senior editor: The senior editor, also often known as the executive editor, has put in at least five years on the job. He probably has a few junior editors he's mentoring and may assign writers and illustrators to projects he initiates. Along with acquiring, commissioning, and editing, he reviews contracts, hires and fires staffers, and works closely with publicity and marketing departments.

Editor-in-chief: An editor-in-chief or editorial director is a dedicated professional with at least seven to ten years in publishing. She has her own authors and illustrators as well as responsibility for the overall development of the title lists each season. Along with more pay, more respect, and a reputation (everyone who's been around a while in publishing gets one of those), she has responsibility for the financial success of her books. She may also manage the department's budget. There's a lot more administrative work and staff management at this level, but she

still gets to handpick books to edit during the year to keep her editorial skills honed.

Publisher: If the editorial director isn't responsible for the budget, then the publisher surely is. Often culled from talented sales or marketing staff, publishers don't always have hands-on editorial experience (though many do), but they do have a keen instinct for what will sell and what won't — if they don't have this instinct, they don't last very long in their lofty positions. Publishers manage the entire editorial, production, and art departments and are often the ones who wield the big guns when a publishing house is trying to seduce new talent or sign on a hot, new license. The publisher, together with the sales and marketing directors, determines a title's initial print run and the monies the publisher will ultimately spend to market and publicize a title. Yes, indeed, the publisher is Zeus: He sits on the throne and wields the lightning.

The editorial department is responsible for creating, identifying, and buying (acquiring) new titles and then developing them into a finished form that can be handed off to production for printing and then to sales for distribution to bookstores. Until it comes time to work with the public relations department to generate consumer interest in the book, the vast majority of author interactions are with people in the editorial department.

Before your manuscript finds its way to the printed page, it will be edited by your publisher's editorial department. In most cases, your primary editorial contact, your editor, deals with the overall story structure, word choices, and writing style. A copyeditor looks at the nitty-gritty of your grammar, spelling, bolding or italicizing, continuity of details, and so on. The proofreader makes sure all these changes have been incorporated into the final text, as well as looking for errors in layout such as extra spaces between words, a paragraph that's not indented, and other word design issues. Sometimes the copyeditor and proofreader are the same person. The editors also consider broader issues, such as whether you need to seek permission for incorporating someone else's work (such as a snippet from a poem or song, or a character that is copyrighted by some other author or company) into your own and whether the illustrations fit the text.

After your manuscript is edited, it is sent to you for review. In the days when manuscripts were typewritten instead of computer processed, manuscripts were edited by hand, using a system of symbols (called *proofreaders' marks*) that signified such actions as inserting a word, applying a bold or italicized typeface, closing up the space between two words, and so on. Today, many manuscripts are edited within the computer files in which they were created, using the word-processing software's ability to track changes. You can then accept or reject the changes as you desire. Most editors still have to work with hardcopy proof sheets during some point in a book's pre-press life, which means that they will be using proofreaders' marks. Look in any good dictionary under *proofreaders' marks* to decipher them.

Editors may also have *queries* — questions — for you to answer within the manuscript. For example, your editor may wonder if you didn't mean to call that purple polka-dotted dinosaur in your story an Apatosaurus instead of a Tyrannosaurus when the context clearly suggests an Apatosaurus.

Your job after receiving the edited manuscript is to rewrite it, responding to the edits and queries in the process. Your editors are professional editors — they do this for a living day in and day out — so, chances are their edits will be right on target. But, as the book's author, you are expected to defend your word usage if you feel strongly that you've made the right choices. In this case, you need to respond with your own rationale as to why your approach should be kept intact.

Job titles, like age-level book specifications in children's publishing, overlap duty-wise from publishing house to publishing house. In some houses, an associate editor is equal in experience to the editorial director; in others he defines the lowest echelon of entry-level. The larger the publisher, the more titles published, the more personnel needed to manage them, and thus the longer the chain of command from top to bottom.

The production process

After you return your rewritten manuscript to the publisher, and after a copy-editor has made sure everyone's changes have been incorporated, it will go into *production*. In some cases, you'll have one last chance to look at your book before it is published. At this final author review, you receive page proofs of your book to approve. The *page proofs* or *galley proofs* show you exactly what the pages of your book will look like when it is published. If you want to make any changes, speak now or forever hold your peace.

The *production director* is probably the person most crucial to the editor's creative success. This person helps determine the materials used in the creation of the book. From the type of paper or board used, to the range of touch and feel materials made available, to the affordable and creative packaging alternatives — the production director has to juggle everything she knows about what materials cost with all the specific and otherworldly demands made on her by the editor who, if she had her druthers, would fashion her book out of solid platinum with a diamond encrusted spine.

Juggling the numbers on a spreadsheet often referred to as a *P&L* (profit and loss statement), the production director costs out the editor's materials preferences (type of paper, hard or soft cover, and so on) while figuring out how many books can be printed and at what cost per book. It may sound like a tedious job, but in reality, if a production director is a highly creative sort, she can make or break many a book — especially where novelty books are concerned, because often a novelty book's success is dependent on the cool and unique materials used in its manufacturing.

After she determines which materials are affordable and provides samples to the editor, the production director (or the managing editor at some houses) will oversee the book's journey from a digital file through the production process at the printing and assembly plant and into the warehouses as a finished book. After the book's *specs* (size, materials, paper type, and so on) are determined, the book goes to the art department for illustrations (if they haven't come with the manuscript) and for layout.

What happens in the art department

After your manuscript has been acquired, and the format specifications priced and finalized, the editor handling the book and the art director sit down. If the book is illustrated, they go over the illustrations and decide whether any could use improvement and what would work best for a cover. If there are no illustrations yet, they go over their top choices for who should illustrate the book. If there is only one clear choice that they both agree on, then they contact that illustrator and hope he has an opening in his schedule. If the timing is not right, they move on to another choice. When more than one illustrator's name comes up, they are contacted in order of preference until the perfect (arranged) marriage is settled.

The art director then assigns the book to a *book designer,* whose job is to come up with an overall design for the book and its cover. The elements considered include cover design, type design, endpapers (if any), chapter heads (if any), page layout, and other artistic considerations that may be format-specific (see Chapter 2 for details on parts of a book). For example, if it is a picture book, the designer works with the illustrator to make sure there is a pleasing mixture of single-page art, vignettes, and full-spread art and decide whether the pages ought to have a border treatment. It is the illustrator who initially decides what image goes on what page, but his instincts and experience combined with the designer's result in what you ultimately see throughout the book.

When writers get a say, and when they don't

If your first book miraculously sells out and is *reprinted* (the magic word for everyone involved, meaning it gets a second printing or more), and your second book does likewise (proving that you are not prone to the sophomore curse), then you have clout and may get a say in what your next book's illustrations look like or how it is designed. Your clout is directly proportional to how much say you have in the process: The more clout you have, the more people listen to you.

This process sounds largely undemocratic — and it is — but that's not necessarily bad. During the process of writing and having a few books published, you become more experienced. You absorb more. And with experience come the incisive questions and visionary suggestions that really open up the discussion and make you the sort of writer the publisher wants to hear from. There are instances (and entire boutique publishing companies) that prove this process wrong, and we say amen to them. But the chances are good that you will end up with a larger publisher who abides by the rule of not listening much to the whims of new writers.

Some technical issues a designer may deal with include scanning the art into the software program used by the publisher and positioning it on the page with the type, assuring that the image will extend to the edge of the finished piece, considering any special colors such as gold or silver or any fun materials such as foil or fabric, and indicating page sizes to the printer. If the cover is to have *embossing* (creating a raised impression on the surface) or *debossing* (creating a sunken impression on the surface) at the printing stage, the designer has to work with the specific typeface that looks good with those techniques. In short, the book designer is the one responsible for taking the manuscript and the art plus the production specifications and making the book a satisfying product for the reader.

If you aren't the illustrator, chances are you won't get to see or hear about any of the process happening in the art department. It's really up to the editor if she wants to share what's going on with the illustrations with you. Most likely, she will not have the time to give you a courtesy look. If you are the illustrator as well (or if you've partnered with one), you or the illustrator will, of course, be in touch with the art director throughout the art production process. The illustrator and the art director form a team through this process whose goal is to create the best images for the manuscript, ones that add yet another dimension of meaning and style to the book.

After the art is completed, the images are scanned into a computer and into the layout created by the book designer. When all tweaks have been made regarding sizing and placement of the art and text, the digitized files and the original art are sent to the printer to begin the printing process. If you are the illustrator, you get to see it before it goes to the printer. If not, you might get to see it when the *first proofsheets* (the first color version of the pages, often referred to as *first proofs*) come back for checking. At this point, everyone from the editor in charge of the project, the copyeditor, the book designer, the art director, and the production director all check over the proofs to make sure the images and the words came out the way they expected. They might even send them to you to check, but that depends on both the schedule and the practices of the house. Changes, major or minor, lead to a second set of proofs and on and on until it's perfect.

The book then goes on to get printed. If it is a novelty book with special paper mechanisms, or if it includes the packaging of a book-plus item (see Chapter 2 for novelty formats), then the proofsheets get built into a 3-D dummy so that the publisher can make sure everything works the way it should and make adjustments if not. Right before the book is bound to the cover, especially if it is a picture book, *F&Gs* (folded and gathered sheets from the actual print run made ready for binding but not yet bound) are sent to the publishing house. At this stage, these pages are simply informational, a pre-bound copy of the book that can be sent to you, the writer, the illustrator, reviewers, or others who might be interested in seeing the book before it is bound and shipped to the warehouse for distribution to bookstores and other selling venues. This is when the marketing and publicity machines really start to make their presence known.

Editors and art directors detest creativity by committee. At least those worth their creative salt can't stand it. The more subjective opinions that have to be taken into consideration in the creative process, the more diluted the vision oftentimes becomes — and the worse the finished product (your book) ultimately is. So let the editorial and art pros do what they are paid to do and you do what you're best at: Getting on with writing your *next* book or devising some very cool marketing and publicity stunts for this one (see Chapter 19), because that's exactly where your book is going to really need your help.

Marketing and publicity

Ever wonder what the difference is between marketing and public relations (PR)? Well, here's the short version. The *marketing* department is the one that gets your book into all the different venues it needs to be in, and the *PR team* lets everyone know about it. Because no matter how fabulous your book is, no matter how lovely the illustrations are, no matter how great the matte paper and the embossed cover are — it all matters not one whit if the book is nowhere to be found and no one knows it's there.

Choosing your battles

Chuck Murphy is a rarity in the children's book world. Not only does he write children's books, he also illustrates and designs them and even engineers the paper to be used in the pop-ups or pull-tabs or other paper mechanisms for them. It's highly unusual to wear so many hats in this dog-eat-dog children's book world, but Chuck enjoys his varied duties. See what he has to say about it.

WCBFD: Is there a special satisfaction you get from being able to both write and illustrate your books?

CM: Yes, certainly. Most of my work so far has been in mechanical and pop-up books. The process of moving from idea to manuscript to mechanisms and layout and finally illustration is pretty complex. Being able to design the book right from the roughest concept to the finished illustrations allows me to juggle those tasks while keeping focused on my original vision for the book. I like having that control over the finished book.

WCBFD: How does being a writer/illustrator/designer all rolled into one make it easier or harder when working with publishers?

CM: The process is *much* easier. It cuts the number of memos in half at least. Things just move a lot faster with fewer people involved. Of course, the bad news is that if there are problems or mistakes, there's only one person to blame. (Obviously, that would be the editor — just kidding!)

WCBFD: Can you relate an anecdote of a particularly difficult moment you've had with a publisher? What did you do to work through it?

CM: Surprisingly, the difficulties I've encountered with publishers are not creative ones, but are almost always about money. Like many creative professionals that I know, I am uncomfortable bargaining over the monetary value of my work. So the continual problem I encounter is negotiating the financial aspects of a publishing contract.

I work through it by pretending to myself that I am a tough author's agent. Of course, the smart thing to do would be to actually sign on with an agent, but so far I've managed on my own.

WCBFD: Are there any special issues you have to deal with when illustrating other authors' works?

CM: Yeah, suppressing my desire to rewrite the whole thing. Once I get past that, it's a matter of getting into the author's head a bit.

WCBFD: What do you do when you and a publisher's art director don't see eye to eye?

CM: Switch eyes. That's actually not a joke. Often a third party's opinion can be helpful. Of course, the third party has to be someone both of you respect. Barring that, I've discovered that being able to verbally defend your creative choices is quite valuable. And it's very important to pick your battles. Nobody wants to work with a prima donna.

WCBFD: How do you deal with those times when your vision of a book is beyond what your editor can comprehend?

CM: I create books for toddlers to kindergarteners. What's not to get? Actually, since I've done quite a few of these kinds of books, my editors know what to expect from my work.

WCBFD: Which contract issues are most important to you and why?

CM: The contracts can be very intimidating and really do require an attorney's review. For pop-up books especially, foreign rights are very important, because these editions can sometimes double the sales numbers. Some publishers insist on worldwide rights, but put practically no effort into selling foreign editions. Also, the publisher will sometimes want to put all of your earned royalties into a "pool" covering any and all titles that you may have with that publisher. This is just not acceptable.

WCBFD: Do you have any pet peeves when it comes to the book business?

CM: Art directors who want the flavor-of-the-month art styles, or "edgy" art for five year-olds!

WCBFD: Why children's books?

CM: The short answer is that I have worked in several forms of advertising and commercial design, and I often wondered if what I was doing was of any use to anyone. In the 30 years or so that I've been creating books for children, that question just doesn't come up.

What marketing does

The marketing department is responsible for generating all the materials used to sell the book as well as riding herd on trade shows and particular kinds of promotional efforts. Here are some things they are responsible for:

- **Sell sheets:** Single sheets of paper with all the information pertinent to a title, such as cover, price, author and illustrator bios, and ISBN and bar-code numbers.

- **Book displays:** Metal or plastic racks and corrugated displays that appear on retailer floors, the design of which the marketing department (in conjunction with the sales reps) oversees, along with determining the book mixes and quantities that go in them.

- **Cross promotions:** Usually done with licensed titles, these are promotions in which a Harry Potter (for instance) book is paired with a Harry Potter costume to increase customer awareness of both items at (let's just say) Halloween.

- **Account-specific promotions:** Promotions at store level, such as a gift with purchase (like posters or sticker kits), buy-one-get-one free, or buy 2 get $1 off deals. These help place a book in the bookstore and can also help the sell-through of a book (*sell-through* means that the book is actually purchased by a customer).

- **Catalogs:** Four-color printed booklets that features every title the publishing house offers for a particular season.

- **Trade shows:** These are the big children's publishing trade shows, such as BookExpo America (www.bookexpoamerica.com), the Bologna and Frankfurt book fairs, as well as all the library association (ALA) conventions, where the publishing-house marketing people can make an appearance and tout their latest offerings.

Catalogs are usually the first of the materials to be produced, as they need to be sent out to bookstores and libraries well in advance of the publication date of the book. Trade shows have dates fixed well in advance, so books are scheduled in as they become available. As the publication date nears, and book details are finalized, sell sheets are produced, and account-specific and cross promotions are buttoned up. Generally, authors (especially beginning writers) have very little to do with the good folks in marketing, except perhaps to receive a copy of the spring or fall catalog in the mail. This means that they have little or no say in the contents of these materials (they may never even see them) or in the nature or kinds of promotions that the marketing folks pursue.

What publicity does

When it comes to the *publicity* or *public relations* department, the story is quite different. Although the marketing department does most of its work in-house with the sales team, the publicity department is more hands-on and they work with the top writers, illustrators, and media. Public relations include

- Setting up author appearances and signings; setting up book tours
- Getting articles written in magazines and newspapers; placing advertising in trade magazines, such as *Publishers Weekly*
- Generating Web site features
- Sending out press releases about new books and book-related licensed products
- Sending out promotional copies to major media outlets and reviewers in the hopes of getting attention and copy
- Generating radio interviews

And this is where you can help. Be sure to check out Chapter 19 for a complete discussion on how to promote your book like a pro.

What to Expect After Your Book Is Published

The publishing process can be a long one — longer and more involved than most first-time authors ever imagined. But one day you'll wake up to a knock on your door. Standing there will be an overnight delivery person with a copy of your book in his hand. Your book is published!

Now what?

Well, now it's time for you and your publisher to sell it. (In fact, your publisher will have already started the selling process well before your book hits the printing press. See the previous section on marketing and publicity to find out how.) And if you want to put extra effort into promoting your book on your own, definitely check out Chapter 19. But first, make sure you know what to expect.

Dispelling the myths

A number of myths about selling a brand-new children's book drive the expectations of authors and publishers. We list some of the more common ones here:

✔ **Books sell themselves.** This is one of those myths very common to many authors-to-be. Regardless of the fact that your brand-new book may have a flashy cover, a snappy title, a top-notch illustrator, a compelling story line, a ready-made fan club among your family and friends, or any number of other favorable attributes, it is in competition with hundreds — perhaps thousands — of similar new products released to the public every year. Books don't sell themselves; people sell books, primarily through their marketing and PR efforts. But even with all the marketing and PR in the world, if the book doesn't get the buzz it deserves and it doesn't catch on in the marketplace — and you've only got a few months at most to get the attention of customers — it will likely die a slow and lonely death.

✔ **Publishers do all the marketing.** Many authors — especially new ones — erroneously think that the division of labor in publishing is very clear: It's the author's job to write the book and the publisher's job to sell it. That's not exactly how the business works. Actually, while your publisher will carry out at least the minimum marketing and publicity necessary, such as getting your book into catalogs, talking up your book to potential buyers (primarily, those working for bookstores and libraries), and sending out press releases, your publisher also expects you to do your share of selling, too.

✔ **Writers do all the marketing.** Many publishers select particular authors in the hopes that, through their contacts or presence in the media (such as writing a weekly newspaper column), or because of their reputations (such as being a nationally recognized expert in childhood development), or because of their unique selling platforms (such as hosting a popular children's television show), they will be able to sell a lot of books with little or no involvement on the part of the publisher. Even so, a publishing company won't expect the writer to do everything. The truth is that although a particular author may be in a unique position to sell a particular book better than most, it's unlikely that he'll be able to do it all on his own without the help and support of his publisher.

✔ **All successful writers get to go on book tours.** The reality is that book tours are reserved for the fabulously successful children's book authors and illustrators (can you say at least 500,000 copies sold?) and are actually few and far between. The cost of these jaunts — which include transportation from venue to venue, hotels, meals, local personal assistants and drivers, and incidentals — are simply prohibitive, unless so much revenue is being generated by the star author or illustrator that the publisher feels the book's sales will further benefit from the publicity generated by a tour. Even if your first book sells well and is reprinted, your publisher probably won't spring for a book tour until you've had a string of successes.

✔ **You can quit your day job now.** Very few children's book authors and illustrators make a living at it. It takes many books, lots of sales, and the persistence to continually produce high-quality books. If you become prolific and successful, you may one day be able to spend all day, every day, honing your craft.

Partnering with your publisher

The reality of book marketing and publicity is that you and your publisher are in a partnership; it is in both of your interests for your book to sell well, so you should both do everything you can to publicize and promote it. For you — the author of a children's book — this means that you should

✔ Arrange for readings and signings in bookstores.

✔ Try to get interviewed by local newspaper and television reporters.

✔ Put your book in the running for awards and prizes.

✔ Offer to do readings in schools and libraries.

✔ Hire your own publicist, if you really want to create a buzz.

✔ Do some crazy, off-the-wall publicity stunts.

The simple fact is this: There's no such thing as too much publicity. The more publicity your book gets — whether it's you or your publisher that generates it — the better your book will sell. And that's a result that's in the interest of both you and your publisher.

Don't wait for your publisher to do everything related to the marketing and publicizing of your book. There's a lot you can do yourself to help put your book on the road to success. For more details on doing your own publicity, be sure to check out Chapters 19 and 21.

Chapter 19

Donning Your Publicity Cap

· ·

In This Chapter

▶ Publicizing your book yourself

▶ Doing book tours, in-store signings, and more

▶ Hiring a publicist to help you

· ·

Getting your book onto a bookstore shelf is only one part of the thrill of being a published children's book author. The other part — which is just as important — is getting your book *off* the bookstore shelf and into the hands of a child. And you must play a big part in making that happen.

In this chapter, we discuss publicizing and promoting your books. Not only do we address some of the tried-and-true techniques for building a buzz around your books, we take a good look the pros and cons of hiring a professional publicist and doing book tours, readings, and more.

Doing Your Own Publicity

You can have the greatest idea for a children's book ever — it can be amply illustrated, lusciously lyrical, and beautifully conceived — but that doesn't mean your particular piece of kid candy is going to sell. Unfortunately, more than a few great children's books have failed to reach their intended audiences, often because the intended audience never heard about the book in the first place and therefore didn't buy it.

And that's what publicity is all about — getting the word out to the people who may be interested in buying your book.

Put together a publicity plan

The thought of doing your own book publicity can be both exciting and overwhelming. Today, you have an almost unlimited number of potential media (and nonmedia) opportunities available to publicize your book. Some of the major categories of opportunities include

- Advertising
- Awards and prizes
- Bestseller lists
- Blogs (Web logs)
- Book reviews
- Internet chats
- Magazines
- Newsletters
- Newspapers
- Public appearances (in schools, bookstores, shopping malls, trade shows, concerts, and more)
- Radio
- Television

Of course, some of these possibilities offer a greater payoff for your investment of time and money than others. And that's really what a good publicity campaign is all about — getting the most exposure for your book with whatever budget you have available.

Every great publicity campaign begins with a plan, a written description of the specific things you'll do to promote your book — like sending out press releases and press kits, doing radio interviews, local book signings, and so forth — and when you'll do them.

So, where do you, as an aspiring, motivated, and energized children's book author, start? With some simple questions:

✔ Will your publisher create a press release and send it out to a wide variety of media contacts across the nation?

✔ Will your publisher assign a publicist to work on scheduling radio and television interviews or set up book signings at bookstores in your area?

✔ Will your publisher send you out on a book tour or buy advertising for your book in newspapers in the top 25 media markets or in national magazines aimed at parents?

✔ What kind of publicity can you do that won't duplicate what your publisher plans to do that can leverage and supplement your publisher's efforts?

If, for example, your publisher plans to create and send out a press release, are there people you know who should receive it? Great! Send the names and contact information to your publisher. If your publisher plans to assign a publicist to schedule radio and television interviews, offer to create a list of eight to ten questions and answers that hosts can use to interview you.

But regardless of what your publisher does on your book's behalf, you can do many things to supplement your publisher's promotional efforts. In the following sections, we consider some of the most common (and most effective) parts of your publicity plan.

Not every media outlet is interested in what you have to offer. Whether you're sending out press kits or trying to get booked for an interview on a radio show, make sure you target the places that have an interest in what you have to say. Make sure your book is interesting, topical, or relevant to the media outlet you're targeting. For example, if your children's book is about a young girl's journey of self-discovery in 18th Century England, then you probably shouldn't bother sending your press release to producers of sports radio talk shows or agriculture reports. You're wasting your time and money, and you're wasting the time of whoever gets your press release.

Send out press releases

The lowest common denominator for most any effort to publicize a book is the tried-and-true press release. A *press release* (also known as a *media* or *news* release) is simply a brief, written notice of some newsworthy event — in this case, the publication of your book — that is sent to anyone and everyone you think may be even remotely interested in mentioning your children's book in their newspaper, television show, or other media outlet.

Press release basics

A press release is most often one — and never more than two — pages in length. Work hard to keep it to only one page. The key parts of a well-written press release contain the following:

- ✔ **Release date:** The media will want to know how soon they can release articles or stories based on your press release. When publicizing any book, you don't want to put your publicity campaign into high gear too early; that is, more than a month or two before the book is published and available for purchase. Pushing your book too soon will only result in frustrated customers who can't find your book when they go looking for it in bookstores. (The exception to this is magazines, which often work up to six months in advance; you'll want to take this into account because if you wait until your release date, it'll no longer be timely.) When you *are* ready to get the word out about your book, your press release heading should read (in capital letters): FOR IMMEDIATE RELEASE.

- ✔ **Headline:** Here's your big opportunity to get your reader's attention with a punchy, one-sentence hook that will make your audience want to read more. Be creative and have fun. Capitalize the first letter of all the words your headline.

- ✔ **City, state, date (when you're sending out the release):** Your reader wants to know where you are and how timely the press release is (news gets stale fast).

- ✔ **Introductory paragraph:** Here's another opportunity to get your reader's attention and have them yearning to learn more. Write a strong introductory paragraph that includes who, what, when, where, why, and how about your book — as concisely as possible.

- ✔ **Body:** This is the heart of your press release, where you provide more detail about what your book is about and why it's so darn special. The body should be at least two paragraphs long (but remember — keep your press release to no more than a page).

- ✔ **Biography:** A brief biography of the book's author — you.

- ✔ **Detailed contact information:** The name, address, phone number, fax number, Web site URL, and e-mail address of the person to contact for more information about the book.

Here's what a press release using the preceding elements might look like:

FOR IMMEDIATE RELEASE

New Kid's Book Digs Deep Into the Past

Chicago, IL, January 5, 2010 — Bestselling children's book author Divvy Bobivy digs deep into the Egyptian pyramids in her new book *Who Built the Pyramids?* published by Acme Press in January 2010 and available now for $9.99 at Barnes & Noble, Borders, Amazon.com, and fine book retailers nationwide.

In what promises to be her next blockbuster children's book, Divvy Bobivy blows the lid off centuries of myths and misinformation surrounding the mysterious Egyptian pyramids. An amateur student of archaeology, Bobivy has long wanted to write a book that would bring ancient history to life for its young readers, while finding out the truth behind these mysterious structures. Says Bobivy, "I've long had a fascination with the pyramids — where they came from, who built them, how they were built. This book brings it all together for me, in a fun and fact-filled way."

Author Bobivy has tapped into a huge potential audience with her latest book. A recent study by researchers at Tinker Toy Tech shows that 79 percent of all readers age 8 to 12 years are interested in learning more about the ancient pyramids. This group of influential potential readers numbers in the millions.

For additional information, contact Banana Fanna at 312-555-1212.

About Divvy Bobivy: Divvy Bobivy is a bestselling children's book author who has written or co-written more than 25 titles, including the blockbusters *What's That Smell?* and *Baby, You Can Drive My Car.*

CONTACT INFORMATION:

Banana Fanna

ABC Book Promoters

312-555-1212 (voice)

312-555-1213 (fax)

banana@abcbookpromoters.com

www.abcbookpromoters.com

Where to send your press release

Now that you've got your press release, what do you do with it? Our advice is to send it (via mail, fax, or e-mail) to anyone you think may have an interest in reading it. This includes newspaper reporters, radio talk show hosts and producers, Webmasters, magazine editors, bookstore owners, and all your personal contacts, as well.

Address the press release to a specific individual in an organization. A press release addressed to a specific person has a much better chance of landing on someone's desk and getting read, which means that you have a much better chance of getting the media attention you seek.

In addition to your own list of places to send your press release, you may also consider sending it out over the Web. Though not specifically devoted to publicizing books, a few of the most effective of these outlets include:

- ✔ www.businesswire.com
- ✔ www.internet.com
- ✔ www.prnewswire.com
- ✔ www.prweb.com

Put together a press kit

If you really want to get noticed by the media, you have a couple of choices: You can sit at your desk or in your office, staring at your phone and waiting for it to ring — or you can take action. If you've already prepared and released a press release — great! If not, that's the first thing you or your publisher should do to publicize your book.

If you really want to get someone in the media interested in your new book, then you may have to take an additional step: preparing a press kit.

A *press kit* is a collection of press materials that is sent to the media (radio, television, newspapers, magazines, Web sites) to get them interested in covering your book. The press kit is actually a folder containing some of the most important documents relating to your book, including things like

- ✔ A one- to two-page press release that describes your book as breaking news (see the preceding section).

- ✔ A two-paragraph to one-page bio with interesting tidbits describing you and your background: "As a nationally syndicated columnist, Divvy has been interviewed on *The Oprah Winfrey Show* and CNN. . . ."

✔ A bulleted fact sheet or essay-style backgrounder about your book: "Two years of research showed that pandas don't actually prefer bamboo leaves. . . ."

✔ A FAQ (frequently asked questions) or eight to ten suggested questions the reporter could/should ask you during an interview: "How did bells become so important to the story?" or "As a full-time mom, how do you find time to write?"

✔ Copies of past press clippings (to show that you're newsworthy) and/or a list of past and future signings/events/shows (showing relevance, competence, and experience).

✔ A sample article (basically, a short version of your press release) that a busy reporter could print verbatim if she desired.

✔ Photos, including headshots of the author, illustrator, and/or book cover.

✔ A copy of your book (depending on how many free books you negotiated for in your contract, see Chapter 17).

✔ Giveaways such as bookmarks, posters, or pencils that your publisher may produce to get word-of-mouth advertising (media folks love freebies).

It takes time and money to put together a winning press kit. You can save a lot of money by writing the material yourself, printing it using your own computer and printer, and then making copies at a local copy store.

A press kit is expensive — especially if you include a copy of your book — so carefully target your recipients.

If you have your own Web site (something we highly recommend and discuss later in this chapter), be sure to make a downloadable version of your press kit readily available to your online visitors. The beauty of putting your press kit on your Web site is that it's available anytime, anyplace, and you get to save the considerable cost of making copies and mailing them out to who knows where. Another plus: You can make changes and updates quickly and easily. The best approach is to use a program that allows you to convert the pages of your press kit into documents that can be easily displayed, downloaded, and printed by visitors to your site.

Book radio and television spots

In the bang-for-the-buck department, it's hard to beat getting interviewed on a radio or television show. Shows on major radio and television stations reach a very large audience. If you get the call for an interview with Katie Couric on *Today* or Larry King on CNN, you'll probably think you've died and gone to heaven.

You simply can't buy this kind of exposure for your book. But what you or your publisher *can* buy is the publicity campaign behind your book that gets it in front of the producers or hosts who are constantly on the lookout for interesting people with fascinating stories.

Here are some tips for getting booked for radio or television interviews:

- **Understand your market.** Nothing turns off a radio or television producer, program director, *booker* (a person who's job it is to sign up people to interview or feature), or host than being approached by someone who seems to have no idea what the show is about and who the audience is. Research the stations, networks, and shows you're interested in — get their schedules and check out their Web sites. And tune in. Don't even think about pitching yourself before you have done your research.

- **Have a hook.** Why should the radio or television producer or radio host book you for this show? What is it about you or your book that is going to turn their audience on? If you want to be booked, you've got to have a hook — the aspect of your story that is going to rivet viewers and listeners and keep them from changing the station. What's your hook?

- **Be selective.** Don't send your press release out to 1,000 random radio and television stations — instead, pick out 15 to 25 to specifically target with your message. Work those prospects thoroughly and then select another batch of stations. Be sure the show is appropriate for your topic and that it will reach a large enough audience to be worth your effort. (A cable access-only show that plays at 3:30 a.m. on Sunday mornings, for example, may not be the best use of your time, unless you're seeking some on-air practice time.)

- **Target a live human.** Mailing your press release to your list of radio and television stations without naming the specific person it should go to is a one-way ticket to the nearest trash can. Instead, target a specific show, get the name and fax number or e-mail address for whoever books guests (usually a producer, program director, or booker — sometimes the host), and send your press release to that person directly.

- **Be persistent, accessible, and flexible.** You never know when you'll get the call for an interview or appearance. Be persistent — stay in the minds of those doing the booking for your targeted show by sending a press release every once in a while — and be accessible and flexible in the event the show needs someone to fill in unexpectedly (like when another guest fails to show or has to cancel an appearance).

Build a Web site for your book

Today, building a Web site to display, promote, and sell your book is considered an important element in an effective publicity campaign. And although the process of building a site was, until only a few years ago, an arcane and often difficult (and expensive) undertaking, a number of simple and low-cost options are available to the budding Webmaster.

Options for building your book's site

The easiest and least expensive of these options is to set up a site with a basic Web hosting provider such as GeoCities (www.geocities.com) or America Online (www.aol.com). Such providers offer a variety of simplified tools and templates to help you get your site up and running in no time, with no need for special technical knowledge or skill on your part — simply choose a site style that catches your fancy, fill in the blanks, click the button that puts it live over the Web, and you're all set. Sites such as these may not allow you to create your own domain name (for example, redcaboose.com), or may do so only if you pay for the privilege.

The other major option for building a Web site — more expensive and not quite as easy — is to use a dedicated Web hosting service such as Dotster (www.dotster.com) or Hostway (www.hostway.com). These sites allow you to search for the domain name of your dreams, reserve it, and then build a site around it using either their templates or your own Web site design created with software such as Microsoft FrontPage, Adobe GoLive, or Macromedia Dreamweaver.

If you're uncomfortable with the idea of building your own Web site, there are plenty of people out there ready, willing, and able to help you out. Seen a site you really like? Find out who built it. You'll often find a plug for the designer at the bottom of the home page.

A well-designed site can be a powerful advertisement for your book and — best of all — it's available 24 hours a day, seven days a week, and can be viewed by potential book buyers anywhere in the world. While it may not sell as many books as a string of book signings or radio interviews, your Web site gives you the home base on which you can build the other elements of your promotions plan.

Driving traffic to your book's site

It's important to have a Web site ready in time for your book's publication. But just because you have a Web site doesn't mean people are going to find it. Just building one is good, but it's not enough. If you hope to be successful, you need the right kind of traffic.

Traffic — visitors to your Web site — is what takes your site from just a pretty compilation of your achievements to a potential moneymaker, with links to online stores that carry your books or even your own warehouse full of self-published books. Here are a few ways to make sure your Web site is an effective publicity tool for your children's book:

✔ **Register with the most visited search engines.** There are hundreds of search engines available, but you shouldn't waste your time with the vast majority of them. Our advice is to stick with the top ten (not in any particular order):

  • Google (www.google.com)

  • Information.com (www.information.com)

  • MSN (www.msn.com)

  • Yahoo! (www.yahoo.com)

  • Overture (www.overture.com)

  • America Online (www.aol.com)

  • Ask Jeeves (www.askjeeves.com)

  • Lycos Networks (www.lycos.com)

  • WebSearch.com (www.websearch.com)

  • MyWay.com (www.myway.com)

✔ **Create interesting content.** Go beyond making your Web site just a place to list your resume, post your cover, and buy your book. Strive to make it unique and compelling. Try new ideas geared toward both children and their parents. Why not consider dot-to-dot games? Or word searches and word scrambles using characters and places from your book? What about an area where kids could color in black-and-white versions of your characters or an interactive cartoon game that brings your characters alive? (Make sure to get permission from the copyright holder of the illustrations in your book.) Ask yourself what kind of content will attract busy Web surfers and get them to come back again for more. Take the time to create the kind of content you or your children would like to find on another (famous) author's Web site.

✔ **Exchange links.** Are there sites out there that are somehow related to what you do but aren't in direct competition? If so, ask their Webmasters to place a link to your site in exchange for putting a link to their site on yours. Encourage your book-selling posse — your publisher, agent, and publicist, for starters — to all have links to your site.

✔ **Register with pay-per-click search engines.** Certain search engines offer a service in which your site is featured more prominently placed further up the food chain than other competitors' sites, based on the keywords someone types into the search engine. Google and Overture search engines offer this additional service (Google's is known as Google Adwords: www.adwords.google.com). For example, if your home-based business is breeding show dogs, you could have a small ad with a link show up anytime someone searches the keywords *show dog breeders* — all for a price, of course. But you pay only when someone does a search using your keywords and then clicks on your ad, and how much you pay depends on how popular the keywords are: more keyword competition means higher prices. Although the price per click can run anywhere from 5¢ to $100 in the case of Google Adwords, a typical price is in the range of 20¢ to $1 dollar per click.

✔ **Start an affiliate program.** You can also offer other Web site owners a commission on the sales they send your way. The big sites like Amazon make affiliate programs a central part of their selling models, driving more traffic to their sites and increasing their sales. You can do this, too. Check out a variety of affiliate programs to see how to set up your own program and how commissions are structured, including Amazon (www. amazon.com), **Barnes & Noble** (www.bn.com), and the Apple iTunes site (www.apple.com/itunes/affiliates).

Book Tours, In-Store Signings, Readings, and More

In addition to sending out press releases, doing newspaper, radio, and television advertisements, and the like, you can do a number of other things to draw attention to your book.

The book tour myth

Many new book authors have the impression that one of the first things their publisher is going to do after a book is published is send the author out on a multi-city book tour, complete with media handlers, tour guides, escorts, and travel expenses. Yeah, right. Truth be told, few authors are ever bankrolled by their publishers to make a cross-country book tour. Sure, if you're an established, bestselling children's book author, you may be able to wrangle a book tour out of your publisher. For most new writers, though, the extent of the book tour will probably be from one end of their home city to the other.

There's an alternative, however: You can create your own book tour. When you're planning to visit another town or city, line up some publicity while you're there. You can do a little or a lot; it's up to you.

- Drop by some bookstores and sign some books.
- Do some readings at local schools and libraries.
- Schedule a radio or television interview or two.
- Make yourself available to local print media.

Preparing for media interviews

We hope that you do get to the point where you have lots of author events to attend and tons of media attention. Bitsy Kemper, of Kemper Communications, a PR and marketing firm, has some advice about how to prepare for those all-important media interviews.

Before your interview:

- Find out who watches the show so you can spin your messages to them.

- Decide what you want people to remember. Refine and rehearse your sound bytes so that if the audience remembers only one thing, it's your slyly-repeated sound byte, "I'll be signing books tomorrow night at BK Books, downtown." When the interviewer is ready to end the interview, repeat, "Thanks, Bob, see you tomorrow at BK Books." The audience will remember your book is sold there, even if they don't make it to the signing.

- Ask in advance whether the station can do a visual/graphic for you (sometimes called a Chyron — (pronounced ky-ron) — which refers to a particular brand of character generator), with the specifics of your book or your event. E-mail them the facts a few days ahead, with a graphic of the book cover, and they should be able to create a slide to show before, during, or after the interview.

- Get some rest the night before. One of our interviews on CNN took place at about 6 a.m. I had to get there at 5 for makeup, and I had been up tossing and turning since 3. I was so tired, I swear I slurred my words!

- Pick out your clothes and make sure they fit. No loud or busy patterns like hound's-tooth or horizontal stripes (cameras hate that). All white is boring.

- Practice your hair and makeup beforehand. Odds are you'll be on your own, because most stations don't provide anything but a crammed bathroom mirror. Makeup should be a touch darker, and perhaps a touch heavier than you normally wear. If you don't normally wear any, borrow some from a friend who can help you out and practice putting it on a few days before the show. Always pat some neutral powder on last. Men, too! Foreheads and balding heads especially get shiny under the heat of the lights and the pressure of nerves.

- You may think how you're dressed won't matter on radio, but it will. People who get dressed up tend to feel, and act, more professional.

- Practice being interviewed in front of a mirror, hire a PR professional for expert advice specific to your situation, or check out interview tips on the Internet.

At the interview:

✔ Arrive 15 minutes earlier than they say to be there.

✔ Walk in ready to go. Hair already done, makeup finished, clothes clean.

✔ Speaking of makeup and hair: You may not want to hear this, but looks count. You don't have to be a hottie to be successful, but a good impression certainly helps. Make a true effort on your appearance.

✔ Be yourself. Yes, you need to prepare. But don't try to be someone else — it's too much work.

✔ Smile. Even on radio.

✔ Notes are okay to have with you, but don't read word for word. Use them for reference.

✔ Don't forget a copy of your book!

✔ And for Pete's sake, look in the mirror before you go on air!

After the interview:

✔ Send a handwritten thank-you note to the interviewer and to the station director or segment producer if you worked with them beforehand.

✔ Immediately start thinking of ways to get yourself back on the air.

With a little advance planning, you can accomplish a lot — all on your own schedule.

Bookstores and libraries

You should never be shy when it comes to calling a bookstore or library to set up a book signing or a reading. Bookstores — and the people who own and run them — love to set up these kinds of events, and most will welcome you with open arms.

Here's something to consider: 99.9 percent of those who work at bookstores and libraries love books. They love reading them, love discovering new titles, and love recommending favorites to customers, patrons, friends, and relatives. And perhaps the only thing they love more than books are the people who write them.

Truth be told, outside of the occasional book signing or reading, bookstore and library employees don't get to meet very many authors — especially in bookstores that aren't in big cities. So, when one drops in and makes his presence known, employees almost fall all over one another to introduce themselves and provide support in whatever ways they can. This support includes gathering your books together for you to sign, applying "Autographed" stickers to the front of the signed books, placing your books in a better position (face out on the shelf, in the front window, or by the cash register), and just generally treating you like a celebrity.

Signings and readings

One of the key ways that children's book authors get publicity is to do book signings and readings.

✔ **Book signings:** A *book signing* is when the author visits a bookstore and signs books for customers. Book signings can either be informal, where you drop in unannounced and sign what books of yours happen to be in stock, or formal, where the bookstore sets up a signing event on a specific date for you to chat with customers and sign books. These formal signings are often advertised by the bookstore, and — if your book is popular — they can draw quite a crowd. Sometimes, you may be asked to give a talk about your book before you actually start signing.

Be sure to bring a couple of fresh, fine-point, permanent markers in whatever color you like — they're great for signing books.

✔ **Book readings:** A *book reading* is just that: an event at a bookstore, library, or school where you read your book (or excerpts of it, depending on its length) to whoever decides to show up and listen. Readings are generally scheduled well in advance so that they can be fit into the organizations' routines and so that they can be announced far enough in advance to generate interest in the event.

Whatever kinds of events you decide to pursue, simply call the organization and ask for the person in charge of arranging author events. You'll soon be on your way to getting the word out about your book.

Hiring Your Own Publicist

Authors love to write books, but many aren't similarly inclined to publicize and market them. Selling books may be something you aren't comfortable with or know anything about.

For these reasons and more, consider hiring a professional book publicist. A good publicist isn't cheap, but she can make the difference between a book that sells a few copies and a book that sells a few hundred thousand copies.

What a publicist can do

The most important thing a publicist can do for you is get your foot in the door at a media outlet (newspaper, magazine, radio, television, Web site), generating enough interest to get you scheduled for an interview, profile, or other article. Specifically, among other things, a good *book publicist* can

✔ Draft and distribute press releases, press kits, and brochures.

✔ Set up interviews with print journalists.

✔ Schedule live and phone-in radio and television interviews.

✔ Build buzz through his network of media contacts.

✔ Arrange book signings and readings.

✔ Submit your book to reviewers.

✔ Schedule appearances at conferences and seminars.

✔ Submit your book for consideration for awards and prizes.

When it comes to publicity, a publicist can do just about anything you'd ever need this side of writing your book. What you have your publicist do for you will be limited only by what your publisher plans to do and the size of your bank account.

Finding the right publicist

Hooking up with the right publicist is a little like dating — you really don't know how things are going to work out until you spend a little time together, maybe get out to a restaurant or two, see a movie, and go bowling. Well, you can probably skip the restaurant, movie, and bowling with your new publicist, but you do need to spend some time working together before you know whether you've got the basis for a long-term relationship to develop and blossom.

If you decide to hire your own publicist, be sure that she has the following:

✔ **Significant experience promoting children's books:** A wide variety of publicists are out there vying for your account. And although many of them may have general experience in publicity and public relations, fewer have specific experience in publicizing books, and even fewer in publicizing children's books. Don't fool around; hire publicists who have a solid track record of experience in publicizing children's books.

✔ **Established media contacts:** In the publicity business, the Golden Rolodex — an extensive network of media contacts — is everything. Your ideal publicist has a well-developed list of media contacts that she can take your book to.

✔ **Creativity:** The best publicists do more than just one or two of the same old things (for example, only mailing out press releases) to publicize a book. They're always trying out new and creative ways to get the media's attention — and to draw attention to you and your book.

✔ **An assertive but pleasant manner:** You want a publicist who is going to actively publicize your book — making calls, mailing, faxing, e-mailing — but not in an overly aggressive manner that will turn off your media contacts. Assertive is good; aggressive is bad. Someone with a good voice who is pleasant to work with can get you a lot more interviews than someone your media contacts try to hide from.

✔ **Time for you:** When you're paying someone your hard-earned money, you should be treated like the valued and respected client you are. You should not be kept on permanent hold when you call, your voice and e-mail messages should be responded to promptly, and you should always be treated professionally — with dignity and respect.

✔ **A personality that meshes with your own:** This is someone with whom you are entrusting your newest pride and joy — your book — and you not only need to trust this person implicitly, you need to get along with her. Spend some time with your prospective publicist — on the phone, over lunch — before you sign on the dotted line.

✔ **A knowledge of industry trends:** Books are a business, and the business of books is in constant change. Your publicist should be up-to-date on the latest trends.

Find the publicist you like the most

Odds are you've seen Bitsy Kemper on CNN or quoted in everything from *Investor's Business Daily* to *Parenting* magazine. Maybe you've heard her on national radio or on TV or read her work in one of the countless newspapers she's appeared in. Now running Kemper Communications, Bitsy asserts that public relations and marketing are her passions — not just her job.

WCBFD: How does someone go about selecting and hiring a publicist?

BK: When you chose your own doctor, you did your homework. You wanted a truly qualified professional. On first meeting, you sized 'em up and down (maybe not in an obvious way), wondering, "Will this person do what it takes to keep me well?"

Expertise surely was a main factor in your final decision. But when it came right down to it, you picked *the one you liked the most*. Even if he or she didn't have the best interpersonal skills or the most years of experience, there was something that made you confident a long-standing relationship would be fruitful.

Choosing a publicist, book promoter, or PR person is very similar. Do your homework. A lot of it. Get a client list and talk to at least two clients. But never assume a list of successful writers means that publicist was the reason behind it. Similarly, don't assume a list of "nobodies" means the publicist stinks. Some publicists won't give out names, so ask for samples of press materials they have personally written or overseen (not something someone in their office did — what *they* did). Ask for press clippings of past media hits, with dates, of clients they have booked.

Think about how they talk and respond to you. Is this a relationship you want to set in motion? You'll be spending a lot of time together. No matter how accomplished they might be, don't pick 'em if you don't like 'em. It's so much easier to work with someone you like and respect.

WCBFD: What are the most effective approaches to promoting a book?

BK: While there's no silver bullet, there are many ways to better ensure success. The first is breadth — going everywhere, trying every angle. Get coverage around Thanksgiving on your book about fashion ("What did the pilgrims *really* wear?"), pitch a story about your critique group the same month your new book comes out, sponsor an essay contest on resolving teen conflict with your book as one example of a friendly solution. Pick a few different angles based on audience demographics.

The second approach is depth — building a personal relationship with the news director or reporter so they learn to trust you (and are more likely to return your call next time). Know when the TV station or paper is going to do their annual firehouse story and suggest they come to a local school where kids will be reading your nonfiction book about why fire burns (get the school's okay first!). The media loves a chance to get a shot of kids reading or having fun learning, but it has to be a "new" reason.

WCBFD: How do you ensure that your message is heard in a very crowded (and noisy) world?

BK: The best way to break through the noise is to do your homework. Get creative. Be prepared. Make sure your press kit is tiptop: current, relevant, and error free. Don't send a book about talking bunnies to a nonfiction reviewer. Don't do a book signing at a store that doesn't carry your book. The better you understand your market, the better you know how to speak to them in their own language. Know whom you are talking to, know their preferences, know

their track record, know their deadlines. Or make sure your publicist does.

WCBFD: What advantages does a professional publicist have in promoting a book over someone who is just learning?

BK: A professional publicist has something a newbie simply doesn't: contacts. It's like showing up in a foreign city and needing to get from the busy airport to a small office in an overcrowded high-rise development before anyone else does. An experienced publicist has the map. The *proven* map, not last year's edition. And odds are they can drive pretty fast. Think of the money you'll save in gas.

WCBFD: What else can a publicist or PR person do for me?

BK: A PR professional should be able to offer other services beyond booking you on the 6 o'clock news. You need to be prepared for the interview, as does the interviewer. Practice the answers, in sound bytes, to the list of suggested interview questions that should be in your press kit: why you or your book is unique, and so on.

Can your publicist find out whether the reporter has kids, and if so, what age? (***Note:*** Leaving a signed copy of your book made out to their child's name can go a long way.) They should not only give you an address and phone number, but directions as well. Make-up tips. Sound bytes. Realistic expectations. Bookings for the town your in-laws live in so you can pop in on vacation.

Remember, not everything is media-worthy, no matter how good your book is, or how creative you might get. But a PR professional can help give you your best shot.

To find a publicist, ask other children's book authors for referrals. If you belong to a group like the Society for Children's Book Writers and Illustrators, ask around. See whether you can get referrals from your literary agent, your editor, a friend or relative, or someone else you trust who's connected to the business.

Getting the most for your money

You don't want to shell out a ton of money to a publicist without getting results in return. After you've made the decision to engage a publicist, and after you've found a good one, you need to ensure you get your money's worth. Here are a few tips for doing just that:

- ✔ **Don't wait until the last minute.** Your publicist needs time to work his magic — the more time you give him, the better he can do (and the less he'll spend on overnight delivery services). Ideally, you should engage a publicist at least three months before your book is published — six months is even better.

- ✔ **Get a proposal.** Be sure your publicist-to-be gives you a written proposal detailing exactly what services she'll provide and exactly when they'll be delivered.

- ✔ **Set a fixed price and ceiling.** Publicists usually work in one of two ways: a fixed price for an entire marketing campaign or a fixed hourly rate. If you go with the latter, be sure that you set a ceiling price that your publicist may not exceed without first obtaining your written approval.

- ✔ **Put it in writing.** All agreements with your publicist should be in writing.

- ✔ **Get reports.** Require your publicist to provide regular (weekly, monthly) reports of what he has done on behalf of your book — phone calls made, press releases sent, producers contacted, and so forth.

- ✔ **Assess and reengage (or say good-bye).** Take time to periodically take stock of where you're at: Has the publicist done what he promised? What are the results? If you're happy, continue the relationship. If not, don't hesitate to fire your publicist and find a new one.

A good publicist can be your best friend. By taking care of the business side of things now, your relationship can proceed on a firm foundation of trust. And that's good for you and for your book.

Part VI
The Part of Tens

The 5th Wave   By Rich Tennant

Is this the "Rejected Authors Sweat Out Their Aggressions" Aerobics Class?

In this part . . .

Here are a couple of quick reference chapters to help you negotiate writing and selling a children's book. Not only are these short-and-sweet chapters great for generating ideas or solving problems, but they're also fun to read. We cover classic children's book storylines and give you tips on the very best ways to promote your book.

Chapter 20

More than Ten Great Sources for Storylines

Certain premises for storylines can be employed time and again. Whether your take on an existing story sounds derivative is up to you and your writing skill. But ever since we writers started scratching our stories on the walls of caves, or sitting around a fire listening to a tale told with a good cup of tea, we've been sharing our experiences and imaginings with others. And some of these experiences and imaginings are more universal than others. They may have happened to us, or to a friend, or perhaps we heard them told as children and the tales still captivate us. Some are just great stories with action and adventure, good and evil, magic and exploration. And some are pure urban (or rural) myth.

To find out whether anyone owns a story, and whether you can retell it in your words without getting in trouble, use this fairly reliable test: If you can find three different sources of adaptations or retellings in the public domain then you can fairly assume the story is up for grabs. (A story falls into *public domain* if it is a creative work that is no longer protected by copyright and can be used by anyone.)

But make sure to actually get your hands on the three actual books the story comes from (online sources cannot always be relied upon to correctly credit material). Check the copyright and permissions pages and ascertain that they haven't obtained permission from someone else to use the story — because if they did, they would have to credit it, and if the credit is in the book, they may have had to pay for the privilege of using it or adapting it — something you may not want to do. And a word of caution: If you choose fairy tales, go back to the originals and not to the Disney adaptations, because certain additions to the Disney tales are not public domain.

In this chapter, we list some fabulous resources for storylines that you're welcome to pilfer and tinker with to your heart's content because no one — and everyone — owns them.

Classic fairy tales, fables, folk tales from around the world, mythological tales, Bible stories, and nursery rhymes are all great places to find good storylines in need of retelling in your voice. Entire libraries contain tales from peoples all over the globe, some shared across cultures and languages — and many with their own versions of essentially the same stories. Satisfying and familiar, new and interesting, these stories can provide numerous chances for a retelling that emphasizes humor (always great for kids) and learning, by introducing children to other storytelling topics and styles from other cultures. Adapting one of these stories in a new voice or with a twist can be a fun exercise — and not just an exercise because many adaptations, both serious and fractured, have become classic children's books themselves. We won't tell you the premise of every single classic story here, but we will give you a few to whet your appetite.

Fairy Tales

Fairy tales are, of course, fanciful and imaginary stories about people, animals, things, or magical beings who have magical powers. They are always made up and are intended to amuse and entertain. They have satisfying themes, such as good triumphing over evil. Fairy tales follow certain conventions: There is no question who the good guys are, magic often abounds, and the bad guys usually get their due. Although these and other conventions can make fairy tales somewhat predictable, that predictability and familiarity provide the perfect set-up for deviations.

For example, what if you were to take the well-known tale of Goldilocks and set it in the present day with a young bear who breaks into a house of humans? Or how about a tale about a young male Sleeping Beauty instead of a female one? Here are a few choice fairy tales boiled down to their storyline premises:

- **Cinderella:** A young woman, trapped in her own house as a scullery maid, overcomes her timidity and becomes a princess despite the efforts of her evil stepmother and stepsisters.

- **The Frog Prince:** A desperate, frog-detesting princess makes a deal with a frog who then forces her to be his companion.

- **The Golden Goose:** A kindhearted simpleton wins the heart of a princess through a series of unfortunate accidents.

- **The Magic Tinderbox:** A witch entices a soldier to fetch a magic tinderbox which he then steals, using it to fulfill his own dreams.

- **Rapunzel:** A couple makes an unfortunate deal with a witch who takes their child and locks her in a tower; the child's hair grows long enough to reach the ground and let in unwanted strangers

✔ **Rumplestiltskin:** A little man spins straw into gold in exchange for a princess's first child.

✔ **The Three Little Pigs:** Three porcine antiheroes learn the value of building homes that can withstand the hot air of one bad wolf.

✔ **The Ugly Duckling:** The hero of this tale is shunned by all for being a weird bird, only to show them all up in the end.

Fables

Fables are stories that have a point, a lesson that's supposed to help the reader live better, understand something about a specific culture, or comprehend the natural world. Fables are heavy-handed morality tales in which animals and humans are taught obvious little lessons. Although we don't advise preaching to children in your haste to teach them everything you know or believe (a very common mistake made by first-time writers), we do think fables provide interesting moral dilemmas and lessons that can be disguised by good writing. Here are some pretty popular fables:

✔ **The Ass and His Purchaser:** A person is known by the company he keeps.

✔ **The Birds, the Beasts, and the Bat:** He who plays both sides against the middle ends up friendless.

✔ **The Buffoon and the Countryman:** We often praise the imitator and deride the real thing.

✔ **The Cock and the Pearl:** Precious items are reserved for those who can value them.

✔ **The Dancing Monkeys:** Not everything you see is what it appears to be.

✔ **The Dogs and the Fox:** It's easy to kick someone who's down.

✔ **The Eagle and the Fox:** Do unto others as you would have them do unto you.

✔ **The Father and His Sons:** United we stand, divided we fall.

✔ **The Fox and the Woodcutter:** There is as much malice in a sly wink as there is in a mean word.

✔ **The Tortoise and the Hare:** Slow and steady wins the race.

✔ **The Lion and the Mouse:** Little friends can prove to be great friends, or size doesn't matter.

✔ **The Shipwrecked Imposter:** Liars deceive no one but themselves.

✔ **The Two Dogs:** Children aren't to blame for the faults of their parents.

Although we repeat the original titles here, we don't suggest that you submit an adapted fable to a publisher using the word *ass* in the title or the text. Why? Because although children of a certain age will find it hilarious, the gatekeepers (publishers who acquire the manuscripts in the first place, booksellers who stock the books, librarians who shelve them, and then parents who buy the finished product — more about them in Chapter 3) may not share your delightfully childlike sense of humor. On the other hand, the story of how *Walter the Farting Dog* (North Atlantic) was published (read the sidebar interview in Chapter 17) flies in the face of all convention.

Fables provide life lessons in proper behavior and human nature. They also open the door to storylines based on teaching lessons in the most obvious of ways, for how much more obvious can you get than a stated moral at the end of a story? Unless you're writing a traditional fable in the traditional format, which includes a fable-like title and an obviously spelled out moral at the end, avoid preaching to children. They don't like lectures any more than you do. If you must have a moral to your story, it's better to be subtle about it, elegantly writing it into your plot and character development and letting the reader discern its validity on her own.

Folk Tales

Folk tales involve the traditional beliefs, practices, lessons, legends, and tales of a culture or a people passed down orally through stories. Folk tales have ways of explaining basic natural truths for each culture, such as where the world came from, why humans have power over animals, why animals act the way they do, why the seasons change, and so on. They tend mostly to be based in the natural world, but, like fables, they can also focus on human behavior; however, they rarely have that preachy, moralistic tone of fables. Often, folk tales require the characters to use their wits to solve a problem.

- ✔ **Anansi Tales:** Also referred to as Trickster Tales, these stories about Anansi (sometimes a spider, sometimes a monkey) involve a protagonist who cleverly gets what he's after, no matter what the consequences.

- ✔ **The Birth of Finn MacCoul:** A young boy is saved by his grandmother who teaches him how to be a great warrior and starts him on his heroic journey.

- ✔ **The Bremen Town Musicians:** A donkey, dog, cat, and rooster set off to become famous musicians but get waylaid by a bunch of robbers.

- **The Cock and the Mouse:** A cock, in search of some nuts to eat with his friend the mouse, gets hurt and must enlist the help of a long line of people, animals, and objects to be cured.

- **The Lad Who Went to the North Wind:** A boy goes to the north wind to ask for the return of items the north wind has spirited away, but ends up with other treasures instead.

Mythology and Mythological Heroes

The Greeks and Romans (and every other ancient culture) developed heroes and antiheroes that populated exciting stories of adventure, magic, and power — covering every imaginable activity, behavior, hope, and emotion that humans or immortals could conceive. These mythologies, regardless of origin, have been adopted into nearly every culture and religion in the world in some way or another. These myths represent experiences that are universal in nature, and therefore myths are a fabulous source for storylines. Here are some of the more famous gods and heroes who figure prominently in the canon.

- **Apollo:** Only minutes after his birth, he slew a mighty dragon and later grew up to protect cattle and keep the wolves away. He is also a twin to his sister, Artemis.

- **Athena:** The goddess of war who sprang from her father Zeus's head, she won a competition to see which of the gods could provide the most noble gift; Athena is also known as the goddess of peace, inventor of the flute, and bearer of the loom.

- **Hermes:** Son of Zeus and the mountain nymph Maia, he is the messenger of the gods, equipped with a staff, winged shoes, and hat. As a small boy, he stole a herd of cattle belonging to his brother.

- **Psyche:** A young girl named Psyche is chosen by Eros, the god of love, to be his bride, but his jealous mother, Venus, forces her to accomplish some seemingly impossible tasks before she will allow the marriage to take place.

- **Zeus:** The ruler of all the gods, Zeus hurled his father and other unwanteds away and ruled the world with his brothers Poseidon and Hades. God of weather, he lived on Mount Olympus, from which he would throw thunderbolts.

Nursery Rhymes

These little ditties from our childhood are great sources for characters and storylines. Imagine Mary, Mary Quite Contrary as the star of her own hip-hop troupe. Or what if Little Miss Muffet was not arachnophobic and befriended the spider — then what? Jack and Jill had a lot of exercise to do, but how would they have approached the hill if one of them were physically challenged? Nursery rhymes are also perfect for getting you in that kid-space, rhyming, upbeat, funtime, storyline-writing mood. Here are a few:

- Baa Baa Black Sheep
- Georgie Porgie
- Hey, Diddle Diddle
- Humpty Dumpty
- Jack and Jill
- Little Miss Muffet
- Mary, Mary, Quite Contrary
- Rub a Dub Dub
- Three Blind Mice

Bible Stories

The Bible, both the Five Books of Moses and the New Testament, is full of exciting stories. Miracles were born in the Bible, and Bible stories provide great storylines for children's books. Behold some of the most popular ones:

- **Daniel in the Lion's Den:** A pious Daniel is thrown into a lion's den by a bunch of jealous townsmen and is saved by the God he loves.

- **David and Goliath:** A young boy takes on a huge soldier and saves Israel's army from being taken into slavery.

- **Fishes and Loaves:** With five barley loaves and two small fish, Jesus feeds 5,000 hungry people.

- **Jacob and the Coat of Many Colors:** An old man gives his favorite son a colorful coat, thus inciting the envy of his brothers who plot to get rid of him.

✔ **Jesus at the Temple:** The 12-year-old boy Jesus is accidentally left behind in a temple in Jerusalem, where he astounds a group of professors with the depth of his wisdom and knowledge.

✔ **Jonah and the Whale:** A man hears the voice of God commanding him to pass on God's teachings and decides to try to ignore it. He flees to the sea, where God chases him down and teaches him who's boss by allowing him to survive being swallowed by a whale.

✔ **Noah and the Flood:** Disgusted by what he has wrought, God decides to wipe out mankind, save the righteous Noah, his family, and a male and female of every species of animal on earth.

✔ **Samson and Delilah:** The strongest man on earth falls in love with one of the most deceitful women on earth, who gives away his most sacred secret for her own gain.

Sibling Issues

Certain experiences in a child's life are definitive. Those involving siblings can even be life altering. What better storyline for a sibling in need than one that revolves around issues facing siblings?

✔ Disabled or sick siblings

✔ New baby

✔ Rivalry and/or strong connections between siblings

✔ Sibling babysitters

✔ First borns, middle borns, babies of the family

✔ Multiple birth siblings versus singletons

✔ Adopted siblings

✔ Favoritism — real or imagined

✔ Inseparable siblings

✔ Flattery or copycatting?

✔ Taking a sibling's stuff

Family Changes

Most children must face changes that alter the delicate balances of the family unit in subtle and not-so-subtle ways. Because children seem to thrive with structure (better to allow them to fly free and experiment in the world), and family is the most basic and important structure in their lives, any issue facing a family affects them. How do children react and feel about the following issues:

- Separation or divorce
- Remarriage
- Nontraditional families (gay, lesbian, transgender, or bisexual parents, or two single parents not romantically involved combining households)
- Move to a new neighborhood
- New school
- New caretaker
- Latchkey situation
- Grandparent or other relative moving in

Any of these situations could be the basis for a storyline appealing to children and their parents. Think of situations that your family faced as you were growing up or situations that made you feel unsure or uncomfortable. Chances are, you could write a book to help some other child who feels the same way you did.

First Experiences

Few things are more touching than thinking about a child facing an experience for the first time. For some reason, we sentimentalize (as in "How cute!") these situations, when in actuality, such experiences are more often exhilarating or frightening (or something in between) to a child. In other words, anything but *cute!*

Many books out there are about the first day at school, but you may be able to write a better one. Or you can write something about any of the following topics:

- First trip to dentist
- First playdate
- First bicycle
- First haircut

- First pair of glasses
- First best friend
- First sleepover
- First crush
- First team sport
- First phone call
- First time in trouble at school

The list of these is endless. Again, scour your memories for some memorable firsts in your own life or in the lives of your family members for some potent storyline material.

Common Childhood Fantasies

Which of us hasn't wished that we lived in different circumstances? Or that we were a different person altogether? Children move in and out of their fantasy worlds many times during a given day. More importantly, fantasies are great starting points for interesting storylines. Here are some that Lisa and Peter came up with:

- **Adoption:** I must have been adopted, and I have a better family somewhere on this planet.
- **Astronaut:** I can drive this airship deep into space to explore the cosmos and maybe even meet aliens.
- **Beautiful Dancer/Singer/Entertainer:** I am the star of the show.
- **Fairy/Princess/Bride:** I am such a special person.
- **Mad Scientist:** I can create anything in my laboratory (pronounced with a trill: la-BORRRR-a-torrrr-ee).
- **Magical powers:** I know I have some, if I could just figure out the access code.
- **Monster:** I am all-powerful and can scare away anyone I please.
- **Sailor/Pirate:** I sail the seas.
- **Secret Agent/Spy/Super Hero:** I have been hired by my country to save the world from . . .
- **Talking to/Understanding Animals:** Call me Dr. Doolittle.
- **Wishes:** If I could have all the wishes I wished for . . .

Friendship and Social Issues

From the first time they attend a "Mom and Me" or "Dad and Me" class to their first playdates, children are thrust into social situations that become more and more important to them as they get older. Soon friends supplant parents as favorite people to spend time with. So if you can think of a ton of issues that face families, imagine a child trying to figure out all the ins and outs of being a friend. Just take yourself back to junior high school or high school days and it should all come rushing back to you. Here are some issues kids are concerned with:

- Old best friends and new best friends
- Boyfriend/girlfriend getting in the middle of friendship
- Religious/racial/cultural differences
- Depression/anxiety/suicide
- Peer pressure
- Cheating
- Smoking, drugs, alcohol
- Sports(wo)manship
- Eating disorders
- Inequalities in privilege
- Popularity

Growing Pains (Emotional and Behavioral)

Here we get into experiences with feelings that most children don't have any way of knowing how to deal with. Even the tiniest children experience new and powerful emotions all the time and don't know how to handle them. Some children seem to just barely survive, whereas others make these experiences seem easy. But wouldn't it be great if there were wonderful stories starring someone we could relate to who has to deal with these issues in their own lives? Then we could explore options without leaving the comfort of our favorite secret fort. Some of these topics include:

- Losing a friend
- Feeling inadequate
- Feeling aggression versus assertiveness

- Being shy
- Being left out
- Being disabled
- Getting along with others
- Hitting, biting, scratching, spitting, pushing
- Having a good or bad attitude
- Using a particular tone of voice
- Feeling fears
- Having nightmares
- Experiencing sleeping or napping troubles

Bodies and Their Functions

These issues face not just the wee ones, as you may imagine, but bigger children as well. In the last decade, quite a few books about bodily functions that were considered taboo in polite society have become raging bestsellers. Consider storylines about:

- The uses of your five senses
- Potty training
- Poo-poo, pee-pee, passing gas (and the equipment that makes it possible)
- Burping
- Puberty: body hair, menstruation, breasts, and all the rest
- Body types and differences
- Acne
- Boogers, vomit, and other interesting and chunky bodily matter
- Disease and sickness

Historical Figures, Historical Moments

Sure, some history teachers could bore the prickles off a porcupine, but history is filled with great stories about heroes and heroines, villains and do-gooders, and just plain old folks like you and us. Have you ever felt captivated by a time in history? Have you ever wondered what it felt like to be in the shoes of an especially fascinating historical figure? If you've failed to comb your American or World History textbooks in a while, here are some ideas of people in the public sphere who may warrant a second look:

- Presidents, dead and alive
- Record breakers
- Pioneers
- Holocaust survivors
- Salem, Massachusetts and the Witchcraft Trials in the 1600s
- Slavery and the Emancipation Proclamation
- Civil rights activists
- Inventors of vaccines and other medical advances
- Tribal peoples in third-world countries
- Especially talented choreographers and dancers
- Famous writers and poets
- September 11, 2001

Nature and Science

Stories with natural or scientific premises are highly coveted by publishers. Especially if they are fictional. And even if they are not, if they are well-written, you have a good chance of being published. Teachers, librarians, and parents are always looking for material to supplement what is taught in school — material that does not reek of lessons to be learned or homework to be done. If you can couch learning about trees and plants in a story about a young boy's adventures in the Amazon, then you are onto something good. Think about storylines revolving around the following topics:

- Fossils
- Dinosaurs
- Trees and plants
- Spacecraft
- World geographical changes
- Earthquakes
- Storms
- Volcanoes

Now choose one of these and start writing already!

Chapter 21

Ten Best Ways to Promote Your Story

In This Chapter

▶ Doing book readings

▶ Getting on the air

▶ Hiring a publicist

*I*t's one thing to write a children's book and have it published, and it's another thing altogether to sell it. And to sell it you must promote it. Your publisher will likely do far less to promote your new book than you may expect, perhaps sending out a stack of press releases to the general media and a limited number of copies of your book to key reviewers, as well as perhaps bundling it with other titles for bookseller promotions. That's about it.

If you want your book to stay in print for more than a couple of years, you have to build a strong track record of sales, particularly within the large chains (Barnes & Noble, Borders, and — increasingly — big-box retailers like Wal-Mart, Target, Costco, and Sam's Club). You can't rely on your publisher to make this happen; as an author, you need to create your own buzz and do whatever you can to promote and sell your books. In this chapter, we go over ten of the best ways to do that. And don't forget to check out our discussion on publicizing your book in Chapter 19.

Create a Web Site

Although you certainly can get by without a Web site, you'll find that having one can be a very effective way to promote and sell your book — especially as word of mouth builds, and curious people begin to try to find out more about your book online. You can sell your book through your site, or create links to other sites that sell it — or both. With online payment services like PayPal, people can buy your book using a charge card and you can receive the proceeds quickly and easily. If nothing else, your Web site will serve as a kind of online brochure — always standing ready to tell visitors more about your book and about you.

Creating your own Web site doesn't have to be an expensive proposition. Popular Web-hosting services like Hostway, Cedant, Interland, Network Solutions, and Dotster offer easy-to-use templates to create your own Web site. Or, if you have a bit of spare change squirreled away, you can always hire someone to build the site for you.

Build a Platform

By building a platform, we don't mean going to your local home-improvement store and buying a stack of lumber and a hammer and nails; we mean putting together a solid foundation of activities that will automatically market your book and result in additional sales. One sturdy plank in a well-built marketing platform for an aspiring children's book author would be, for example, to write a regular column about the trials and tribulations of parenthood, and to get this column nationally syndicated so that it appears on a weekly basis in newspapers across the country. Besides building your name recognition, the weekly column provides you with an excellent opportunity to plug your book — if only in the tagline that says something like "Suzy Harris is author of the popular children's book *Wind on the Water.*"

Other activities to build your marketing platform could include doing regular readings at bookstores across the city you live in, offering a once-a-month Bedtime Story Reading Hour at your local bookstore (with your books on a table nearby for anyone who may be interested, of course!), presenting a seminar on how to write a children's book, starting a local-access radio or television show featuring children's books or stories, and much more. Building a platform not only helps you sell your current books, it makes you more attractive to publishers when you pitch future books. It is therefore a very wise use of your time and money.

Send Sample Copies

One thing that your publisher should do is send sample copies of your book to people who will either write and publish an enthusiastic review or who will buy lots and lots of copies to stock in their library system. If, however, your publisher doesn't do the job — or only does half the job — you need to step in and do your own mailing. If you can get your publisher to be as enthusiastic about your publicity ideas as you are, you may be able to get them to provide you with the free copies of your book to do promotional mailings. Hey, if your sales pitch is exceptional, you may even be able to get them to cover postage — but don't hold your breath.

Consider creating a spreadsheet to keep track of whom you send samples to and when you contact them. That way you won't alienate potential allies by being a pest!

In deciding to whom you should send copies of your book, consider who will offer you the most publicity for the least amount of effort on your part. If you can get a syndicated columnist or national radio talk show host to mention your book, then this is a very high return for your efforts. Send copies to people like this, along with your local media contacts (the ones you get to know or are introduced to by name), and organizations that sponsor book awards and prizes. Then follow up with an occasional, unobtrusive reminder by e-mail or a phone call. Hey, it's your career. Don't be shy! (Besides, many of the costs of mailings are tax deductible. Talk to your accountant about how to keep accurate records.)

Get in Your Local Newspaper

Newspapers love to profile local authors, probably because their subscribers enjoy reading these kinds of stories. Get your book and a press release in front of the editor in charge of the local news section of your newspapers, and then follow up with a phone call.

And don't ignore community weeklies, church or temple newsletters, and local magazines, especially magazines targeted to parents. They will often be happy to review your book after they become aware of it (and making them aware is *your* job). Communities and their local publications take pride in their local successes and tend not to be as jaded as their national counterparts, opening up lots of opportunities for you to get interviewed and for your book to be featured — cover shot, author photo, and all.

Do Readings in Stores, Schools, and Libraries

Think a big book chain like Barnes & Noble or Borders — or your local independent bookstore — wouldn't want to waste its time on a new, less-than-famous author like you? We have some news for you.

Bookstores *love* authors. They love authors to drop by and sign books. (Peter always carries a blue Sharpie felt-tip pen with him so that he'll be ready to sign books at the drop of a hat.) They love to schmooze with authors, and they love to schedule children's book authors to do readings. To do a reading in a bookstore, contact the owner — if it's a small independent — or the community relations manager or community relations coordinator if it's a large chain. Believe us; they will be happy to hear from you! Follow a similar process to schedule readings in schools and in libraries. In the case of a school, you should call the school's office and ask how you can set up a reading. For a library, call the librarian to find out the process of getting signed up for a reading.

Whichever approach you take, be sure to invite the local media to join you at the reading. Although they may not send out a reporter or camera crew, it's a possibility.

Get on Local Radio and TV

Here's a news flash: Your local radio and television stations are constantly on the lookout for stories with a hometown flavor that will appeal to their audiences. That's good news for you, because, as a local author, there's a very good chance that you'll be able to line up a guest appearance on any number of radio and television stations — especially if you or your book have a unique or compelling journalistic angle.

What makes for a unique or compelling angle for a local radio or television station? If you're a published author, news media in your area may be interested in showing you off as "one of our own." Or maybe your book is set at a site that figures prominently in local history. If your children's book includes references to The Alamo, Independence Hall, or Alcatraz Island, for example, contact the stations in Texas, Pennsylvania, or San Francisco to set up an interview. Or maybe your book is based on a true story — something interesting that really happened in a community. Wherever your book takes place, the people and media in the neighborhood may be interested in knowing about it.

The best way to approach your local radio or television station is the direct approach. Write an e-mail message that pitches your book. (You'll find contact information for most radio and television stations within their Web sites.) Then follow up your message a few days later with a phone call. Offer to provide the station with a copy of your book. If you don't get an immediate response, don't give up — if you keep working at it, there's a good chance you'll eventually get their attention, and a valuable opportunity to promote your book in the process.

Perform (G-Rated) Publicity Stunts

Ever feel like doing something wild and crazy? Well, now's the time! If you really want to get the attention of the media and potential book buyers, a well-planned publicity stunt may be just the ticket. For example, to kindle American interest in his English creation, *Winnie the Pooh* author A. A. Milne hatched a publicity stunt that involved sending the real Pooh (Edward Bear) and friends on a transatlantic tour to the United States. In 1947, Milne's publisher arranged for Pooh and his (stuffed) entourage to visit every major media market in the U.S. The result? A lot of books sold, and a popular children's icon was established.

Publicity stunts are limited only by your imagination. How about having a kite-flying contest tied to your book, or giving away helium-filled balloons imprinted with the name of your book at local shopping centers and malls, or organizing a pumpkin drop from a tall building in the center of town? (Check with the local fire department if you are thinking of doing anything that may be construed as risky.) Again, you are limited only by your imagination and your budget.

Put On a Play

You don't have to limit your book to the printed page; with a bit of work, it can easily be brought to life. Why not consider turning your book into a play that can be staged in your community, or that can be sent on tour? A play will not only entertain audiences, it will help generate interest in your book.

A friend of Lisa's was working on her second middle-grade novel for years, but the timing was off and it was never published. Everyone, including the friend's agent, believed it was wonderful, creative work. So the writer did the next best thing, she approached her child's school and asked if she could write a play based on her novel and oversee the middle-graders putting on a theatrical extravaganza. Well, if you think the teacher jumped at the opportunity, you'd be right!

Everyone involved had a wonderful time, the play was a success (meaning all the parents, relatives, and siblings showed up to see it), and the media even appeared for a quickie local newsbyte. The writer followed up with a cookies and milk wrap-party reading of her book and set up a signing table to offer it to playgoers. Based on the incisive feedback she received from the children during the production, she was able to rewrite the book and eventually see it through to publication. So while this may seem like a very long and winding road to getting published, it still proves the point that you are bound as a writer and a promoter only by the limits of your imagination.

Hire a Publicist

One of the best ways for you to promote your book is to pick up the slack of your publisher's publicity efforts and to hire your own publicist; specifically, a publicist experienced in promoting children's books.

Ask other children's book authors for referrals, or do some research on the Internet to find a good PR representative. Some of the things a good PR representative can (and should) do for you include: sending out press releases and copies of your book, setting up interviews with the media (print, radio, and television), approaching targeted magazines and newspapers to review your book, and much more. (Basically they should be reading this Part of Tens chapter on how to promote your book, and they should do the things we've listed here.) Hiring a PR representative or firm isn't cheap — you'll pay anywhere from several hundred dollars for a bare minimum effort to many thousands of dollars for the full-court press. And you'll need to make a significant financial commitment over a prolonged period of time if you would like your promotional efforts to have an impact on potential buyers.

For more information about children's book publicists, check out Chapter 19 — and make sure not to miss the information in the sidebar interview with communications specialist Bitsy Kemper.

Aim High: Prizes and Awards

Book prizes and awards are great! Not only do they look good on the wall of your home office, but they can help you sell your book. (And they can help get publishing companies interested in your future books, too.) How? When awards organizations publicize their awards — who won in which categories — they also publicize your book at the same time. Not a bad deal. Be on the alert for literary competitions or competitions sponsored by local libraries or governments. Individual states and certain geographical regions often offer book awards and prizes, and there are of course a number of prestigious prizes available on the national level. Visit www.childrenslit.com/award_link.html for a complete list.

Index

Notes

Notes

Notes

Notes

Notes

BUSINESS, CAREERS & PERSONAL FINANCE

0-7645-5307-0   0-7645-5331-3 *†

Also available:
- Accounting For Dummies †
  0-7645-5314-3
- Business Plans Kit For Dummies †
  0-7645-5365-8
- Cover Letters For Dummies
  0-7645-5224-4
- Frugal Living For Dummies
  0-7645-5403-4
- Leadership For Dummies
  0-7645-5176-0
- Managing For Dummies
  0-7645-1771-6

- Marketing For Dummies
  0-7645-5600-2
- Personal Finance For Dummies
  0-7645-2590-5
- Project Management For Dummies
  0-7645-5283-X
- Resumes For Dummies †
  0-7645-5471-9
- Selling For Dummies
  0-7645-5363-1
- Small Business Kit For Dummies
  0-7645-5093-4

HOME & BUSINESS COMPUTER BASICS

0-7645-4074-2   0-7645-3758-X

Also available:
- ACT! 6 For Dummies
  0-7645-2645-6
- iLife '04 All-in-One Desk Reference
  For Dummies
  0-7645-7347-0
- iPAQ For Dummies
  0-7645-6769-1
- Mac OS X Panther Timesaving
  Techniques For Dummies
  0-7645-5812-9
- Macs For Dummies
  0-7645-5656-8

- Microsoft Money 2004 For Dummies
  0-7645-4195-1
- Office 2003 All-in-One Desk Reference
  For Dummies
  0-7645-3883-7
- Outlook 2003 For Dummies
  0-7645-3759-8
- PCs For Dummies
  0-7645-4074-2
- TiVo For Dummies
  0-7645-6923-6
- Upgrading and Fixing PCs For Dummies
  0-7645-1665-5
- Windows XP Timesaving Techniques
  For Dummies
  0-7645-3748-2

FOOD, HOME, GARDEN, HOBBIES, MUSIC & PETS

0-7645-5295-3   0-7645-5232-5

Also available:
- Bass Guitar For Dummies
  0-7645-2487-9
- Diabetes Cookbook For Dummies
  0-7645-5230-9
- Gardening For Dummies *
  0-7645-5130-2
- Guitar For Dummies
  0-7645-5106-X
- Holiday Decorating For Dummies
  0-7645-2570-0
- Home Improvement All-in-One
  For Dummies
  0-7645-5680-0

- Knitting For Dummies
  0-7645-5395-X
- Piano For Dummies
  0-7645-5105-1
- Puppies For Dummies
  0-7645-5255-4
- Scrapbooking For Dummies
  0-7645-7208-3
- Senior Dogs For Dummies
  0-7645-5818-8
- Singing For Dummies
  0-7645-2475-5
- 30-Minute Meals For Dummies
  0-7645-2589-1

INTERNET & DIGITAL MEDIA

0-7645-1664-7   0-7645-6924-4

Also available:
- 2005 Online Shopping Directory
  For Dummies
  0-7645-7495-7
- CD & DVD Recording For Dummies
  0-7645-5956-7
- eBay For Dummies
  0-7645-5654-1
- Fighting Spam For Dummies
  0-7645-5965-6
- Genealogy Online For Dummies
  0-7645-5964-8
- Google For Dummies
  0-7645-4420-9

- Home Recording For Musicians
  For Dummies
  0-7645-1634-5
- The Internet For Dummies
  0-7645-4173-0
- iPod & iTunes For Dummies
  0-7645-7772-7
- Preventing Identity Theft For Dummies
  0-7645-7336-5
- Pro Tools All-in-One Desk Reference
  For Dummies
  0-7645-5714-9
- Roxio Easy Media Creator For Dummies
  0-7645-7131-1

* Separate Canadian edition also available
† Separate U.K. edition also available

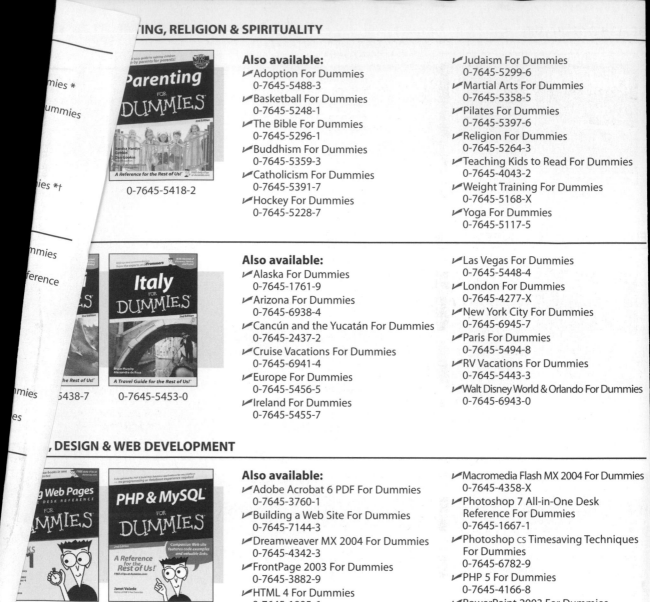

0-7645-6820-5 *†

0-7645-2566-2

Also available:
- Alzheimer's For Dummies
  0-7645-3899-3
- Asthma For Dummies
  0-7645-4233-8
- Controlling Cholesterol For Dummies
  0-7645-5440-9
- Depression For Dummies
  0-7645-3900-0
- Dieting For Dummies
  0-7645-4149-8
- Fertility For Dummies
  0-7645-2549-2

- Fibromyalgia For Dummies
  0-7645-5441-7
- Improving Your Memory For Dummies
  0-7645-5435-2
- Pregnancy For Dummies †
  0-7645-4483-7
- Quitting Smoking For Dummies
  0-7645-2629-4
- Relationships For Dummies
  0-7645-5384-4
- Thyroid For Dummies
  0-7645-5385-2

EDUCATION, HISTORY, REFERENCE & TEST PREPARATION

0-7645-5194-9

0-7645-4186-2

Also available:
- Algebra For Dummies
  0-7645-5325-9
- British History For Dummies
  0-7645-7021-8
- Calculus For Dummies
  0-7645-2498-4
- English Grammar For Dummies
  0-7645-5322-4
- Forensics For Dummies
  0-7645-5580-4
- The GMAT For Dummies
  0-7645-5251-1
- Inglés Para Dummies
  0-7645-5427-1

- Italian For Dummies
  0-7645-5196-5
- Latin For Dummies
  0-7645-5431-X
- Lewis & Clark For Dummies
  0-7645-2545-X
- Research Papers For Dummies
  0-7645-5426-3
- The SAT I For Dummies
  0-7645-7193-1
- Science Fair Projects For Dummies
  0-7645-5460-3
- U.S. History For Dummies
  0-7645-5249-X

Get smart @ dummies.com®

- **Find a full list of Dummies titles**
- **Look into loads of FREE on-site articles**
- **Sign up for FREE eTips e-mailed to you weekly**
- **See what other products carry the Dummies name**
- **Shop directly from the Dummies bookstore**
- **Enter to win new prizes every month!**

* Separate Canadian edition also available

† Separate U.K. edition also available

Available wherever books are sold. For more information or to order direct: U.S. customers visit www.dummies.com or call 1-877-762-2974.
U.K. customers visit www.wileyeurope.com or call 0800 243407. Canadian customers visit www.wiley.ca or call 1-800-567-4797.